THE HOLLYWOOD PROPAGANDA OF WORLD WAR II

Robert Fyne

The Scarecrow Press, Inc.
Lanham, Md., & London
1997

SCARECROW PRESS, INC.

Published in the United States of America
by Scarecrow Press, Inc.
A wholly owned subsidary of
The Rowman & Littlefield Publishing Group, Inc.
4501 Forbes Boulevard, Suite 200, Lanham, Maryland 20706
www.scarecrowpress.com

PO Box 317
Oxford
OX2 9RU, UK

The author acknowledges the Museum of Modern Art for allowing reproduction of these photos, which were originally press photos from: 20th Century-Fox, RKO Radio Pictures, MGM, Universal Studios, Warner Brothers, Paramount Pictures, Columbia Pictures, and Republic Pictures.

British Library Cataloguing in Publication Information Available

Library of Congress Cataloging-in-Publication Data

Fyne, Robert.
　　The Hollywood propaganda of World War II / by Robert Fyne.
　　　　p.　　　cm.
　　Includes filmographies. Includes bibliographical references and index.
　　ISBN 0-8108-2900-2 (cloth : alk. paper) —ISBN 0-8108-3310-7 (pbk. : alk. paper)
　　　　1. World War, 1939–1945—Propaganda. 2. Propaganda, American. 3. World War, 1939–1945—Motion pictures and the war. 4. Motion pictures—United States—History—20th century. I. Title.
D810.P7U368　　　1994
791.43'658—dc20　　　　　　　　　　　　　　　　94–15963

ISBN 0–8108–2900–2 (cloth : alk. paper)
ISBN 0–8108–3310–7 (pbk. : alk. paper)

⊖™ The paper used in this publication meets the minimum requirements of American National Standard for Information Sciences—Permanence of Paper for Printed Library Materials, ANSI Z39.48–1984.
Manufactured in the United States of America.

This book is for
Bridwell Klee Fyne
last surviving member of the
1927 Battin High School
varsity basketball team

CONTENTS

CHAPTER ONE

PROPAGANDA AND HOLLYWOOD

. . . of all the arts, the most important for us is the cinema.—Vladimir Ilyich Lenin

Movies are the lingua franca of the twentieth century.— Gore Vidal

On Thursday, April 21, 1898—the day the United States Congress declared war against Spain—two New York City motion picture entrepreneurs, J. Stuart Blackton and Albert E. Smith, sent a small filming crew to their office, located on the top floor of the old Morse Building. Looking down at the jubilant crowds swelling Nassau and Beekman Streets, and shouting various nationalistic slogans while waving the Red, White, and Blue, both men realized their country was ready for a strong dose of instant patriotism. Within a few hours, this hastily organized production team—now working on the roof—hacked out a one-reeler entitled *Tearing Down the Spanish Flag,* a ludicrous but chauvinistic movie depicting the seizure of a Spanish government installation in Havana by U.S. Army troops, an event that, historically, was still many weeks away.

Soon, thousands of New Yorkers sat in diminutive, cramped, makeshift theaters of vaudeville houses, watching Vitagraph Company's version of the Cuban fighting. For most of these paying viewers, it didn't matter that the events flickering on the screen were fictitious. These audiences wanted to see American soldiers rush their Spanish enemy, capture his stronghold, rip down his flag, and capitulate to Jeffersonian democracy. For a few cents, these moviegoers sitting hundreds of miles from the combat area—fulfilled their vicarious desires for adventure and

1

victory, watching this lopsided view of a war created by the deft hand of a film propagandist.

Over the next few years, the motion picture industry slowly picked up steam as new techniques were developed. By 1903, an American filmmaker, Edwin S. Porter, enthralled spectators with his editing skills in two short melodramas: *Life of an American Fireman* and *The Great Train Robbery*. Both twelve-minute titles contained different modes of action in storylines made cohesive by overlapping one scene with another, shaping a juxtaposition that—later on—was labeled montage. Porter's one-reelers opened the floodgates, fashioning a new artistic form which heralded the growth of the industry and inspired another director, D. W. Griffith, to produce—in 1915—an elaborate Civil War epic, *The Birth of a Nation*.

As a historical entity, *The Birth of a Nation* became the prototype for the war propaganda films that followed. Memorable scenes included the panorama of Sherman's Union Army marching to the sea, artillery duels, hand-to-hand combat, and civilian casualties. Psychological factors, such as Lincoln's assassination at the Ford Theatre or the Little Colonel's abortive battle charge, added a certain realism to the storyline. Within six months after its preview, *The Birth of a Nation* drew large crowds, even though some theaters charged two dollars per ticket, and its impact was enormous. The South saw the film as presenting a states' rights issue plus a justification for the Ku Klux Klan, while Northern liberals argued that the photoplay distorted a glorious Union victory against rebellion. President Wilson's apocryphal comment—that it was writing history in lighting—only added more fuel to the propaganda fire.

Two years later, however, in 1917, the United States' involvement in Europe's Great War allowed the film propagandists to shower the American public with such anti-German titles as Cecil B. De Mille's *Joan the Woman, The Little American* and *Till I Come Back to You*. All three motion pictures depicted the Huns as barbaric, uncivilized and depraved men, who only wanted to violate America's favorite sweetheart, Mary Pickford. Other directors mirroring the same sentiments produced *The Hun Within, The Kaiser—Beast of Berlin, The Evil Eye* and *To Hell with the Kaiser*. A few weeks before the armistice was signed,

Charlie Chaplin released his personal antiwar statement, *Shoulder Arms.*

As an American movie star, Chaplin's earlier two-reelers brought him instant recognition. Audiences everywhere were familiar with *The Rink, The Cure* and *The Pawnshop,* films that employed slapstick, the chase, the pirouette, pathos, the Murphy bed and a gas lamp to achieve their humorous effects. *Shoulder Arms* was a continuation of these themes but in a slightly different format. Military life was satirized, while a strong pacifist position echoed Chaplin's liberal ideas. War, according to the baggy-pants comedian, was a series of petty humiliations ranging from boot camp life to the tedium of standing in the trenches, hoping to shoot a German. Rebellion was a means for survival.

So was ingenuity. To stay afloat, Chaplin, the doughboy fighting on the western front, ran amuck with his many comic strip adventures. In one scene, he camouflaged himself as a tree; in another episode, he escaped down a sewer that was corked by a plump German. Later, the mustachioed soldier, disguised as a chauffeur, captured both the Kaiser and the crown prince, while rescuing a pretty French lass. His heroics, however, were short-lived. He woke up from a sound sleep, still ensconced inside the barracks, realizing that all his adventures were nothing more than allegoric dreams.

When the Great War ended in November 1918, American audiences had seen dozens of silent propaganda pictures that justified their nation's intervention into this global conflict. Moviegoers cheered in unison as they watched reel after reel showing the American doughboy racing across no man's land to reach the German trenches and rout the barbarians from their earth-laden stronghold. At war's end victory was sweet and the filmmakers knew that the clamoring public's gratification appetite was satiated. Now that peace was here, the producers realized, it was time to shelve the wartime film and start grinding out new themes. For a while, the propagandists enjoyed a needed respite.

Over in Russia it was a different story. In October 1917, Lenin's Bolsheviks stormed the czar's Winter Palace and established the dictatorship of the proletariat. Right from the start, Lenin envisioned the propaganda role this new medium could play in bringing the tenets of his revolution to the rural areas. Lenin appreciated that most of the Russian peasantry was illiterate, but they all understood moving pictures. Loaded down with an elaborate gasoline generator, projectionists were dispatched to remote villages where the image of communism was spread on some faded white sheet set up in the main square. While most of the Russians clustered in the nighttime audience did not read or write or use electricity or running water, they all recognized Vladimir Ilyich's personage as he flickered before them, his arm stretched forward, calling for greater sacrifice against the western capitalists.

Within months, a nationalized Soviet film industry was in full swing, complying with Lenin's dictum that newsreels and documentaries were needed to inform the masses of the Revolution. Soon, new directors emerged on the Soviet scene to experiment with the montage format, and in 1925—a year after Lenin's death—Russia's greatest filmmaker, Sergei Eisenstein, produced *The Battleship Potemkin*. With its memorable Odessa steps massacre scene, *Potemkin* embodied the essence of the Bolshevik Revolution as the crew members of this naval vessel overthrew their tyrannical captain—the man who served maggoty meat— and proclaimed power to the people.

As a propaganda film, *Potemkin's* visceral appeal stirred up the masses with its quick cutting from scene to scene, which created a sense of speedy realism. Enthralled audiences watched the elderly woman—her bloodied face and broken spectacles proclaiming the wanton violence of the czar's Cossacks—cry out in anguish as the townspeople, including a man with no legs, ran from the soldier's sabers. Three years later, in 1928, Eisenstein repeated this type of propaganda in *October* (sometimes called *Ten Days that Shook the World*), a film based on John Reed's book about the Bolshevik Revolution. Once again, Eisenstein glorified Lenin's followers by creating a moving picture that enshrined communism.

Other directors added to Lenin's edict of propaganda during the twenties. Vsevolod Pudovkin made *Mother, The End of St. Petersburg* and *Storm over Asia,* while Dziga Vertov created *The Man with a Movie Camera*. Other titles included Abram Room's *Bed and Sofa,* Esfir Shub's *The Fall of the Romanov Dynasty,* Alexander Dovzhenko's *Zvenigora* and *Arsenal,* and Victor Turin's *Turksib*. Each silent motion picture heralded the same message: the triumph of Bolshevism over its enemies—those capitalists, czarists, white guards, imperialists and saboteurs who only wanted to undermine the Revolution. As film propagandists, these Russian directors, with their innovative montage system, took a rudimentary medium and, in a few years, elevated it to a full-blown art form.

Back in the United States, the only 1920s-style revolution was the Volstead Act, the congressional law that prevented Americans from enjoying their favorite alcoholic beverage. While a frustrated public adjusted to the Prohibition ruling, the motion picture industry expanded by leaps and bounds as new companies were formed and elaborate movie palaces constructed to show the array of titles released each week. Popular subjects included such standard themes as the Western, comedy, action and adventure, historical, problem, and war. Since sound was still years away, no thought was given to a musical. For postwar America, the movies offered escapist entertainment to people sitting in a darkened room, watching scenes on a silver screen about a life-style that few of them would ever know.

Gradually, a few titles about the Great War appeared, clamoring for revenge against the defeated enemy. *Why Germany Must Pay* demanded retribution for the execution of an English nurse, Edith Cavell. *Behind the Door* justified the sadistic killing of a German U-boat commander by a U.S. naval officer, while sterilization, public hanging, and extermination were demanded for the Kaiser, his family, and military officials in *Daughter of Destiny, America Must Conquer, After the War,* and *The Kaiser's Finish.* In 1921, Rex Ingram's *The Four Horsemen of the Apocalypse* combined vengeance with sexuality. In this film, Rudolph Valentino's erotic tango dancing oozed Latin sensuality with every dip and twist, while his enemies—the blood-lusting Huns—were routed in some elaborate battle scenes.

As propaganda, these motion pictures summarized the exuberance of America's first victory on the European battlefield, while laying the cinematic groundwork for the films that would follow some twenty years later. Many of the psychological components clarified the issues, reducing the concept of good and evil to simplistic terms, while defining the nature of the enemy. Addressing the emotions of the audience, rather than the intellect, these movies worked as propaganda because the Great War was depicted solely from the point of view of the Allied side, forcing the viewers into believing every frame that flickered before them.

However, by 1925, the motion picture industry began to see the Great War in a different light. The earlier propaganda films—with all the hoopla on American bravery and German bestiality— gradually gave way to new titles that examined the trench warfare in somber terms. King Vidor's *The Big Parade* and Raoul Walsh's *What Price Glory?* took a hard look at the pockmarked battle- fields, and the results echoed General Sherman's pithy "war is hell" pronouncement. William Wellman's *Wings* and Howard Hawks' *The Dawn Patrol* continued this antiwar theme in the air lanes over France, but in 1930, one film said it all—Lewis Milestone's *All Quiet on the Western Front*.

As a pacifistic movie, *All Quiet* (adapted from Erich Maria Remarque's best-selling novel) told the simple story of a German unit on the French front in 1916 that lost one young man after another to mortar attacks, cave-ins, rifle shots, and illness. The film's contradictory theme—when it comes to dying for your country, it's better not to die at all—was echoed by a young German recruit, Lew Ayres, as he watched his friends become routine casualties. There were no gallant charges from the trenches across no man's land, only futility, isolation, and death. In one poignant scene, a German and a Frenchman inadvertently shared a shell hole, discovering their mutual angst regarding the war. This small episode raised the basic question: why fight other men who were so much like yourself?

For many American moviegoers, nurtured during the Great War on a steady diet of anti-Hun, silent propaganda films, *All Quiet* appeared as an open admission that the horror of battle knew no national boundaries. The clean-cut, young German soldiers, fresh from their local gymnasiums, resembled any American fellow walking down Main Street, hand in hand with his steady girl. In their naive way, these German lads sought only friendship and romance, two pursuits that were interrupted when the Kaiser's call to arms dropped them on the European charnel fields. For Lewis Milestone, this motion picture—a sharp departure from any previous film because it included a soundtrack—represented a personal statement calling for the abolition of combat. Probably no other title portrayed the misery associated with battle as graphically as *All Quiet on the Western Front*.

But other movies flickered all over America in the 1930s, providing audiences with their definitive form of popular culture.

More than 80 million people a week traipsed to their neighborhood movie houses—the ''shows'' as they were frequently called—to see their favorite stars in another escapist role, perhaps depicting the good fortune of a pretty salesgirl who married a millionaire, or maybe watching a group of distaff dancers, arranged in a straight line, kick their feet into the air. Hollywood knew the public wanted to forget—at least, for a while—the problems of the Great Depression, and its film moguls provided their customers with that one desired commodity—entertainment. Once in a while, a storyline might contain a direct or subliminal social message, but the cardinal rule was inflexible: every film must have a happy ending.

No wonder propaganda films were virtually unknown. By the mid-Thirties, Hollywood's self-imposed censoring committee—the Hays Office—regulated the contents of all motion pictures, and its omnipotent czar, William Hays, published page after page of proscribed subjects, terms, events and sounds. High on this list were ''national feelings,'' a topic the old World War I propagandists knew quite well. As far as this regulatory committee was concerned, only wholesome American entertainment was allowed for public consumption. Without the Hays Office's imprimatur, no film was permitted in any theater. Propaganda, of course, was basically verboten.

But none of that mattered to John Q. Public, the moviegoer, who sat in the darkened theater responding to those vicarious thrills unfolding on the screen. Fun, excitement, romance, shaggy dog stories—these were what audiences flocked to see in the 1930s. Clark Gable, Douglas Fairbanks, Jr., the Marx Brothers, Marlene Dietrich, Paul Muni, Ronald Colman, Katharine Hepburn, Warner Baxter, and Cary Grant became household words as America's love affair with Hollywood roared along at full throttle. When Fred Astaire and Ginger Rogers showed off their latest terpsichorean skills, audiences broke out in spontaneous applause to show their appreciation. What difference did it make if the inanimate screen couldn't respond to the loud noises created by hands clapping and occasional shrill whistling? It all meant the same thing: Americans were enamored of their movie idols.

How prevalent was fantasy in the viewer's mind? Could a filmgoer differentiate between reality and photoplay? In fact, wasn't it all a strange blend of truth and fiction? Audiences knew, of course, they were watching a storyline created by running some celluloid film through a projector and shown in a darkened room on a large screen. But were the characters on this screen real or fictitious? Which name would audiences ascribe to the characters flickering before them? While watching William Wellman's screwball comedy *Nothing Sacred,* did viewers call the female lead Hazel Flagg or Carole Lombard? In Michael Curtiz's *Charge of the Light Brigade,* what name did moviegoers use when discussing the ill-fated hero—Major Geoffrey Vickers or Errol Flynn?

Most viewers, of course, knew the character by the star's name, not the appellation heard over and over again in the script. In such films as *Dinner at Eight* or *Saratoga,* did audiences refer to the leading female part as Kitty Packard, Carol Clayton, or Jean Harlow? What name first came to mind when viewers blabbed about *The Kid from Spain*—Eddie Williams or Eddie Cantor? The facts seemed obvious—American audiences called the characters in their films by the names of those portraying the characters. Everyone knew that Claude Rains was the Invisible Man, not Jack Griffin; William Powell was the Thin Man, not Nick Charles. Who was the Informer? Gypo Nolan or Victor McLaglen?

This name-switching indicated, perhaps, part of the mystique associated with Hollywood motion pictures and their ineluctable power of persuasion. Putting aside a few cynics, wags, or eggheads, most viewers readily accepted as gospel what flitted before them on the silver screen. When Jimmy Stewart or John Wayne spoke, either in the halls of Congress or from a cramped stagecoach, one thing was certain—their words were ex cathedra. Movie stars always told the truth.

By 1940—as the American economy slowly edged out of the Great Depression—the motion picture industry sustained its phenomenal growth as millions of moviegoers still flocked to their neighborhood shows to watch their favorite stars in another double feature. While the Dream Factory continued to grind out its wonderful escapist fare, one problem would not go away. The war in Europe inched closer and closer to America's shores. As political scientists and militarists perused the world map, the predictions seemed ominous. Even with President Roosevelt's 1940 election promise ringing in their ears, most parents envisioned their sons on a foreign battlefield. Hollywood also knew about the fighting in Spain, witnessed the rise of National Socialism and understood Mussolini's territorial claims. For many directors, itching to enter the fray, it was time to blow the dust off the propagandist manual and return to work.

At first, a few propaganda films trickled out of Hollywood—invoking the wrath of numerous congressional isolationists—which, once again, took potshots at the old German nemesis, now under the rule of a mustachioed autocrat, Adolf Hitler. But December 7, 1941, changed everything. While the American military forces called for volunteers and civilians donated large quantities of blood and pulled down their blackout shades, Hollywood realized that days of escapist entertainment were over. From here on, the motion picture industry, like everyone else, was on a war footing. Hollywood was now part of the fight.

For the next four years, the cameras never stopped churning as one propaganda film after another documented the global conflict. Some of the titles were major productions—*Mrs. Miniver, Yankee Doodle Dandy,* or *Air Force*—with big-name stars and fancy directors. Smaller B-studios made their particular contribution with such obscure listings as *Fall In, Hillbilly Blitzkrieg* and *That Nazty Nuisance.* What was the total count of propaganda films by V-J Day? Probably around 300, not including the numerous serials, documentaries, shorts, and cartoons that supported the war effort.

Right after the Pearl Harbor attack, President Roosevelt cited Hollywood for its role during this wartime period. Claiming that the motion picture was the most effective medium to inform the nation, FDR promised no governmental censorship and called for a continuous output of titles to keep the public abreast regarding the War. By June 1942, after some bureaucratic shuffling around, the Office of War Information—the OWI—became the official watchdog of the film industry. Headed by Elmer Davis, the OWI issued elaborate guidelines, divided into numerous categories, to insure conformity in every photoplay. Like it or not, the Hollywood moguls had to sift through hundreds of pages of official instructions to insure compliance with the federal directives.

For the most part, Hollywood voluntarily adhered to these rule books. Occasionally, a screenplay deviated from OWI's straight and narrow path, causing minor objections from Davis' office. Films depicting goldbricking—for example, *Iceland* or *Abroad with Two Yanks*—received a perfunctory slap on the wrist for poor judgment, while titles portraying ethnic harmony—*Destroyer* or *Destination Tokyo*—earned high praise for their wartime contributions. Other pictures were routine, humdrum melodramas providing entertainment while a subtle reference inserted in the storyline reminded audiences about current events. Like any governmental agency on an emergency footing, the OWI, enmeshed in its own tendentiousness, safeguarded American moviegoers from those ill-conceived, ambiguous or offensive themes that might disrupt morale.

How effective was the OWI? Was this governmental agency really necessary? Could Hollywood regulate itself without federal decree? These questions were debated throughout the War, prompting the liberal faction to cry censorship while the conservative wing advocated adherence to the status quo. The answers, of course, lay somewhere in the middle. For a four-year period the motion picture industry followed the OWI's edicts, producing every title in a standard format. The results were an effective combination of information, patriotism, hero-worship, and propaganda.

When the first World War II propaganda films appeared in early 1942, the moviegoing public needed some good news to offset the ominous events following Pearl Harbor. The Nipponese forces, after numerous attacks on other South Pacific islands, controlled a good portion of that ocean and West Coast residents worried about an impending invasion. In Europe, Hitler's armies occupied much of the Continent, bringing subjugation to millions of people. With such gloom in the air, audiences sought out those Hollywood pictures that reaffirmed their faith in democracy, FDR, and the Almighty. Since propaganda films appealed to groups with homogeneous interests, these titles created a pleasant, fictional world offering the same antidote: as in the previous World War, the Yanks were coming. The early battles were lost, but final victory would belong to America.

Other messages hammered away at similar themes. Military strength, Home Front sacrifices, ethnic harmony, underground resistance, individual heroism, and Allied cooperation all flickered on the screen, and attested to the total victory motif. Film after film depicted Americans routing their enemies and liberating subjugated nations, while audiences cheered and whistled. Some of the motion pictures provided insight into the origins of the War and attempted some cause-and-effect explanation. Many titles lacked continuity and analysis, relying on two-dimensional portrayals, clichés, and stereotypes. What difference did it make? For the war-weary audiences, any title would suffice. As for the propaganda, who would recognize it? Would viewers object to Errol Flynn bombing Germany and then uttering a few pejorative words about the Japanese? If William Bendix resorted to prayer while crouching in his dugout, did this act of faith offend anyone? Who would fault the U.S. Marine Corps and Randolph Scott for blasting the Japanese out of their pillboxes on Makin Island?

When the War ended, Hollywood could easily pat itself on its large back for a job well done. Despite constant criticism from the naysayers, the motion picture industry sustained morale and maintained optimism during the four years of conflict and produced many significant titles. Granted, some of the motion pictures were turkeys, and others suffered from mediocrity, perhaps caused by the logistical problems created by the government's rationing edicts. Film stock was in limited supply, so retakes were curtailed, forcing studios to make do with substandard scenes. Sugar, resin, and balsa were prohibited items, so Hollywood stuntmen could no longer crash through windows (sugar-based), knock a bottle (resin) or break a chair (balsa) over someone's head. Movie stars, technicians, and writers were also scarce as many of the younger men enlisted in the armed forces.

Overall, the propaganda films filled an important void, reassuring audiences about the righteousness of the American cause, while reaffirming the vileness of the Axis camp. Later, some of these titles became classics—*Casablanca* and *Since You Went Away*. Others carried the controversial label—*Mission to Moscow* and *The North Star* for their favorable treatment of communism, or *The Moon Is Down* for its sympathetic portrayal of a Nazi officer. Many of the B-pictures proffered a simple escapism, with far-fetched plots and implausible storylines. Westerns, musicals, second-rate mellers, spy yarns, and slapstick added to the propaganda output, while offering entertainment and fantasy. When moviegoers strolled down to their favorite shows for a few hours of diversion, the War, in many formats, was part of the program.

Since effective wartime propaganda aroused a viewer's sympathy, emotions, and intellect in a manner that remained subtle and

unobtrusive, audiences were unaware of the manipulative qualities of the images on the screen. Did viewers realize the significance of these films? Did anyone perceive that years later, when
Marshal McLuhan expostulated his sensory-tactile-linear theories, these titles were primers in the art of persuasion? Probably
not. For most Americans, sitting in their darkened theaters, these
pictures provided the doses of morale necessary to sustain a nation
enmeshed in a global war.

What were some of the better films? Which pictures retained
their popularity years later as tangible reminders of 1941–1945?
Many titles come to mind but, without question, the best propaganda film of World War II was Twentieth Century-Fox's *The
Purple Heart,* a story of the captured Doolittle flyers and their
ordeal in a civil Japanese court. Fox's *The Fighting Sullivans*
ranked second with its portrayal of the lives and times of the five
Sullivan brothers. Other titles included Columbia's *Sahara* (Ser-
geant Humphrey Bogart took on the German army in the North
African desert); Fox's *Wing and a Prayer* (Commander Don
Ameche steered his aircraft carrier to victory); and MGM's
Bataan (Sergeant Robert Taylor's last stand against the fanatical
Japanese).

Also on the list were MGM's *Thirty Seconds Over Tokyo*
(Colonel Spencer Tracy bombed Tokyo); Universal's *Gung Ho*
(Colonel Randolph Scott's Marine Raiders seized Makin Island);
Republic's *Flying Tigers* (John Wayne blasted the Japanese out of
the China skies); Fox's *Guadalcanal Diary* (the Marines captured
a strategic island in the South Pacific); and Paramount's *Wake
Island* (the Marines defended their outpost to the last man).

As propaganda, these ten films represented the best of Hollywood's persuasive skills. In scene after scene, American audiences saw their enemies routed by their favorite movie star heroes,
while their wives and sweethearts smiled approvingly as the
background strains of "America the Beautiful" conveyed the
righteousness of their cause. Other films, of course, echoed the
same message, but these titles employed taut storylines and in-
depth characterizations, two traits that appealed to viewers'
patriotism, emotions, and self-interest. When John Wayne flew
his pursuit plane into the wild blue yonder, Home Front America
knew one thing for certain: their hearth was safe from all foes,
both real and imaginary.

No other period in cinematic history equalled the output of propaganda films produced during the Second World War. Hollywood's effort contributed to the nation's morale by capitalizing on America's love affair with the movies. The War saw record attendance despite a large federal tax increase on theater admissions. The added money helped to finance the war effort. Audiences now had two reasons to watch a double feature: a night out at the show was both entertaining and patriotic.

CHAPTER TWO

THE GATHERING STORMS

". . . take Hitler, and stick him on the funny page."—Cary
Grant, to his layout editor, in Howard Hawks' 1940 screwball comedy, *The Front Page.*

On February 23, 1939, the Motion Picture Academy of Arts and
Sciences—resplendent with typical hoopla and flair—presented
its annual awards at an elaborate dinner in Los Angeles. For
Hollywood, another banner year was over and on this pleasant
winter evening—the temperature was a balmy 65 degrees in
southern California—the Academy showed off its best work for
1938. Winning the top honor that night was Frank Capra's
lighthearted comedy, *You Can't Take It with You,* a film that
expounded the virtues of the simple life. For the Italian-born
Capra, this was his third Oscar. Bette Davis walked away with the
best actress award for her sizzling performance as *Jezebel,* while
the indomitable Spencer Tracy happily displayed his gold statue
for a superb performance as kindly Father Flanagan in *Boys Town.*
Other motion pictures, likewise, received industry accolades that
evening, but one item was strangely missing. None of the winning
titles even remotely suggested the hostilities raging—in plain
view—across the ocean in faraway Europe.

It wasn't easy to ignore the international crisis. Each day,
newspaper accounts of Nazi Germany's aggression lit up page one
and every Hollywood mogul seated at this gala ceremony, sipping
some vintage French champagne, knew of the significance of
these reports. They all had read, a few months earlier, of
Chamberlain's feeble peace-in-our-times appeasement pronouncement, a pathetic piece of paper that, in a mere twenty days,
on March 15, doomed Czechoslovakia to abrupt capitulation.

Other events were just as ominous: Hitler's militaristic Germany, totally rearmed, was on the move, threatening neighbor nations with its saber-rattling expansion demands. Refugees coming out of the Fatherland recounted new horrors about life in the Third Reich—suspension of civil liberties, late night arrests, deportations to concentration camps, an elaborate propaganda machine, and the strongest air force in the world.

True, a few titles had already filtered out of Hollywood that, in one way or another, touched upon the events now altering the map of Europe. In 1937, Republic produced another B-Western in its popular Three Mesquiteers series, *Range Defenders,* a formula film that pitted the forces of American law and order against a gang of Nazi look-alike thugs—who wore armbands closely akin to the German swastika—threatening to take over the farmers' range. Like any other B-movie, this production caused little commotion. That same year Paramount's *The Last Train from Madrid* became the first picture to deal with the Spanish Civil War; United Artists soon followed with a Walter Wanger production, *Blockade.* Since both titles sided with the Loyalist cause, another controversy ensued because most Americans, unaware of the ideologies in this conflict, couldn't figure out who were the real villains in this complex civil strife, a war involving many foreign volunteer brigade members. Both films, naturally, were box-office failures.

While none of the capitalists gathered at this elaborate ceremony would admit it, all knew that the Hollywood businessman depended on European sales for higher profits, and most 1938 movies distributed abroad contained the necessary escapist themes—themes that basically complemented the existing American isolationism. These films, of course, were mere extensions of similar titles produced during the Great Depression of the 1930s, those motion pictures that eschewed the harsh realities of an American economic system that virtually collapsed overnight by highlighting frivolity and choreography. Fantasy and dance steps, the film titans averred, were the potent ingredients of the box-office success. Politics, aggression, and realpolitik—unlike music—would not soothe the savage audience.

A few weeks after this gala awards soirée, an abrupt change took place. On April 28, 1939, Warner Brothers released its first major anti-Nazi propaganda film, a motion picture that sounded the alarm, rang every clarion, and alerted all law enforcement agencies about the treachery of Third Reich activities in the continental United States. Directed by Anatole Litvak, *Confessions of a Nazi Spy* became a watershed picture that blatantly mentioned the Germans by named and pointed the *j'accusé* finger at Adolf Hitler and his lebensraum policies of expansionism and conspiracy. Other dangers included the sub rosa machinations of the American Bundists operating in large cities, an organization infused with fifth columnists.

The next day, April 29th, the *New York Times* film critic, Frank S. Nugent, summed up the initial reaction to this inflammatory motion picture. "Warner Brothers formally declared war on the Nazis at 8:15 a.m. with the first showing of their *Confessions of a Nazi Spy* at the Strand," he wrote. Clearly, this spring morning launched the beginning of the World War II Hollywood propaganda film genre, a movement that would continue for the next six years.

What was so incendiary and warmongering about this picture? Why did it become so controversial? How did this formula film rile up audiences? The storyline answered these questions. In 1938, a Nazi spy, Francis Lederer, received orders to acquire some military intelligence regarding U.S. Army personnel in the New York City area. He could steal this information because American security was lax, the workers were naive, and most people—living comfortably thousands of miles from the European conflict— were oblivious to the dangers of the New Order.

Right from the opening frames, the theme was highlighted: the vulnerable American public was easy prey for the fifth column activities of Nazi Germany, a group which had been operating stealthily for a least six years. Disguised as fraternal organizations, the Bund (so called from the German word meaning "league") was really a collection of spies and agents provocateurs who regularly stole valuable defense information. These documents were then handed over to their superior, a Nazi bigwig played by the suave British actor, George Sanders.

A predictable plot ensued. The Nazi underling, Francis Lederer, attracted the attention of FBI agent Edward G. Robinson and soon, the law enforcer pieced together the spy network's modus operandi. Then, another Axis agent, Paul Lukas, whose Manhattan medical practice served as the conduit between New York and

Berlin, was caught, and the German revealed everything. This became the confession of a Nazi spy. Lukas bragged: . . . *the Nazis have spies stationed in all the Navy yards—in Brooklyn, in Philadelphia, in Newport News. There are German agents in the airplane and munitions factories at Bristol, Seattle, Boston, Buffalo. There's a spy base in Montreal, Canada. The chief United States inspector, in one of your factories turning out secret airplane parts, is a German spy.''* By itself, this scene— appearing in Spring 1939—offered a frightening appraisal of America's laxity regarding the international conflict.

However, the most revealing aspect of America's shortsightedness was highlighted in the denouement. Brought before a court of law, eighteen German-Americans were charged with violation of the espionage laws. Throughout this trial—it was reminiscent of a New England town meeting—the foreign agents bragged about Third Reich conquests: . . . *Austria is part of Germany; Czechoslovakia is through. Italy is with us; and so is Yugoslavia. Japan is our ally; Hungary is practically ours. Our agents are succeeding in Rumania and Lithuania. France will soon be isolated from all sides.''* The fifth columnists continued their sallies and point after point exposed the vulnerability of America's naive isolation policy. This was a strong indictment, citing years of ill-preparedness, and a frightened hush permeated the courtroom.

The evidence was overwhelming and the Nazi agents were pronounced guilty of all charges; long jail sentences were meted out to this hapless group. Ending on an upbeat tone, the film lauded the skills of the FBI for corralling its enemies. For the time being, at least, America enjoyed a brief respite from its foreign foes. As the first major propaganda film, *Confessions of a Nazi Spy* became Hollywood's *deus ex machina* about the Nazi menace. Employing scare tactics, the film suggested that Axis spies worked everywhere, disrupting the internal security, and plotting the overthrow of basic democratic ideals. But, spearheaded by the skills of the FBI, special agents discovered these fifth columnists, made arrests, and brought them to trial. The film was a blatant glorification of J. Edgar Hoover's federal organization.

It certainly was true, as the *New York Times* reported, that war had been declared on the Nazis with the release of this motion picture. And for the next few months audiences everywhere argued the merits of this controversy. The flag-waving contingency saw the film as a dire warning to prepare for the eventual conflict, while right-wing groups denounced the propaganda aspects. In one instance, a Milwaukee movie house in a predominantly German neighborhood was torched, presumably by a group of pro-Nazi thugs. Bund groups were especially vociferous against Warner Brothers, since actual newsreels of their tactics in the 1938 Washington birthday rally at Madison Square Garden, which painted a pejorative picture of their methods and ambitions, were inserted generously into the storyline of *Confessions*.

A few months later everything changed abruptly: on September 1, 1939, the German army ordered its blitzkrieg against Poland, and in a few days Britain and France formally declared war. This meant that most of the European markets were closed to U.S. film imports. With its eye on purely domestic sales, Hollywood, following the Warner Brothers' lead, began a subtle shift to unabashed patriotism by peddling soft propaganda. Now, all the major studios flung down the gauntlet and the Nazi party and Hitler were mentioned by name and cited in unflattering terms. Putting aside the many B-films which were nothing more than recruitment drives for the American armed forces, numerous major productions took up the call to arms and addressed the issues across the Atlantic. For the next two years—prior to the Pearl Harbor attack—Hollywood would grind out one film after another which, like *Confessions of a Nazi Spy,* was imbrued with propaganda, adjuring America to prepare itself for the global war that certainly was heading its way.

Needless to say, these motion pictures aroused much public awareness with their strident messages, two-dimensional characterizations, and explicit warnings. By January 1940, Warner Brothers released *The Fighting 69th,* an extravagant tribute to the New York National Guard Rainbow Division, a unit whose exploits during the Great War entered the mainstream of American history and folklore. Without question, this film offered a jingoistic, chest-pounding testimony to heroism as personified by the World War I doughboy, the soldier who defended the principles of democracy and religious freedom against the Huns. Nothing could be more apple pie than Pat O'Brien as the famous Irish, Roman Catholic Army chaplain, Father Duffy (his statue stands prominently in New York's Times Square), while James Cagney starred as a young, brash recruit.

Like any propaganda film, the theme was predictable. An obnoxious, loudmouthed soldier (Cagney) must learn the hard way that it takes a group effort to win a battle. After causing the battlefield death of his friend through carelessness, the penitent convert, after talking to Father Duffy, experienced an epiphany. A few moments later, Cagney threw his body on a hand grenade, saving his sergeant and earning his own film immortality. His apotheosis complete, the chaplain adjured all fighting men to remember Cagney's sacrifice for inspirational guidance.

Complete with an all-star cast that included Alan Hale and George Brent, the film contained visceral appeal with its over-the-trenches attack scenes. Time after time, the American dough-boy charged his enemy, drove him out of his embankments into capitulation, proving the indomitable strength of Yankee know-how. The constant theme, we-did-it-before-and-we-can-do-it-again, mirrored America's perceptions in early 1940, and motion picture companies merely pandered to these weaknesses. Frank Nugent, the film critic for the *New York Times,* noted on opening day, January 26th, that the film was having a little trouble making itself heard over the cheers and whistles of a predominantly schoolboyish audience. Again, the tenets of propaganda success-fully gnawed away; American audiences weren't watching this war film; together with the Fighting 69th, they crouched in their trenches ready to race across the field and rout the Hun from his fortifications.

A third Warner Brothers' production that capitalized on the past glories achieved in World War I was *Sergeant York.* Starring the venerable Gary Cooper, this film retold the patriotic story of the Tennessee hillbilly, Alvin York, who literally came out of the hills to join the Army and fought at the 1918 Battle of the Argonne, where his exploits—capturing 132 Germans on a single day—earned him the Congressional Medal of Honor. Overnight, he became a national celebrity when his unit returned stateside and the Warner Brothers' feature caught the excitement of those victorious days. Heavy with corn and using many stock stereo-types—including the turkey shoot—*Sergeant York* embodied everything pure and wholesome. One of the consistent theme songs, permeating many scenes, was the evangelical hymn, "Give Me that Old Time Religion." As for Cooper, the lean actor won an academy award for his straight- arrow performance.

As another propaganda film from Warner's stable, *Sergeant York* contained the necessary ingredients to emote public response. The film slowly traced the modest life story of a poor Tennessee farmhand who wanted to improve himself within the American success story. After a brief setback regarding some bottom land he hoped to purchase, a small miracle occurred. Like Saul on the road to Damascus, Gary Cooper was struck by "lightning" and God's word was revealed. Soon converted to a higher calling, the young sharpshooter averred that he was a pacifist. As with the rowdy bad boy in *The Fighting 69th,* Cooper's transformation was realized after a serious talk with the clergy about German bestiality. Now the young hayseed, nurtured by this ecclesiastical blessing, was off to fight the Huns. This noble cause—both patriotic and religious—demonstrated two components of effective propaganda.

As soon as Warner Brothers opened the floodgates with their anti-German crusade, other companies quickly followed suit, especially since Adolf Hitler had ordered his troops into Poland, forcing its eastern neighbor's capitulation. Now it was easy to refer to the Fuehrer by name and, in many cases, to accuse him of a variety of crimes. A good example was Twentieth Century-Fox's *Man Hunt,* a fictional account of an attempted "assassination" of Adolf Hitler that purported to take place on July 29, 1939. Starring Walter Pidgeon and Joan Bennett and directed by Fritz Lang—the German-born movie maker who had been offered the directorship of the Third Reich's film industry by Reichsminister Joseph Goebbels, but instead fled to the United States—*Man Hunt* stretched the limits of credulity with its off-beat storyline.

In the summer of 1939 a world-famous big game hunter, Walter Pidgeon, crawled undetected through the heavily guarded forest in Berchtesgaden, Germany to within a few hundred yards of a lone figure standing nonchalantly on his spacious veranda. It was the Fuehrer. A few moments later, the English sportsman aligned his target in the crosshairs of his precision rifle and pulled the trigger of the unloaded weapon. A soft click broke the silence and offered the reassurance that the cartridge, if primed and fired, would hit the target. For Walter Pidgeon, the thrill was in the stalking, not in the killing of any prey, and here was the biggest game of all.

Soon, the plot continued in a more traditional format. Captured by Nazi guards, the Englishman's story—detailing the aesthetics of hunting—was rejected and, after a series of convoluted events, involving torture, escape, and smuggling, Pidgeon returned to England, only to learn that the Gestapo was relentlessly pursuing him. Befriended by a streetwalker, pretty Joan Bennett, he resorted to survival skills to outwit the Axis. Later, in the closing moments of *Man Hunt,* Captain Walter Pidgeon, now a member of the British Army, parachuted into Nazi Germany; his mission was to assassinate Adolf Hitler. The voice-over explained the assignment: *". . . somewhere within Germany is a man with a precision rifle and a high degree of intelligence and training that is required to use it. It may be days, months, or even years, but this time he clearly knows his purpose and unflinchingly faces his destiny."*

As a propaganda film, in these still prewar days for the U.S., *Man Hunt* fostered morale for the British people, America's distant ally, a nation that in early 1941 was fighting the Battle of Britain in what was later called their Finest Hour. For Twentieth Century-Fox, *Man Hunt* embodied Hollywood's new policy of denouncing their enemies in no euphemistic terms. Nazi officers routinely bragged about their conquests—*". . . we do not hesitate to destroy in order to create a new world"*—and resorted to murder, torture, and brutality. Hitler, therefore, became a candidate for assassination. In effect, with this motion picture, Hollywood finally came out of the closet and said what most people were thinking: kill Hitler!

Other films, equally outspoken, were produced depicting the stalwart British in their singular fight against the German juggernaut. United Artists' *Foreign Correspondent* offered an elaborate paean to English perseverance in another spy-versus-spy melodrama. Directed by Alfred Hitchcock and starring Joel McCrea and Laraine Day, *Foreign Correspondent* was a strong plea for America to wake up to the reality of Nazism. Twentieth Century-Fox's *A Yank in the RAF* glorified the Battle of Britain by highlighting the flying exploits of Tyrone Power, a volunteer American airman fighting for the Crown.

United Artists' *Sundown,* a topical film depicting fifth column activities in Kenya, warned about the dangers of Nazi aggression in Africa. Starring Bruce Cabot and Gene Tierney, *Sundown* became a minor B-film classic. Directed by Henry Hathaway, the film's propaganda value was enhanced by a wonderful sermon delivered in a bombed-out church in London by the indomitable Sir Cedric Hardwicke. Universal's *Paris Calling,* starring Randolph Scott and Basil Rathbone, highlighted not only the RAF but a British rescue mission as well. A Warner Brothers' B-production, *International Squadron* was another stalwart testimony to the Royal Air Force, this one starring Ronald Reagan as a volunteer fighter pilot whose death added dignity to the British cause.

Other titles touched upon unrest in the Fatherland, reiterating that the Nazi menace, not the German people, was plunging the nation into war. Warner Brothers' *Underground* paired B-actors Jeffrey Lynn and Philip Dorn as two brothers—one a Nazi officer, the other a leader in the underground—whose political differences created family dissension. After finally seeing the light, the Nazi brother quit the party and joined the resistance movement. Likewise, Twentieth Century-Fox's *Four Sons* described the internal strife in a Sudetenland household when one son opposed his brother's Nazi membership. But MGM's *The Mortal Storm* offered a detailed explanation of life in a small Bavarian village where university students disparaged their professor for not teaching National Socialism's racist theories. It starred James Stewart and Robert Young as two school friends who were miles apart concerning the New Order, and the film's propaganda value was strengthened by an elaborate book-burning scene, an event already documented in Hollywood newsreels.

Soon, more local heroes denounced fascism, but in a frivolous way. Abbott and Costello joined three service branches—the Army, Navy, and Air Corps—in a trio of pictures: *Buck Privates, In the Navy,* and *Keep 'em Flying.* All three storylines were mere vehicles for needed recruitment drives. Bob Hope, likewise, saw military duty in *Caught in the Draft,* a B-comedy that attempted to explain the need for conscription, a topic on the minds of most young Americans.

This same idea, adjusting to the needs of the selective service system, was the theme of *You're in the Army Now,* which dressed the schnozzola, Jimmy Durante, in khaki. In Republic's *Rookies on Parade,* Bob Crosby and William Demarest became part of Uncle Sam's Army. Also drafted was William Tracy, the callow recruit with a photographic memory, in United Artists' fifty-minute B-production, *Tanks a Million.* The inscrutable Charlie Chan broke up a Nazi spy ring which was hoping to destroy the defenses around the canal zone in *Charlie Chan in Panama,* while Nick Carter, the popular American gumshoe, smashed a gang of fifth columnists operating a stone's throw from the nation's capital in *Sky Murder.*

For a nation not yet at war, the list of Hollywood's antifascist films seemed endless. John Wayne starred in Republic's *Three Faces West,* a modern-day Western about the hardships of dirt farmers living in the dustbowl, circa 1930, and their eventual trek to the promised land of Oregon. Aiding these new settlers were a Austrian refugee doctor and his pretty daughter, a former well-to-do who had trouble adjusting to Yankee democracy. When her old Nazi boyfriend turned up spouting Third Reich slogans, the propaganda aspect of the film became discernible. In a few moments, the stern father, now a staunch patriot, dispelled the Nazi's rhetoric: *". . . you have become infected with a disease more horrible and malignant than cancer—a disease that will be fatal to you and millions of your countrymen."* This denouncement of the New Order once again warned about the war creeping toward America's shores.

Two other titles—Warner's *Dive Bomber* and Paramount's *I Wanted Wings*—stressed military preparedness by glamorizing the elaborate training for both flight surgeons and aviators. Concomitantly, both storylines reiterated the ongoing theme that it takes a group effort to complete a mission. The same idea was reinforced in RKO's *Parachute Battalion,* another B-recruitment drive production, with Robert Preston and Edmond O'Brien as two fighting men in this elite unit, as well as in MGM's *Flight Command,* a tribute to the volunteers who flew the Navy's Hellcats under the watchful eyes of Robert Taylor and Walter Pidgeon.

Life on the high seas included Paramount's *Mystery Sea Raider,* starring B-actor Onslow Stevens as a Nazi officer preying on British shipping in the North Atlantic. He was no match for Henry Wilcoxon. Similarly, two B-contributions from Columbia warned about Nazi U-boats operating in stealth: *The Phantom Submarine*, with Anita Louise and Bruce Bennett, and *Escape to Glory*, which paired Pat O'Brien and Constance Bennett. Once on shore, Navy life had its breezy moments in Republic's *Sailors on Leave*. Here, Seaman William Lundigan wooed a sailor-hating chanteuse, Linda Hall.

Another effective way to denounce Nazism was to show real-life situations in a nonmilitary setting, with an average person slowly drawn into the conflicts of the New Order. These melodramas included Twentieth Century-Fox's *The Man I Married*, a serious look at the problems confronted by an American citizen, Joan Bennett, who, in 1938, married Francis Lederer, a German national. Arriving in the Fatherland, the pretty Miss Bennett quickly realized this conjugal union was a mistake. Her return to New York, sans husband, was a quiet, subtle reaffirmation of American values. Similarly, United Artists' *So Ends Our Night*, starring Fredric March and Margaret Sullavan, described the plight of exiles and their frustrating peregrination from one country to another. In its singular way, this title became a landmark film because it was the first time an American production uttered the word "Jew" on the soundtrack in such a vile and derogatory tone. Released on January 27, 1941, this film created new standards for directors and screen writers.

Other motion pictures included Paramount's *Arise My Love*, a half-spoof, half-serious look at fascism, using Franco's Spain as the backdrop. Ray Milland and Claudette Colbert, the starring twosome, experience some lighthearted moments while occasionally proffering some interventionist dialogue. And in Paramount's *Hold Back the Dawn*, suave Charles Boyer, a refugee from Europe living in Mexico, employed his amatory skills with Olivia de Havilland to gain legal entry into the United States.

However, it was a Charlie Chaplin production that spurred the greatest brouhaha when it was released in October 1940. United Artists' *The Great Dictator* caricatured the New Order right down to the Fuehrer's mustachioed appearance. Every mannerism of the Third Reich was mimicked. Hitler was lampooned as a clown, a buffoon, a comical figure; his personality defects included insecurity, vanity, and plain stupidity. Adding to the caustic, ad hominem bite was the inclusion of the Italian dictator Mussolini, called Napaloni, played by Jack Oakie.

The plot of *The Great Dictator* had a simplistic storyline and, in a roundabout way, resembled Shakespeare's *A Comedy of Errors.* Charlie Chaplin portrayed a fascist dictator, named Hynkel, ruler of a "fictitious" nation dubbed Tomania. Chaplin wore the fascist armband—the logo contained two x's, known as the "double cross." This insignia, displayed everywhere, resembled Hitler's swastika. Also, the arm salute, with the accompanying "Heil Hynkel," was the mandatory official greeting. Even the public statues held their right arms extended, silently paying homage to the great dictator, their leader responsible for renewed prosperity for the Aryans and abject misery for the Jewish citizens, jammed into their ghetto.

However, an exact double of the dictator resided in a mental institution, where for the past twenty years he had lingered in oblivion, suffering from a Hollywood-induced amnesia. Eventually, this double escaped, found work as a barber and later assumed the role of fascist leader, sending the real Hynkel off to a concentration camp. The film culminated at an elaborate Munich-type rally where the double renounced his former position of aggression and, instead, advocated brotherhood and mutual understanding. However altruistic Chaplin's motives were in writing this fairy tale ending, there was an obvious tone of antiseptic naiveté that permeated each reel. In some scenes, the horror of the Third Reich was minimized to buffoonery and slapstick. In the classic bouncing, global balloon sequence, it reached *reductio ad absurdum.*

To be sure, there were numerous critics of the simplicity found in *The Great Dictator,* and other factions sympathetic to Hitler, plus some national pacifist organizations, who called for an immediate boycott. Chaplin, himself, received many threatening letters and crank phone calls; some theater owners were warned that stink bombs would be lobbed into the audience during the performance. Many years later, Chaplin admitted that he oversimplified some of the major scenes in *The Great Dictator,* and acknowledged that spotty news reports had concealed the actual horror of the concentration camps. Had he known the truth about Hitler's genocidal policies, Chaplin reflected, *The Great Dictator* would never have been made.

In practical terms, however, *The Great Dictator* was a daring film that indicted Nazi Germany for a variety of offenses. Storm troopers randomly assaulted bystanders, including the pretty Paulette Goddard, while mass executions were routinely ordered for political prisoners. The lavish, opulent life-style of high-ranking Nazis contrasted sharply with the squalor of the Jewish ghetto. To add one more insult, Hitler's Minister of Propaganda, Joseph Goebbels, was called Garbitsch (pronounced on the screen as "garbage"), while Field Marshal Hermann Goering did not escape calumny; he was simply "Herring."

But Nazi Germany wasn't the only threat to America's security. Ever since the October 1917 Revolution, Hollywood's depiction of the Soviet Union had been decidedly negative. For many Americans, the terms Nazism, fascism, or communism were synonymous, and the motion picture industry, ever mindful of public sentiment, hacked out one anti-Soviet title after another, denouncing all aspects of Russian life, including their leader Joseph Stalin. In early 1939, MGM's screwball comedy, *Ninotchka,* mocked the Soviet system with its depictions of food shortages, mail censorship, and inadequate housing. By late 1940, little had changed. On December 26th—with the Hitler/Stalin nonaggression pact fresh in their minds—MGM released another major anticommunism film, *Comrade X.* Starring Clark Gable and Hedy Lamarr in the comical roles of thesis/antithesis, *Comrade X* was a devastating attack on all aspects of Soviet life in the ambiguous days of 1939. Russian bureaucrats were portrayed as cynical, corrupt, and obedient to Stalin's every whim. The evils of Bolshevism occupied every scene, reiterating that all Slavs were foes of America. Writing in the *New York Times* that day, Bosley Crowther stated that diplomatic relations between Hollywood and Soviet Russia had been in bad shape for years. Look for a clash of arms, he joked, any day now.

Even though *Ninotchka* was a strong indictment of the Soviet system, it seemed puny when compared to *Comrade X.* Most of *Ninotchka's* storyline took place outside the USSR on the capitalist streets of Paris, so much of the criticism of communism was implied. *Comrade X* eschewed such subtleties. In 1939, tough, no-nonsense American reporter Clark Gable was posted to Moscow, employed by a U.S. wire service, and every story he dispatched was quickly censored. Resorting to trickery—and using a secret code—he wrote the "truth" under the byline Comrade X. Naturally, the inept Russians searched, but could not find, this surreptitious journalist; the film highlighted Gable's expertise in eluding the Secret Police.

High comedy permeated the picture but the real crux was still in the dialogue. In scene after scene, the Soviet government was slandered. Later, the film took a somber tone when Gable and his new Russian wife witnessed the innocent execution of more than 100 peasants on trumped-up charges of counter-revolution. After this scene, Hedy Lamarr, once a strong supporter of communism, repudiated the Leninist system and escaped, with Gable, to the U.S.A., where she wound up in the bleachers in Ebbets Field, yelling *"Kill the Reds!"* (The Cincinnati Reds).

There was a strange footnote to *Comrade X*. Six months after opening day, *Comrade X* continued to draw large audiences in theaters all across the country. But on June 21, 1941, Hitler ordered his Operation Barbarossa attack against Russia and now the balance of alliances clearly shifted; the Soviet Union, by default, became part of the allied camp. MGM's producers realized that this grim satire of Soviet life could not be kept in circulation unless the film was anesthetized to appear as only meek banter between friends. Unwilling to kill this high-grossing Clark Gable picture, the MGM moguls quickly inserted an explanatory foreword, asserting that any spoofing of the Russians in *Comrade X* was intended only as good, clean fun between comrades-in-arms.

Fun or not, America's days of uneasy peace dwindled as the European allies suffered new setbacks: France's capitulation and the Battle of Britain were factual reminders that neutrality and nonintervention were outdated terms. As for Hollywood in the closing days of 1941, the studios continued to churn out anti-fascist titles with new vigor. In the shaky months before Pearl Harbor, Columbia released *You'll Never Get Rich,* while United Artists distributed *International Lady.* Universal's *Swing It Soldier* added to the list; MGM's *Smilin' Through,* Paramount's *World Premier* and *Power Dive* likewise warned of the Axis plot.

In Hollywood's eyes, at least, open warfare was imminent and the numerous films produced between 1939 and Pearl Harbor clearly indicated that the halcyon days of neutrality were finished. The collective message of these propaganda films highlighted Nazi aggression and chided Americans for their political complacency and military lassitude. In clear, blunt, and accusatory dialogue, Hitler's Germany was denounced as a threat to most nations, and their recent aggression, strong military forces, anti-Semitic laws, and undercover activities were reiterated on the screen. To a lesser degree, the other Axis members received the same treatment. Japanese imperial ambitions became the theme of MGM's *They Met in Bombay*, an adventure yarn that pitted Clark Gable, now posing as a British officer, against the Nipponese army in war-torn China. In Universal's *Burma Convoy*, iron-fisted Charles Bickford became the major force in the building of the famed Burma Road, as Japanese agents unsuccessfully attempted to thwart this construction work.

Another casualty to the increased tensions between the United States and Japan was the popular Mr. Moto series. Between 1937 and 1939, Twentieth Century-Fox produced eight B-titles about a Japanese sleuth, Mr. Moto, whose wily skills and inductive reasoning resembled the modus operandi of another Oriental detective, Charlie Chan. Portrayed by the Hungarian-born actor Peter Lorre, wearing exaggerated makeup, the B-films highlighted the Oriental's sagacity as he solved numerous murders in exotic locations. One episode, made in 1937, *Thank You, Mr. Moto*, heaped American praise on the sleuth for solving a difficult homicide case. In *Mr. Moto's Last Warning*, the friendly Japanese detective, now working at the Suez Canal, saved the day by reconciling France and England after a bitter misunderstanding, orchestrated by an unnamed foreign country, threatened to destroy the amity between these two powers. But, in 1939, as the international conflict worsened, these B-adventures became too risky for a major studio to continue; the Mr. Moto series was cancelled.

On another front, the Italians fared much better. While clearly a member of the Axis pact, Mussolini and his Black Shirt fascists unleashed their war machine against Ethiopia and, in Rome, more demands for territorial expansion were heralded by *Il Duce*. But their portrayal on the silver screen, in these pre-Pearl Harbor days, was nonexistent. Hollywood hadn't made up its mind regarding the treatment of a nation that was well-known for its sunny weather, bouncy music, delicious food, and zest for life.

Only one major film, United Artist's *Sundown*, mentioned Italy by name, and it sugarcoated their warmongering deeds. Directed by Henry Hathaway and released on October 20, 1941, *Sundown* depicted the adventures of some upper-crust British officers, stationed at a remote outpost in the African nation of Kenya. Always wary of a fifth column native uprising, the English troops maintained a cautious humanity with the Kenyan nationals and their isolated garrison was a model of democratic benevolence. The African natives, ever appreciative of their British rulers, came before the commandant with routine supplicant requests, and in the opening scene, a senior British major, Bruce Crawford, advanced the money to a Kenyan warrior so that the soldier could purchase his bride.

Included in the retinue serving the British officers was an Italian prisoner of war, Joseph Calleia, living under unusual circumstances. He was the cook for the entire officer corps and each day his singing emanated from the kitchen as he prepared succulent Italian recipes for everyone's enjoyment. Throughout the film, the happy-go-lucky Calleia proclaimed that he was not a prisoner, because he voluntarily surrendered to the English when hostilities broke out in Africa. In less vigorous moments, the Italian chef detailed his civilian life back in Italy. He was a college professor, a teacher of philosophy, and lamented that Mussolini forced him into the army, a situation he detested. At the first opportunity he escaped and came over to the Allied side because, like most of the Italian people living under the heels of the tyrant, he was not a fascist, just a victim of oppression. And while Germany was the clear villain in *Sundown*—the British army was called out to crush a Nazi surprise attack—another theme was the subtle exoneration of Italy from former bellicose acts.

By the fall of 1941, American audiences had seen dozens of these soft propaganda films warning about the Nazi menace, and while some congressional leaders advocated immediate military preparedness, a small but powerful group of isolationists in the lawmaking body, hoping to embarrass both Roosevelt and the interventionists, criticized the motion picture industry for its warmongering pictures. In October 1941, Hollywood found itself on the carpet when Senate Resolution 152 was enacted. This bill called for a thorough and complete investigation of any film propaganda. In the next few weeks, the major producers heard charges that their studios hammered away at the anti-Semitic policies of Hitler because many of the American stars and directors were Jewish—or refugees from European countries who were only interested in drawing America into a foreign war.

Other accusations cited the plethora of English actors in the industry, who were concerned with preserving the British empire for financial reasons. If the United Kingdom collapsed, it was reasoned, this lucrative film market for American exports would disappear. Over and over, the Hollywood moguls read indictments that their studios were capitalizing on international events purely for economic gain. Spearheaded by two isolationist senators, Gerald P. Nye and Bennett Champ, the resolution bill continued its unrelenting attack on Hollywood's intentions right up to the first week in December. Then, on a quiet Sunday afternoon, a time in history that now seems so "long ago and far away," the motion picture industry, after rehearsing in the wings for more than two years, was called on stage for the most important role of its career.

CHAPTER THREE

REMEMBER PEARL HARBOR: HOLLYWOOD ATTACKS JAPAN

". . . go back to your Jap garbage, where you belong"—
Victor McLaglen, as Major Bull Weed, in Twentieth Century-Fox's *China Girl*

On December 7, 1941, the Japanese Air Force attacked the American military base at Pearl Harbor and, with bombs and torpedoes, virtually destroyed most of the ships and aircraft moored at this strategic Hawaiian port. The following afternoon, President Roosevelt delivered his powerful Day of Infamy declaration, and now the United States, a nation that had teetered on the brink of involvement for many months, was officially at war with its Oriental adversary, as well as with Germany and Italy. Overnight, civilian and military organizations mobilized, setting up temporary defense measures, while ordering every American into the fray. This was going to be a long and difficult war and everyone, officials adjured, shared a responsibility, no matter how small, for final victory.

Hollywood, of course, was not caught flat-footed when Roosevelt's words resounded in the halls of Congress. For more than two years, most studios had produced dozens of antifascist films, warning of inevitable war with Nazi Germany, and now the industry's dire prophecy became a reality, not in Europe as these motion pictures often predicted, but at a faraway island in tranquil Hawaii. For the film industry, involved in the national emergency decree, this meant a shift in emphasis from a European enemy to an Oriental foe, a belligerent that, because of size, pigmentation, and facial differences, lent itself to caricature. Hours after the bombs settled at distant Pearl Harbor, the Hollywood cameras were loaded and ready to go.

The first anti-Japanese film to roll off the assembly line appeared on January 19, 1942, just forty-three days after the sneak attack. MGM's *A Yank on the Burma Road* was a typical B-production, hacked out in record time, to capitalize on the Japanese invasion threat in the vulnerable southeast Asian nation of Burma. The film starred Barry Nelson as a former New York City cab driver, now working as a mercenary delivering medical supplies over the tortuous Burma Road to nearby China. When news of Pearl Harbor reached his crew, the good-looking Nelson, assisted by comely Laraine Day, underwent an immediate metamorphosis from businessman to superpatriot. Confronted by landslides, bombed-out bridges, and Japanese forces, the ever-resourceful truck driver—personifying the best in American skill and daring—delivered his needed cargo to his Chinese allies.

As the first film to depict combat, *A Yank on the Burma Road,* like any other B-title, caused little commotion: the American hero and his girlfriend fell in love and lived happily ever after (even though the global conflict was raging), while the Chinese nationals smiled approvingly. As for the invading Japanese, they merely ran up hills into the onslaught of Barry Nelson's machine-gun bullets in the same way American Indians were routinely massacred in the numerous Western films produced in the 1930s. Without question, this first propaganda salvo stood on shaky ground.

Soon, an entire collection of B-titles appeared prompting the war against Japan. Monogram's *Black Dragons* put Oriental agents on American soil in a new version of the horror genre. This movie featured Bela Lugosi (famous for his Dracula role) as a Nazi plastic surgeon who changed the appearance of six Japanese to resemble six American entrepreneurs, in the hope that these "Americans" could undermine important defense work in their own factories. The FBI, always on guard, broke up this scheme. Twentieth Century-Fox's *Secret Agent of Japan* pitted British nationals against Japanese infiltrators operating in Shanghai, while handsome Preston Foster, interested only in selling oil to the highest bidder, looked the other way. When the war broke out, the American outcast, with some romantic help from Lynn Bari, realized his folly and began to wave the Red, White, and Blue.

Columbia's *Two Yanks in Trinidad,* with Pat O'Brien and Brian Donlevy, became a routine comedy-adventure yarn, depicting the unsavory antics of two petty hoodlums who inadvertently enlisted into the service. When news of Pearl Harbor reached their Trinidad base, the two gangsters-turned-patriots jumped into the fight, wrecking an Axis plan to blow up the fleet. Republic's *Remember Pearl Harbor* starred cowboy hero Red Barry, now in Uncle Sam's Army, who routed some enemy agents operating in the Philippines. In Twentieth Century Fox's *Little Tokyo, U.S.A.,* Preston Foster, as a Los Angeles lawman, exposed a Japanese spy ring working in the City of Angels.

However, a major film production, like gestation, required nine months of planning, and by August 1942, the first significant title, imbued with every element of propaganda, appeared. Unlike the B-quickies that were hacked out in a matter of weeks—many were a mere sixty minutes long and lacked any characterization— Paramount's *Wake Island* was a carefully crafted testimony, gleaned from the recent war headlines, to the Marine Corps for its brave but tragic defense of Wake Island, a small atoll in the Pacific between Hawaii and the Marianas. An all-star cast including Brian Donlevy, MacDonald Carey, Robert Preston, William Bendix, and Walter Abel, provided numerous subplots—comedy, romance, conflict between civilian and military, love of animals, and devotion to duty.

The story of *Wake Island* held no surprises because this military defense effort had ended in capitulation to the Japanese on December 22, 1941, just three weeks after the Pearl Harbor attack. In recreating the events of those last few days, Paramount walked a tenuous line between fact and fiction. Naturally, the subplots were contrived, but the loss of the island was a staggering blow for America's morale. Hollywood, however, would manipulate that surrender into strong film propaganda, containing every element necessary to motivate moviegoers to praise their country and laud the honor of its Marines, while debasing the bestial Japanese invaders. Like any well-defined motion picture, *Wake Island* had a slow start, gradually developing its characters, allowing the audience to fill in whatever was missing from the plot and form personal allegiances with certain actors. This technique, of course, is used every day in contemporary television soap operas.

It was early December 1942 as *Wake Island* began, and life on
this tiny but strategic military island appeared peaceful but
cautious. Commanding this post was Major Brian Donlevy, a
career officer whose fairness, strength, and acumen were re-
spected by all the jarheads. Frequently, the major looked the other
way when one of his charges committed some lighthearted
peccadillo; he was the typical father figure in propaganda films,
calling many of his younger privates ''son'' as he offered paternal
advice on numerous matters.

Complicating military life was the arrival of rough-and-tumble
Robert Preston, a hard-hitting construction boss in charge of a
civilian crew hired to build a new runway. For Preston, the only
important matter was adherence to the tight schedule required for
the completion of this airfield and his smart aleck remark—he
called his assignment a Boy Scout operation—underlined his
haughtiness. Within hours, the inevitable conflict arose between
the rash, loudmouthed civilian and the straight-arrow military
commander. Preston did not want to hear the major's argument
that cooperation, not grandstanding, would speed up the job. At
this point, a primary theme developed in the storyline—the
brashness of an individual who badmouthed any military edict.
Later, as in every propaganda film that employed this motif, the
recalcitrant would see the error of his ways and perform some
penitent act.

The plot moved along. Arriving on the island was a Japanese
emissary played by the omniscient Richard Loo, the Hawaiian-
born character actor, noted for his numerous roles as the Oriental
nemesis. Sitting at the dinner table with the Marines, this stealthy
ambassador praised President Roosevelt and toasted peace between the two nations. This ironic gesture—another form of
subtle propaganda—set the stage for the treachery that followed.

For the enlisted men, living in their open-air tents, a mood of
frivolity, not politics, existed, especially since one of their
number, William Bendix, had completed his service and was
mustering out. Planning to own a chicken farm and marry his
sweetheart, Mabel, when he returned to the mainland, the Brooklynite fought off the playful jabs of his buddies; in his spare time
he cared affectionately for his pet dog, Skipper. As in many
propaganda films, the presence of a mascot became a tangible

reminder of those emotions associated with less trying days back home.

Two other characters added to the Marines' diversity in *Wake Island:* MacDonald Carey, a young aviator, recently married and devoted to his young wife, and Mikhail Rasumny, a Polish refugee, now a sergeant in the Marine Corps, with unpleasant memories of his family back in Warsaw. But in a few days, everyone's life became disrupted as news of the Pearl Harbor attack flashed over the air waves. Within hours, elaborate defense plans were implemented to ward off the impending invasion and all differences were reconciled. The major and the contractor aligned and the civilian's expertise as a construction supervisor proved invaluable. William Bendix was reinstated into the Corps and, with his mascot, awaited the enemy attack, while the pursuit pilot, MacDonald Carey, stood poised, ready for his first sortie.

The inevitable soon happened. The Japanese fleet arrived but the initial enemy offensive was thwarted because Major Donlevy, employing what he called an "old Chinese trick," permitted the ships to advance close to the island before he ordered the Marines to fire. Thoroughly disoriented, the Nipponese admirals retreated, allowing the beleaguered Americans their first victory. But the outnumbered Marines could not maintain the advantage. Mac-Donald Carey was killed on his first air mission and, later, Navy pilot Damian O'Flynn was machine-gunned by a Japanese plane as he parachuted from his disabled aircraft. This propaganda scene, designed to create even greater hatred of the Japanese, was repeated in many other motion pictures.

Soon, all became hopeless for the American defenders. On their second attack, the Japanese landed their ground forces on the island and the small groups of Marines, now clustered in their private foxholes, were killed off by the sinister-looking enemies. Both Major Brian Donlevy, who earlier had radioed the Nipponese to "come and get us," and the construction boss also perished. The film ended on an upbeat note as a voice-over announced that the Marine defenders may have lost their first battle, but they would not lose the last.

As the first major American propaganda film of World War II, *Wake Island* was superb in every detail. The Japanese were two-dimensional caricatures of hate and destruction and in the

closing minutes were caricatured as wild-eyed simians bayonet-
ing helpless Marines. In another scene, a radio operator was shot
at point-blank range by a crazed Nipponese officer. Replete with
numerous acts of heroism and relieved with minor episodes of
comedy, the picture contained enough visceral appeal to urge the
American forces to victory, even though it was rooted in defeat.
When first shown at the Quantico Marine Base in Virginia, a large
audience of approximately 2,000 Marines stood up and cheered
the film, vowing retribution. *Wake Island* became an effective
vehicle for the Corps' enlistment drive, which was operating at
full force throughout the nation.

After *Wake Island* defined most of the tenets basic to the World
War II propaganda genre, other major films quickly followed,
continuing to glorify American prowess while vilifying Japanese
treachery in a manner that improved with each new production.
Republic's *Flying Tigers* depicted the adventures of the men of
the American Volunteer Group—the AVG—who fought the
Japanese in China before war had been declared. Starring John
Wayne as the legendary Pappy Boyington, the film opened on
September 23, 1942, a time when the war news from the Pacific
theater was still uncertain. As in any propaganda picture, the
storyline of *Flying Tigers* provided those important vicarious
thrills necessary to sustain or improve morale on the Home Front.

It was late autumn 1941 and the situation was grim for the
Chinese people as Japanese bombers methodically struck at their
cities, attacking hospitals and schools, killing helpless men,
women, and children. Immediately, the cruelty of the Nipponese
invaders was delineated and their wanton disregard for civilization became an ominous warning. Many other World War II
propaganda films contained elaborate scenes depicting the Japanese (but not the Nazis) bombing hospitals. A notable example
was found in *So Proudly We Hail* (nurse: *". . . they're machine-
gunning; they're strafing the hospitals! The beasts, the slimy
beasts"*). A similar scene appeared in *Cry Havoc* (nurse: *". . .
they're flying low and machine-gunning the open wards"*). Also,
in *China Sky* a mission hospital, operated by Dr. Randolph Scott,
was destroyed at regular intervals (Scott: *". . . yes, they hit the
hospital quite often"*). In *Somewhere I'll Find You*, newspaperman Clark Gable, stationed in Manila, wired his editor with a

similar report (Gable: *". . . the Nippos bombed Field Hospital Number Three"*).

However, in the midst of this strife, a small group of American mercenaries—the Flying Tigers—challenged the Japanese at every turn and the numerous dogfights end victoriously for the outnumbered volunteer group. As their commander, John Wayne cautioned his pilots, reiterating the importance of a team effort, not individual grandstanding, in winning a war (Wayne, to airmen: *". . . wait until you look back over your shoulder and see a Jap sitting on your tail in a ship you can't outmaneuver. Then, you'll see what I'm talking about"*).

This strong message was intended for an ill-disciplined, adventurous extrovert, good-looking John Carroll, who on more than one occasion broke formation for a solo attack. Later, a tragedy taught the loner the errors of grandstanding. On a routine patrol flight, Carroll's poor judgment caused his wingman to bail out over enemy territory and another cinematic theme was highlighted: the shooting down of an American flyer in his parachute. Carroll watched as the enemy Zero approached the hapless descending pilot, firing unrelentingly until the airman's limp body proclaimed his death. As the plane pulled away, the Japanese pilot's face was alive with glee and excitement. He had killed another American.

Being helplessly attacked by a Japanese airplane while parachuting to safety was another visual cliché commonly found in these propaganda films. Intended to rile up American audiences against their Oriental enemy, the efficacy of such scenes was obvious because it depicted the Japanese as savage, inhuman, sadistic—belligerents lacking any moral code or ideals. Probably the most violent act occurred in Howard Hawks' *Air Force* when an escaping airman, parachuting to a Pacific island, was first taunted by a Japanese pilot before being gunned down. This entire scene radicalized another loner, John Garfield, who like John Carroll in *Flying Tigers* now understood the group concept. Also, in *Wake Island* Navy pilot Damian O'Flynn was shot down in his parachute harness while a group of Marines watched in horror. They, too, became radicalized.

Now was the time for John Carroll's martyrdom. Ordered to blow up a strategic railroad bridge, Commander John Wayne took

off on this perilous mission in a cargo plane, only to find a
stowaway—his recalcitrant friend, John Carroll. Angry at first,
Wayne was placated by his pal's glib remarks. Soon, they reached
their destination and obliterated the target. However, enemy fire
hit their cabin and the two men prepared to bail out. Wayne
jumped first, but Carroll, now wounded and bleeding profusely,
returned to the cockpit and maneuvered the burning airplane into
a Japanese military train, destroying its cargo and killing many
enemy soldiers.

Here was another visual cliché; this time the emphasis was
heroism. Returning to the cockpit after the last crew member had
parachuted, in order to perform some glorified deed, was a common
scene in Hollywood propaganda films. Other examples included
John Garfield in *Air Force* and Spencer Tracy in *A Guy Named Joe*.
In a similar vein, lone pilots frequently crashed their aircraft into
military targets. Rosalind Russell, in *Flight for Freedom,* dove into
the ocean so that her martyr's death would enable Navy fliers to
photograph Japanese military installations. In *Wing and a Prayer,*
Ensign Kevin O'Shea plunged his pursuit plane into the path of a
Japanese torpedo to save his aircraft carrier from being destroyed; in
The North Star, Comrade Dana Andrews crashed his damaged
airplane into a row of Nazi tanks to prevent an attack on his
Ukrainian village; while CRAF pilot James Cagney, in *Captains of
the Clouds,* steered head-on into a German aircraft to save his
squadron. In *Pilot No. 5,* Airman Franchot Tone plowed his pursuit
plane onto the deck of a Japanese aircraft carrier. And Lt. George
Murphy in *Bataan* rammed his crippled aircraft into a strategic
Japanese-held bridge, killing many enemy soldiers.

Even though a popular B-studio produced *Flying Tigers,* it was
a major propaganda film by any standards. The volunteer airmen
represented a cross-section of everything that was wholesome and
their eclectic backgrounds reaffirmed the collective, group concept. Since the United States drew its manpower from every
corner of the land, all the fighting components were heterogeneous. John Wayne's team revealed the squadron's diversity: one
man was from Brooklyn, another from Texas. One airman came
from Maine, another from Michigan. There were, however, no
Black pilots flying for John Wayne.

On the other hand, the Chinese people were strong allies, doing
their part to rid their land of the Japanese scourge. To emphasize

this point, a letter of praise and thanks, addressed to the American people and "signed" by Generalissimo Chiang Kai-shek, was included in the opening titles. This document—an open admission from the Chinese government—acknowledged the role of the Flying Tigers.

Another propaganda film that highlighted the collective nature of the men assigned to aerial combat was Warner Brothers' *Air Force,* a modern-day flying epic that depicted the adventures of a lone B-17 bomber from the time it left San Francisco, on December 6, 1942, until it arrived, days later, at a South Pacific island, poised for its offense against Japan. As in *Flying Tigers,* the crew members represented a cross-section of American life, education, and religion, with each man responsible for an important job to keep the aircraft functioning.

The opening scene—depicting this crew on a routine flight from California to Hawaii, checking and rechecking their positions, making routine radio calls for aviation information, and verifying the date (it is December 6th)—symbolically portrayed America at peace. The mood on the aircraft was tranquil, almost lethargic, with each man reflecting on his hopes and ambitions. The stereotypical bad boy—this time played by John Garfield—personified the same chip-on-the-shoulder attitude exhibited by James Cagney (*The Fighting 69th*) and John Carroll (*Flying Tigers*), annoying others by bragging about their own superiority. A senior sergeant was happy to learn that his Army Corps son was now a fighter pilot, somewhere in the Pacific; a Jewish corporal maintained the aircraft in typical tiptop condition. While the Wasps commanded the large aircraft, named *Mary Ann,* the entire community was wholesome, dedicated, even innocent, and the propaganda message was subtle and unobtrusive—Americans were a happy breed, wanting only contentment and tranquillity.

This Norman Rockwell idyll quickly disintegrated as garbled radio messages, coming out of Pearl Harbor on this bright Sunday morning, described the sneak attack in progress. Forced to alter their course, the airmen finally arrived at a safe island and emerged from the security of their aircraft's womb into the hostile, belligerent world of combat. The Japanese, of course, were responsible for this war, but now the crew confronted the high cost of their country's ill-preparedness and political naiveté. A Marine officer blamed the military defeat on the Japanese fifth columnists, who destroyed strategic ground installations when the first bombs were dropped. A Japanese airplane killed an American pilot parachuting from his damaged aircraft, and enemy snipers chipped away at the aircrew at regular intervals. But, like America itself, the *Mary Ann* would prevail. True, many lives were lost—the senior pilot expired in a deathbed scene as he deliriously called for takeoff instructions that his crew cautiously called out—but like the legendary phoenix, the Air Corps would rise again.

As another major propaganda film, *Air Force* employed many stock devices to show American wholesomeness, while condemning the Japanese treachery. A young crew member introduced his mother to his commander in a scene right out of an Andy Hardy movie. This pilot, the typical father figure, reassured the woman of the righteousness of the youth's place on the flight team. Later, the senior sergeant's placid world fell apart when he learned that his son was one of the first pilots to die during the attack. Saddened by this news, the sergeant (the veteran character actor, Harry Carey) demonstrated dignity and pride, rather than remorse. As for the Nipponese, a barrage of racial epithets pervaded the film: "*. . . fried Nip going down.*"

There was little attempt to assuage the blatant hatred of the Japanese. News accounts depicting their atrocities were widely disseminated and each story offered more proof of Japanese animality. As far as the script writers were concerned, the Japanese were savage and inhuman, a foe that needed eradication. This theme— the bestiality of the Japanese—was the storyline of MGM's *Bataan,* a tragedy taken from then-current headlines. Similar in content to *Wake Island*—another last stand picture— *Bataan* was more graphic about this U.S. surrender. Historically, this tiny garrison located in the Philippines, capitulated soon after Pearl Harbor, resulting in the infamous Death March, an event recorded two years later in RKO's *Back to Bataan.* This type of propaganda, the victory-through-defeat motif, was very effective.

The opening scenes in *Bataan* restated the wantonness of the invaders. A Japanese Zero dove toward a crowd of civilians, shooting indiscriminately, and then strafed an ambulance, destroying it. An American GI cradled an infant in his arms—the mother was dead—harboring the baby from the numerous bullets that were ricocheting everywhere. An elderly couple, staggering from a hospital, was felled by a bomb explosion. Another wounded soldier, his eyes bandaged, groped along helplessly until a burning wooden beam crushed him; he, too, was dead. Confusion and bedlam suffused the entire village. Adding to the disarray was the rapid retreat of U.S. Army forces, now ordered to a new battlefront.

Buying time became a primary military objective in *Bataan* as a combat officer explained that a rear guard defense was necessary so that General MacArthur could escape to Australia. A ragtag group—including a Navy musician, a professional boxer, a tanker, a demolition expert, a seminary student, a cook, a signal man, and a chemical expert—became a special unit, ordered to blow up a bridge. But this small group could not overcome the superior Japanese strength and each day the squad lost one member after another, fallen heroes downed by banzai charges, infiltration, and sniper fire. In these harrowing days, each man— they were the standard ethnic mix of propaganda films—found new strength in his nation, his President, and the American way-of-life. Each death chipped away at the cohesiveness of the defense and the final scenes, depicting a half-crazed Robert Taylor, firing his machine-gun from the hip and calling the Japanese racist names, reaffirmed that victory was also found in defeat.

As a morale-building film, *Bataan* contained every ingredient possible to glorify the American cause. A fighter pilot rammed his aircraft into a strategic bridge to prevent enemy forces from crossing. Another GI was tortured by the Japanese, his mutilated body thrown in the dense jungle. This same scene, depicting Japanese cruelty in the underbrush, was used in *Marine Raiders*. In that movie Captain Robert Ryan found one of his squad members tied to a tree, tortured to death by the Japanese.

Religious prayers and martial music emphasized the American value system: in one poignant moment, a dying soldier made his confession in his native Spanish; another GI gave his supply of quinine to a wounded friend. This homogeneity in *Bataan* established a cross-section of cultures, mores, and values, suggesting that the Pacific war was the people's war. This meant that a Black man, Kenneth Epps, became an equal member of the squad and his presence exemplified the democratic principles espoused by the propaganda. Historically, of course, the military service was not integrated and Black men were routinely relegated into segregated units performing menial tasks.

Basically, Black people did not fare well in many of the propaganda films and glaring examples of racism were common. In *Cry Havoc,* a coquettish nurse justified her flirtation with a married man by reminding her tormentors that she was free, White, and twenty-one. Even *Casablanca* fell short of racial harmony. Entering the Cafe Américaine, Ingrid Bergman noticed the piano player, Sam, and inquired about the name of the "boy" playing the instrument. Throughout the film, Sam (Dudley Wilson) was the loyal servant/musician for Bogart, and on every occasion referred to him as "Boss." In *Crash Dive* a Black mess helper, Ben Carter, played an updated military Stepin Fetchit role; watching the White sailors rub black greasepaint over their face, in preparation for a late night raid, he found humor in his exemption from this camouflage.

What was the purpose of *Bataan?* On one level, the film was a realistic attempt to show a military defeat. In its glorification of the heroics of this small squad, a microcosm of everything noble and brave, the propaganda message was subtle, but constant: the first battle was lost, but this tragedy allowed American forces, under the command of General MacArthur, to reassemble. It was a matter of time before the Marines took offensive action to revenge the Japanese onslaught. On another level, *Bataan* hammered away at a primary theme—the nature of the enemy. The Japanese committed one atrocity after another and their bestiality would rile stateside audiences every time. Americans being captured, brutally tortured and painfully killed by the Japanese was a common feature of wartime films. The most gruesome episode occurred in Warner Brothers' *Objective Burma,* when Captain Errol Flynn discovered the mutilated corpses of one of his squads in an Indo-China hut.

Another title that conformed to the OWI philosophy—a directive that required small groups to display cultural diversity—was Twentieth Century-Fox's elaborate paean to the Marine Corps, *Guadalcanal Diary.* Based on the best-selling book by Richard Tregaskis, the film was a half-true, half-fictional version of an important invasion, in August 1942, of a South Pacific island— the first step on the slow but steady road to victory. Unlike *Bataan,* this propaganda film concentrated on the offensive actions of the Corps, culminating with the capture of this enemy stronghold.

Permeating the many combat scenes in *Guadalcanal Diary* was an effective religious motif, demonstrating that while the Marines were forced to fight a dirty war, they had not surrendered their ethical values. Similar in concept to *The Fighting 69th* (but without the malcontent role), this film traced the adventures of a Roman Catholic priest, Preston Foster, wearing olive drab khakis, as he administered God's word to the faithful, now fighting for the preservation of their Judeo-Christian beliefs.

It is no coincidence that *Guadalcanal Diary* began on a lazy Sunday morning, in July 1942, aboard a Navy transport ship where a large assortment of Marines—the pride of American prowess—relaxed informally in cramped conditions that, surprisingly, bothered no one. They were a mixed bag, all living in harmony: some read, others wrote letters back home to sweethearts or mothers; still others discussed baseball, former girlfriends, good old stovetop cooking, or simply horsed around. Off to the side, a nondenominational service attracted hundreds of followers and popular songs resounded in harmonic unison: ''Rock of Ages'' and the cowboy ballad, ''Home on the Range,'' displayed a wholesome, gee-whiz timbre as this all-male, all-White chorus reaffirmed the glories of the Almighty and nature.

One leatherneck, with a strong baritone voice, bragged about his musical training: his father, a cantor back home, taught him to sing for his neighborhood synagogue. The mood was tranquil, democratic, even antiseptic, and the omniscient narrator reminded the audience that here was America at is pristine best; the Marines squeezed onto this troop vessel were a heterogeneous lot, coming from every state in the Union, subscribing to various religious faiths, and each with myriad interests and talents. In short, they represented the eclectic nature of the republic itself.

What are some of the propaganda elements in this lazy, pastoral setting? First, this peaceful scene on the ship—not one man was hostile toward another—reiterated the doctrine that Americans were not warmongers, unfriendly, or belligerent. As a nation of diversified people, they preferred to live in peace with their neighbors, as the lazy pace aboard this ship demonstrated. Most of the Marines seemed innocent, naive, clean-cut and determined. It was their responsibility to put an end to Japanese expansionism.

Later, deep inside the ship's windowless hull, the enlisted men, oblivious to the annoyances of tight bunk space, maintained this harmony. A solo harmonica wailed out a current jitterbug tune, and two Marines playfully danced to the beat while their pals cheered them on. Here, like the crew of the *Mary Ann* in *Air Force,* these ground pounders were safe inside the womb of military security, content in the knowledge that their leaders would not fail them.

As for the officers, they displayed wisdom, understanding, acumen, and fairness. The senior colonel longed for a copy of ''L'il Abner,'' the popular Al Capp comic strip, so he could learn about Mammy Yokum's latest escapade. Two other officers reflected on their undergraduate life together and this taut scene delineated subtly the social stratification of the Marine Corps. The leaders—the officers—were college graduates, chosen for their intelligence, while the enlisted men represented lower-class America, drawing its manpower from every working-class occupation found in civilian life. The officers bunked two men to a room, while dozens of lower-ranked Marines were jammed into a tight living space down below, but this only elaborated the propaganda proviso: officers needed ''room'' to think, so they would not make any mistakes in combat, while the enlisted men, their needs somewhat prosaic, required only a safety valve environment to let off steam. Since neither group objected to these arrangements, they were, *ipso facto,* a tangible symbol of *semper fidelis.*

Even though space was at a premium for the enlisted men, there was still room for their canine mascot Suey an animal entrusted to the tender care of former Flatbush cab driver, William Bendix. This small detail—keeping a pet dog as a mascot—was a propaganda device utilized many times in other World War II films. In *Counter-Attack,* the Russian dog, Marsha, parachuted into battle with the Soviet troops and later saved the life of Comrade Paul Muni, by leading the Russians to the cellar where he was buried; other dogs included Ahab, the mascot in *The Story of G.I. Joe;* Skipper, the canine pet in *Wake Island;* and Tripoli, the bomber crew's charge in *Air Force.* Another dog, Little Joe, was cared for by the airmen in *God Is My Co-Pilot* and possessed certain olfactory skills (''. . . *Little Joe, here, can smell a Jap ten miles off* ''). The feline world was represented in *Action in the*

North Atlantic, where Peaches, the pet cat was first rescued, but later drowned, the result of Nazi hostilities.

Just as the Marines' mascot Suey in *Guadalcanal Diary* represented the former civilian world of home and hearth, other icons were present. William Bendix concocted a unique blackjack he called the "Flatbush Issue," a weapon he would put to good use, while a Marine officer lined his helmet with a wholesome portrait of his wife and family. Later, this headpiece, almost a religious shrine, rolled into the sand, after a Japanese sniper's bullet ended his life. To add to the propaganda value of this poignant death, Japanese soldiers rushed out of their jungle hiding place to bayonet the lifeless body.

Still, at the heart of *Guadalcanal Diary* was the characterization of the military chaplain, Father Preston Foster, whose good nature and easygoing personality endeared him to virtually everyone. A Notre Dame graduate, the genial priest astounded the faithful with some fancy heel-and-toe footwork as he pranced the Irish Jig before a cheering crowd of Marines who were suffering from some invasion day jitters. Later, he volunteered for the first attack wave on Guadalcanal Beach because, he explained, *". . . that's when I'll be needed the most."* His talents seemed inexhaustible as he ministered to the injured, performed the last rites, and helped the medical team with rudimentary first aid. His religious teachings—his numerous homilies and prayers punctuated *Guadalcanal Diary*—rubbed off on more than one Marine. In an elaborate foxhole scene, a group of harried marines crouched close to the ground in their makeshift shelter as Japanese bombs fell precariously nearby. For William Bendix, the simple soul from Brooklyn, the ardent baseball fan of the "Bums," this enemy air attack became a moment of unabashed piety. His short but cogent prayer, imploring the Almighty for deliverance, redefined the nature of propaganda.

But there is more to *Guadalcanal Diary* than religious inculcation. Once on shore the leathernecks, whose task was to establish a beachhead and secure the island, confronted the daily drudgery of warfare. Their Japanese adversary—a ruthless and slimy enemy, hiding in trees, coiled like poisonous snakes, ready to strike—created an atmosphere of nervous tension. Where were the Japanese? Why didn't they come out and fight? These two questions were on the Americans' minds as they moved cautiously inland. Initially, some random contact was made; a deserted Japanese village was located, complete with leftover food still on the stoves. Then the suspense abated as enemy snipers slowly emerged, their evil looking faces, reflected by moonlight, caricatures of subhuman life. As monkeys clustered in an arboreal setting, so did the Japanese. The enemy, the Marines averred, were not civilized humans, they were animals, and as such needed exterminating.

But how primitive were the Japanese? Were they really a prehistoric culture, devoid of refinement and humanism? To find out the Marines must engage in combat. One small squad was decimated after a scrawny Japanese prisoner—on the pretext of arranging a mass surrender—led the Americans into an ambush. The entire scene resembled the last moments of *Bataan* as, one by one, the Marines were killed off, their bodies left lying placidly in the hot sand. While young Anthony Quinn, cast as the energetic Hispanic, survived the massacre—he ran into the ocean and swam to safety—the rest of the Americans could not rest in peace because the Japanese rushed forward and, again, defiled the bodies with numerous bayonet thrusts. The savage nature of the Japanese, devoid of any decency, was blatantly revealed in this small episode. Not only did the Japanese slaughter the Americans, they sacrificed their own soldier, the man leading the Marines into the ambush. He was a nonentity.

The propaganda value of this scene was significant because it established the need for retribution. The Marines took the offensive and located the Japanese hiding in some natural caves. Like simians, the enemy crouched deep inside these large orifices, safe from a frontal attack. But the Marines were trained in all facets of jungle warfare. Employing precision teamwork, the Americans lowered explosives into these caves; moments later, all the Japanese were dead. The final victory belonged to the leathernecks.

As an important propaganda film, *Guadalcanal Diary* touched on other issues beside combat and victory. Baseball, as American as apple pie, represented the ever-present ties with life back in the neighborhood. During the 1942 World Series, the Yankees and the Cardinals squared off for the fall classic and every Marine gathered around the short-wave radio to cheer for his team. Contrasted to the business of war, this scene reaffirmed the basic values of Americans and, in broader terms, presented another reason for fighting the Japanese.

In the same vein, the issue of morale became a sounding board in *Guadalcanal Diary,* especially important was mail call. During a welcomed respite, the postal system caught up with the squad and each man was elated as envelopes were torn open from friends, relatives, and sweethearts back home. Some letters were amusing; others, kind and supportive. One letter, in particular, was a moving account of the civilians donating blood at the local high school. Off to the side, however, a sad episode developed in the middle of all this jubilation; one Marine, angry and lonesome, walked away dejected because there was no mail for him. As propaganda, this scene was pitched toward movie audiences and its message was implicit: write to your serviceman, today! Also, remember to give blood!

On the other hand, *Guadalcanal Diary's* main propaganda value lay in its emphasis on the nature of the dirty war in the Pacific theater and its reminder that the Japanese, holed up in their pillboxes or aloft in the trees, were a tenacious, inhuman enemy. The Marine Corps, the first to fight, the message went, were responsible for capturing every island on the way to Tokyo. Guadalcanal became the first step on that long road to victory, and others would follow.

Another film that continued the adulation of the leatherneck's adventures was Universal's *Gung Ho,* a half-fiction, half-fact account of Colonel Carlson's daring raid on the Japanese-held fortress at Makin Island, on August 17, 1942. Similar, in many ways to *Guadalcanal Diary,* this motion picture paired Randolph Scott and J. Carrol Naish as two father-figure officers who took raw recruits stationed in San Diego and, after rigorous training in the hot California sun, turned them into a collective fighting machine, worthy of the title, Marine Raiders—men imbued with an esprit de corps summed up in two Chinese words: gung ho (working together).

As another flag-waving film adhering to the OWI directives, *Gung Ho* presented every conceivable reason American boys were fighting in the South Pacific. According to Colonel Randolph Scott, the Japanese plan for world conquest festered for many years prior to the Pearl Harbor attack, and most Americans were too complacent to understand the expansionist policies involving China. Now that the Japanese had seized many strategic islands in the Pacific, the U.S. must pay for its shortsightedness—it must send the Marines into a jungle war, requiring specialized training, to drive these Oriental invaders out.

As volunteers for this daring raid, the Marines were scrupulously picked: one man was an ordained minister who believed the Japanese needed eradicating; another wanted to revenge his brother's death at Pearl Harbor; a third fought both in Spain and Greece and hated all fascists; another was anxious for a fight, while one somber-faced Marine wanted only to avenge his sister's violation during the Rape of Manila. Another answer was more succinct: *". . . I just don't like Japs."*

But the two officers were the leading players in this military drama and their paternal roles were everywhere evident. Throughout the stateside training, the young Marines referred to their commander, Randolph Scott, as the "Old Man," and generally stared in awe at his mere presence. In reciprocal fashion, Colonel Scott called his troops "boys," restating the father/son motif, and rewarded them for exemplary conduct: (*". . . sit down, boys, make yourselves comfortable, the smoking lamp is lit"*). On a daily basis, Scott emphasized the man-to-man equality of his outfit, bragging that officers and enlisted personnel shared the same lodging and meals and that suggestions from any rank were welcomed. During one of his homiletic lectures, Scott averred that some Marines would eventually die for democracy, but for now they were to practice according to these principles: when in battle, do the unexpected; go one step further to outwit the Japanese; and always remember—gung ho.

As for his second-in-charge, Lt. J. Carrol Naish, his paternal relationship with the volunteers was equally strong, but as a junior officer, he was more relaxed and frequently offered moral advice. His name, Lt. Cristoforos (Christ), was more than coincidental given the underlying religious messages found in *Gung Ho.* In *Guadalcanal Diary,* another junior officer, Captain Cross (crucifixion) played a similar role—dispensing aphoristic military instructions to his younger charges—and his death, by a Japanese ambush on a pristine beach, established his martyrdom.

Soon, the basic training ended and the dramatis personae were picked up for a lightning one-day raid. The Marines selected represented the diversity of American life and, in accordance with

OWI standards, the typical Hollywood stereotypes: one of these men, "Pig Iron" (his legal name was never mentioned), was a streetwise millworker from a large city; another volunteer, dubbed "Rube," was a farmland hayseed who spent much of his time dreaming of the four hogs his family owned; "Frankie Montana" was another Brooklynite, who learned his marksmanship by tossing bottles at umpires officiating at Ebbets Field; "Transport" was an easygoing Jewish top sergeant, whose malapropisms added levity to many situations; and, lastly, to supply some minor comic relief, two stepbrothers (David Bruce and Noah Beery, Jr.), competed for the affection of a toothsome girl who lived near the training base. The sweetheart—Grace McDonald—never made up her mind regarding these suitors.

So far the storyline of *Gung Ho* followed a semidocumentary format—similar to the *March of Time* series—utilizing a voice-over narrator explaining all facets of Marine training. With methodical precision, the leathernecks studied the ruthless nature of the enemy they would soon face. Show no compassion, they learned, kill or be killed! Destroy the Japanese; put an end to their warmongering policies. This motif—Japanese barbarism—was a central idea in most propaganda films and the narration in *Gung Ho* offered a tangible reminder that the Marine Corps was keeping the enemy from invading the California beaches. This homage was another theme throughout the film and, combined with the all-for-one motif, reiterated the righteousness of this raiding party.

But the high-spirited Marines contained their own vulnerability. Trained to fight a jungle war, they first had to enter the unknown world of submarine travel and the spatial demands of this trip, restricting each man to mere inches of movement, chipped away at morale and discipline. As an elaborate earth mother snugly nurturing its human cargo, the underwater vessel's slow travel speed contrasted sharply with the high level of intensity these men displayed. Like coiled wires ready to spring, the leathernecks wanted to seize the island and destroy the enemy. Instead, they were thwarted by the monotonous, almost lethargic mood created by unnatural confinement in small bunks, bundled one on top of another. To assuage this problem, the two father figures slunk along the narrow passages, and their paternalistic banter reaffirmed the doctrine that, as Raiders, they would endure all discomfort. True, Marines were not meant to be huddled into such incommodious quarters, but when they were released the spirit of gung ho would prevail.

As a propaganda device, American vulnerability worked well because it confirmed a basic human instinct: success is always achieved by the forces that are outnumbered or that have to function in difficult circumstances. When confronted by an adversary that clearly represents evil, the opposing side, no matter how small, will win because of the righteousness of its cause. In *Gung Ho,* the Marines took pride in reiterating that only 200 men were involved in this surprise raid against an enemy that probably numbered close to 1,000. This meant that American forces must perform admirably—they must fight harder, run faster, and think quickly—because the survival of their country, their homes, their families now rested on their shoulders. The Japanese started the war, but the leathernecks would finish it.

When the Raiders finally reached Makin Island, they gathered in small rafts and paddled slowly but efficaciously towards the unfriendly shores. As knights in shining armor, led by their own paladin, the Marines embarked on another messianic task. Reaching the shoreline, they jumped out of their small boats and lay flat on the warm sand in a scene that suggested atonement for the carnage that was inevitable. Like the Marines in *Guadalcanal Diary,* these Americans were cautious but determined and as they quickly moved into the interior, the propaganda value was obvious. Where were the Japanese? Why didn't they attack? The tension grew until, finally, the enemy appeared. Hiding in treetops or submerged in pillboxes, the Japanese, wearing thick eyeglasses, resembled simians from some antediluvian time zone and as they fired upon the Marines, their wide-open mouths and their barbaric yelps defined their primitive characterization, elaborating their subhuman qualities. Adding to the caricature were the Japanese officers, little men dressed fastidiously, waving their samurai swords in the air like circus performers, lacking real authority or competency.

In contrast, the young Americans performed with precision and organization and slowly the strategic points were destroyed. The Marines' mission—"not a Jap left alive on the island"—reached culmination after Randolph Scott employed some military subterfuge that caused Japanese pilots to fire upon their own troops. As propaganda, this small scene was superb. While the Marines fought the hidden enemy deep in the jungle, two leathernecks painted the American flag on a deserted Japanese command post, and after feigning a retreat the Marines drew the enemy back to this area. When the Zeroes appeared, they opened fire on this building, destroying their own troops.

The implication of such an attack was obvious: Japanese soldiers possessed such poor vision that they could not distinguish friend from foe. As enemies, they were reduced to cartoon figures with large teeth and bulging, thick lenses which distorted not only their faces but their view of reality. Even in *Flying Tigers,* one of the pilots reminded his buddies that he *". . . didn't take this job to be a target for a bunch of four-eyed Japs."* While in *Guadalcanal Diary,* William Bendix, a salty leatherneck, fired his weapon into the underbrush, ostensibly at a Nipponese soldier: *". . . I could have sworn I saw those buck teeth."*

While the enemy resembled caricatures, the Marines were dignified and merciful. But their kindness backfired after three haggard Japanese surrendered but then fired a concealed machine-gun, killing one American. Later, another Japanese, playing possum in a medical area, attempted to shoot the medical officer; his effort was thwarted by some deft knife throwing by Robert Mitchum. Both examples carried the same propaganda message: do not trust the Japanese, do not believe their false promises of surrender. A similar scene in *Guadalcanal Diary,* in which Japanese soldiers wanted to give up, also resulted in the death of unsuspecting Marines, and the same show-no-quarter message was restated. In another instance, when the Raiders were pinned down in a ditch as an enemy sniper in a pillbox fired at them, a young private, Harold Landon, quickly removed his shirt and gear, pulled the pins out of two hand-grenades with his teeth, zigzagged through the jungle, and hurled the two explosives, destroying the enemy fortification. The motive was clear: death to all Japanese.

Finally, the objectives were completed: the installations destroyed and the enemy decimated. The Marines buried their casualties and evacuated their wounded back to the submarine, moments before a Japanese invasion fleet arrived. Safely under the water, back inside the cavernous womb that now nurtured the victorious leathernecks, the two father figures became more subdued, even demurred as they eulogized the fallen men left on this small island. The closing scene added to the propaganda message. Here, Randolph Scott performed an ecclesiastical role: *". . . it is for us at this moment, with the memory of the sacrifice of our brothers still fresh, to dedicate our hearts, our minds and our bodies to the great task that is still ahead."* Adding to this apostrophe were the musical strains of "The Battle Hymn of the Republic," played in a martial beat, as the Marines, proud of their success, beamed at each other.

This ending, resembling the stereotypical cowboy hero riding-off-into-the-sunset motif, was the trademark of director Ray Enright. As a filmmaker, Enright's reputation rested on his many formula-type B-Western yarns, and in many ways *Gung Ho* exhibited the style, texture, and composition of this genre. Like a typical Western, *Gung Ho* pitted the forces of good versus evil, but in a more dramatic setting. In the stereotypical cowboy movie, the man-in-white always won because his cause was noble and just. Here, in a 1942 Pacific island shoot-out, the men in khaki represented the same virtues.

If Westerns were altered into propaganda films, why not update a swashbuckling tale into a modern naval adventure? If the Marines could fight the Japanese on remote islands, the Navy, likewise, could dispatch a lone ship out on the high seas, in search of the Japanese armada and, after some cat-and-mouse tactics, eventually destroy it. This was the theme of Twentieth Century-Fox's *Wing and a Prayer,* an elaborate tribute to the sailors who manned the decks of an aircraft carrier during the precarious days right after the Pearl Harbor attack. Released in July 1944, Henry Hathaway's *Wing and a Prayer* became a major motion picture that dramatized naval operations on a large scale, culminating with victory at the Battle of Midway.

As a propaganda film, *Wing and a Prayer* fulfilled the OWI rules depicting the portrayal of naval officers involved with command decisions, individuals who understood that "heavy is the head that wears the crown" and the responsibility that a ship's captain must bear. To highlight this idea, much of the footage was shot aboard the U.S.S *Yorktown,* a newly commissioned aircraft carrier, during its shakedown cruise in the Caribbean. The result was Hollywood's interpretation of the microcosm that is life aboard a large ship, with hundreds of sailors from all walks of life clustered together, and functioning as a fighting machine under the directive of a single man, whose daily orders were actually life-and-death instructions to the pilots who flew the torpedo planes against the Japanese. Unlike other films that depicted the intricacies of a small group working together in cramped conditions—*Air Force* or *Bataan,* for example—*Wing and a Prayer* emphasized the larger picture of seafaring life, sprawled out to resemble a cinematic diorama.

The plot of *Wing and a Prayer* developed along traditional lines. The opening scenes depicted America's worst naval defeat, Pearl Harbor, and the final action produced an elaborate victory at Midway, where the Japanese fleet was routed. As propaganda, this type of thesis/antithesis arrangement restated a basic American principle—we lost the first battle, but not the last. This point was irrevocable: as the film averred, it was the Japanese sneak attack that started the war in the Pacific. The American Navy, however, would finish it.

To highlight this point, the movie started with the typical voice-over narrative creating a documentary atmosphere—the same technique that *Gung Ho* and *Guadalcanal Diary* employed. This way, the needed exposition developed and the authoritative tone for the next ninety minutes was established. The omniscient, unseen voice summarized the bitter defeat of December 7th, explaining that one aircraft carrier escaped and now that vessel—safe on the high seas—had a new mission carefully crafted by naval intelligence: it must reappear at various checkpoints to create the illusion that several ships were on the ocean. Under no circumstances should the carrier take an offensive posture—it must not attack the Japanese.

For the pilots stationed on the carrier this order was anathema because it suggested vulnerability. Why not fight, they asked; what were we waiting for? How much longer could we take this? In charge of this squadron was Lt. Commander Dana Andrews, an easygoing individual who instilled in his flyers the importance of obeying military directives. For Andrews, this became a daily chore because his airmen, according to OWI requirements, represented a cross-section of American culture and values and this heterogeneity was, naturally, a complex matter when men (without women) were placed aboard an elaborate fighting machine in the middle of an ocean during a major war. Initially, the squadron did not fare well with Commander Don Ameche—one pilot ignored the wave-off signal from the flight deck and landed precariously—but this only demonstrated the nature of propaganda. Show Americans making mistakes; this way, they learned from their errors and, later, developed maturity and acumen.

Other problems frustrated this mammoth vessel: a young turret gunner confided that he was underage when he enlisted but his words fell on deaf ears because his buddy, a flight mechanic, confessed to being overage. While the two men worried about their birth certificates being scrutinized, another pilot suffered from fainting spells and faced the possibility of being grounded. But this was the nature of the American response to Pearl Harbor—age and health were unimportant; the real issue was not personal comfort, but the eradication of the Japanese.

True, there was some pleasure and camaraderie aboard ship: one sailor grew some vegetables, using chemicals and Yankee know-how; another flyer was a Hollywood movie star and the crew delighted in reading his fan mail and hearing his stories about the leading ladies he kissed. But overshadowing this frivolity was the domineering presence of the quasi-martinet Don Ameche, the officer who enforced military regulations to the letter. Here was the essence of warfare—battles were won through planning and discipline, and the commander, alone, bore this responsibility. If isolation was the price for victory, the commander paid his dues.

So "stoicism" became another word in the lexicon of film propaganda, standing alongside "heroism," "bravery," and "martyrdom." As Don Ameche realized, this trait was unavoidable if orders were to be obeyed. Occasionally, his human side surfaced—he lamented the necessity of writing letters to the relatives of deceased sailors—but as a leader he sent airmen on dangerous assignments, ever mindful they might not return.

But patience was eventually rewarded and after interminable weeks of roaming the ocean, the fortunes of war were reversed— the attack order was sounded. Immediately, the crew became a finely tuned instrument, transmogrified from its frustration into a squadron ready for action; the Battle of Midway had started. Navy aircraft, their propellers straining, flew off the carrier decks, heading for the Japanese fleet miles away, while anxious sailors scoured the sky, watching for enemy Zeroes. The momentum reached crescendo when the first hostile airplane was spotted.

For Commander Don Ameche, the primary concern was to protect the ship against the Japanese attack planes emerging out of the morning sunlight. Like miniature beeps on contemporary electronic games, the enemy Zeroes descended towards the lone carrier but were destroyed in midair moments before they reached their intended target. Here was another component of effective propaganda. Audiences sat in movie theaters for many reasons, including the vicarious thrill of huddling with a gun crew, lining up another bandit in the cross hairs, and blasting the enemy aircraft to smithereens, seconds before it crashed on the flight deck.

For many viewers, watching *Wing and a Prayer* was tantamount to playing a 1940s pinball machine game, because the rules were the same: do not allow the enemy to penetrate your defense, safeguard the perimeter, be alert at all times. Occasionally, an enemy aircraft hit the ship, but the response was quick and heroic—American sailors rescued their buddies and extinguished all fires. In human terms, the price was high to preserve the ship. For Ensign Kevin O'Shea it became a sacrifice for God and country; he rammed his aircraft into the path of a torpedo which was heading straight for the carrier's hull.

But this was how democratic life functioned aboard a large ship whose mission was to keep the Japanese from invading California. A certain ethos developed, with attack pilots seen in terms that resembled apotheosis, while the aircraft carrier itself was revered, nurtured and protected no matter how great the cost. Self-sacrifice was part of the scheme of things aboard this giant vessel; ramming a Japanese torpedo heading for the unprotected bow was a ritualistic obligation that flyers accepted.

Similarly, when another pilot became lost while airborne, he observed radio silence because communication would reveal the ship's position to the enemy. In this case, the airman understood that he would exhaust his gasoline supply and crash into the sea. Later, two of the three crew members were rescued; the one casualty was accepted because, again, the carrier—a tangible symbol of the righteousness of the American cause, viewed purely in anthropomorphic terms—could not be compromised. Ironically, when Japanese pilots rammed their aircraft they were seen as religious fanatics, adhering to a cruel and paganish deity; when Americans sacrificed themselves they were heroic, dignified, eternal.

Even though self-sacrifice was an integral component of propaganda, there was no substitute for total victory. When Americans sat in darkened movie houses watching films produced under federal guidelines, there was a need to remind them of Joe Louis' aphorism that victory was predestined for the Allied forces because God favored their side. Show defeat occasionally, the OWI directives asserted, but always point the way to the final moment of triumph.

Historically, of course, no military successes occurred during the early months of conflict. Right after Pearl Harbor, American losses were dismal as island after island fell in the Pacific theater and Japanese forces slowly encroached toward Australia's northern coast. The British and Dutch surrendered their ocean territories, while over on the U.S. mainland, California residents, amid rumors that enemy submarines were near, prepared for the worst. But on April 18th, 1942, a little light broke through the gloom. A propaganda coup was pulled off—the Army Air Corps bombed Tokyo.

Overnight, new heroes were extolled as the events of this daring raid unfolded. Conceived and implemented by the flamboyant Air Corps officer, Colonel James Doolittle, sixteen B-25s gingerly lifted off from a Navy carrier, the U.S.S. *Hornet,* and flew the 600 westward miles to the Japanese capital, where ten aircraft dropped their bombs over predetermined targets. Four other Japanese cities—Yokohama, Yokosuka, Nagoya, and Kobe—were attacked by the remaining six aircrews. After this surprise raid—it caught the Japanese military off-guard—Doolittle's squadron finally reached safety in China; a few perished in crash landings, others were captured by the Japanese and one hapless crew, that ran out of gasoline and touched down on Soviet soil, was interned by the Soviets. Almost overnight, Doolittle became a household hero, his exploits heralded everywhere. Adding to the jubilation was President Roosevelt's statement that the bombers had taken off from Shangri-La, the mythical land of youth and enchantment described in James Hilton's popular novel, *Lost Horizon.*

For Hollywood, always looking for new themes, the Doolittle raid represented manna from heaven. By July 1943, the first film depicting this attack flickered on the American screen. RKO's *Behind the Rising Sun* was a distorted version of the Tokyo bombing, which showed the Doolittle Raiders leaving the city simmering in smoking ruins. In actuality, the city suffered little damage, but the propaganda value of such a storyline was obvious. For the first time, American audiences snatched an eyewitness account of their first victory, an event that gave new meaning to the term Old Glory. Soon other titles appeared that in one way or another referred to the Doolittle raid or the bombing of Tokyo: *Destination Tokyo,* a submarine adventure, gave a fictional account of the reconnaissance work necessary for the attack, while *God Is My Co-Pilot,* in a discursive manner, employed elaborate poetic license in portraying a massive bombing mission against Tokyo, a raid that originated from the Allied airfields in China. But two other films—*Thirty Seconds over Tokyo* and *The Purple Heart*—captured the spirit and hardships associated with the Doolittle flight in a real and poignant fashion. Both storylines, in essence, redefined the meaning of propaganda.

Because the Doolittle raid raised the national morale to such tangible heights, Hollywood devoted its best personnel to recreating this historic military operation. In producing *Thirty Seconds over Tokyo,* MGM picked the indomitable Spencer Tracy to star in the leading role; not only did the veteran actor resemble the aviation hero, he captured the voice and mannerisms down to a tee. In restructuring Captain Ted Lawson's literary account of the attack, the National Book Award winner, Dalton Trumbo—whose propaganda screen credits included *A Guy Named Joe* and *Tender Comrade*—produced another of his crafted scripts, and Van Johnson, the fair-haired boy of the distaff viewers, took the role of Captain Lawson. Robert Walker played another of his "innocents abroad" roles and Robert Mitchum portrayed the hard-as-nails aviator, while reliable Benson Fong's Chinese national, who aided the flyers, was another stereotype in his long career as the obliging Oriental.

The storyline of *Thirty Seconds* was divided into three even sections, classified as the home, the attack, and—finally—the sacrifice for democracy. By using such discrete parts, the propaganda effect began in low gear and culminated with an elaborate patriotic paean to the American way-of-life, complete with conjugal fidelity. The first section depicted the standard exposition necessary for any plot development: it was January 1942, one of the darkest hours in American history. The Japanese had destroyed the fleet at Pearl Harbor and captured numerous military installations.

But the American generals were not asleep and a daring offense was nurtured on the drawing board. Under the leadership of Colonel Doolittle, the Army Air Corps would launch sixteen B-25s off a carrier and bomb Tokyo. If successful, it would provide the needed shot-in-the-arm to bolster morale. It would also give a new dimension to the role of airpower in the global war, because bombers had never flown off from the deck of any ship. Since this was a dangerous assignment, a call was issued for volunteers and soon an array of aviators assembled at a Florida training base.

Who were these flyers? What propelled them to select a secret mission that would take them out of the country? What were their motives in joining this elite squadron? As always, each airman was stamped from the OWI mold as again the best of American prowess—an eclectic group, of course—answered Doolittle's call to colors. Van Johnson was the leading character and his boyish ways—he was married only six months ago—endeared him to his colleagues. A skillful pilot, Johnson was reminded to keep secret the details of all military training, even from his wife, pregnant Phyllis Thaxter. For Johnson, the only important issues were his home and country, two ideals he swore to protect.

Joining his aircrew was turret gunner Robert Walker, a young, naive GI from Billings, Montana, whose pithy observations always revolved around some comparison between his hometown and wherever he might be at the moment. Personifying the best of youthful innocence, this same Robert Walker role was seen in *Bataan, See Here, Private Hargrove, Since You Went Away,* and *The Clock.* This stereotypical character was predictable and its message consistent: American youth were pure and nonbelligerent; when called up to war, their innocence did not wash off. Even when airborne, the genial Robert Walker became nauseated as he stood, symbolically, near his machine-guns, weapons of potent destruction; again, the point was hammered home—war was not a natural state for Americans, but when their security was threatened, they would fight.

The volunteers, generally, were simple and carefree. Some horsed around in the barracks, playing sophomoric pranks, while others sang simplistic tunes, reaffirming the wholesomeness of life back home. One melody, "The Eyes of Texas," was repeated as a tribute to the state's unique regionalism. Some wrote letters, others catnapped, and one or two pondered the inexplicable: why are we here? What is our mission? Moments later, some important news was announced: Colonel Doolittle was in charge of the secret training mission. A hush quickly permeated the large room. Doolittle—the name rang out like an apotheosis and each man realized something big was afoot as they stood in rapt homage to this aviation giant. As propaganda, this was another example of the father-figure image; here was the messianic leader, the officer who would organize the battle and lead his charges to the promised-land of victory.

But the attack was not imminent; the training, Doolittle stressed, would be intense, and each day aircrews practiced new forms of flying, learning to take off from a short runway. As always, American aviators benefited through hard work and perseverance, two traits that enhanced the propaganda message of any motion picture. Concomitantly, the wives and sweethearts, while oblivious to the military implications of the numerous sorties, offered support and reiterated the wholesomeness of American womanhood, reaffirming the sanctity of the home and family. For Van Johnson, coddling his pregnant wife, the purity of conjugal life, complete with antiseptic twin beds, restated the need for such a dangerous mission. Not only was democracy at stake in this global war, but the survival of a foundation—the home   rested with the success of these raiders. To fail now was tantamount to enslaving American women to a vicious and savage enemy.

Doolittle was a man of action. Dramatically, he assembled his crews in the middle of the night and sent them off, hedge-hopping to a naval station in California where, to everyone's surprise, the sixteen bombers were hoisted onto an aircraft carrier, the *Hornet.* Quickly, the ship embarked and the airmen, now charges of the Navy, realized that the attack was near. Roaming through the intricate innards of the carrier, searching for their living quarters, the flyers revealed their naiveté: symbolically, they were lost at sea, but with the help of their new brothers-in-arms, their Navy buddies, they adapted quickly to shipboard life. The spirit of cooperation and teamwork—two traits that Doolittle insisted on—were tangible propaganda reminders that this joint military operation succeeded if everyone worked in harmony. Life on board this large ship resembled the easygoing idyllic world that everyone left behind, back on Main Street. For the men now

stationed on this floating behemoth, the aircraft carrier represented their home/womb.

But the purpose of propaganda was to raise the national
conscience by elaborating military victories, not to portray
domestic bliss. Dramatically, the film shifted into a new mode—
the attack segment. Historically, the aircraft carrier was spotted by
a small Japanese fishing boat on the morning of April 18, 1942.
Fearful that the mainland would be warned, Doolittle immediately
issued the attack order and the crews sprang into action, some
eighteen hours earlier than planned. Cinematically, the launching
of these bombers became one of the crowning achievements of the
film. The pilots rushed to their parked aircraft as the blaring
sounds of the loudspeakers emphasized the dangers of the operation. One question permeated the screen: can a bomber take off in
such a small space. The exercise had been perfected on a cozy
Florida airfield; could it work now? All eyes were on Doolittle;
could Spencer Tracy lead his country to victory?

As propaganda, this elaborate scene, highlighting the precarious take-off of Doolittle's Raiders from the deck of a swaying
aircraft carrier, had few equals in the World War II film genre. At
issue now was American technology, and the final examination
awaited each airman lined up in formation. But for Doolittle, this
launching was the airman's proverbial piece-of-cake. Sitting in
his cockpit, the epitome of sang-froid, Spencer Tracy roared down
the short flight deck and efficiently headed off into the wild blue
yonder. Immediately, the ship's personnel responded with loud
applause. Doolittle's safe departure acted as the inspiration for the
entire squadron; soon each plane lifted off from the carrier, the
squadron's destination—due west. But for Captain Van Johnson,
sitting in his *Ruptured Duck,* there was cause for alarm. As in any
good Hollywood thriller, a moment of suspense always worked in
a crisis. Here the pilot stared woefully at his left engine as he
frantically manipulated the dials on his dashboard; the motor did
not start. Now what? Would Van Johnson lose his impending
moment of glory?

Of course, the film was taken from the book of the same name,
written by Captain Ted Lawson, the character that Van Johnson
depicted, so, naturally, the engine must start. Unless Van Johnson
became airborne, there would be no record of the historic thirty
seconds and, by extension, no plot, no book, no movie. As

propaganda, however, this was an effective scene. Everyone seated in the audience knew the frustration of an automobile that would not start. For the American driver, watching this Hollywood scene, there was a moment of empathy—almost a spiritual uplifting—when Johnson's engine turned over, because for the American motorist, who basically viewed his car in anthropomorphic terms, the loud noise, coupled with the spinning propeller, became an exhilarated sigh of relief. Now, the driver/audience was reassured; now we were back on the road, now we were clicking on all cylinders. When Van Johnson's B-25 became airborne and streaked out towards Japan, the strength and dignity of American airpower was formidable. This small scene was a real-life situation that all Americans understood. Momentarily, it placed every driver inside the cramped cockpit of a B-25.

After such a dramatic scene, a propaganda film must lessen its intensity to sustain its creative emotion. The outbound flight became routine as the *Ruptured Duck* headed towards the Japanese capital with no further problems. Once, a Japanese fishing vessel waved to the surprised airmen, but this small episode only restated the basic ignorance of the Oriental enemy and poked fun at his myopia. Reaching the coastline, the B-25 approached Tokyo on target and witnessed some burning oil tanks that had been bombed by another aircrew. With deft precision, the *Ruptured Duck* traversed the city and—for the next thirty seconds— dropped its incendiaries directly on target, blowing up buildings and igniting large fires.

On two occasions, Japanese planes were spotted overhead but they did not attack the American bomber. As the crew exclaimed, the Japanese pilots could not see their American adversary— another reference to the poor vision that, according to Hollywood, was symptomatic of all Japanese. Quickly, the aircraft turned westward; they had bombed Tokyo and escaped unscathed.

Since *Thirty Seconds over Tokyo* was a historical account of this famous Doolittle raid, the film's plot followed a certain format to sustain its basic verisimilitude. At this junction, the movie reached its third section, the sacrifice for democracy. When the *Ruptured Duck* passed the Chinese coastline, it crash landed in the dark of night. Soon, the crew were picked up by Chinese guerrillas and, along with other rescued crew members, taken from one hiding place to another. They had many close calls; the

Japanese were everywhere, but Chiang Kai-shek's nationals eluded their enemy at every turn. Reprisals were common, but the Chinese were determined to save their American friends, the gallant pilots who bombed Tokyo.

One tragedy marred the escape route of the airmen. Van Johnson's leg was amputated following injuries sustained in the crash landing of his B-25. (This was likewise true for Captain Ted Lawson, the author of *Thirty Seconds over Tokyo.*) For Johnson, this problem became a moment of triumph rather than defeat. As the pilot expatiated, over and over, this was the sacrifice for democracy, necessary for total victory. Just look at the hardships endured by the Chinese, he reflected. The high price of war touched everyone.

Eventually, the airmen reached Washington, D.C. and united with their spiritual leader, now General Doolittle. In a firm but tender voice, the general ordered his captain back to duty at a stateside base, to train other men for similar raids over Tokyo. His handicap, Doolittle stated, was not an impediment to the hard work that would follow. As a concluding propaganda statement, this small scene was superb. Sitting in his wheelchair, the good-looking Van Johnson, personifying the best of youth and innocence, came to terms with the hard facts associated with the War. His sacrifice, like those of many other servicemen, was the price for democracy. But heroism was always rewarded. A few seconds later, his pregnant wife, looking loving and demure, entered his hospital room and the tearful reunion brought the film to its saccharine conclusion. The facts were clear: Americans would fight to preserve their home and democracy; some would die and others be wounded, but their women remained steadfast.

This was the cohesive propaganda ingredient of *Thirty Seconds over Tokyo*—the aircrew was never alone, never isolated from family and friends, never kept in the dark about important matters. During the training session, the wives and girlfriends were always close by, supplying the needed succor and companionship; later, when they were traveling on the high seas, heading for their target, the airmen were befriended by their colleagues, the men of the Navy, who viewed the pilots in heroic terms. After bailing out in China, the Raiders were picked up by the nationalists and secretly transported to safety in relative comfort and security. Throughout the film, this motif became the permeating idea—as servicemen you were not alone, someone would watch over you, someone would protect you! This, of course, was a reiteration of a basic American value: stand by your military; don't abandon our boys in the service, guard them at all costs.

But while fourteen of the sixteen Doolittle aircrews eventually found their way back to safety and public acclaim, a worse fate befell the flyers of two missing airplanes; they were eventually captured by the Japanese near their bailout sites. The Japanese military, enraged by this daring bombing attack, sought immediate revenge and reprisal. After a quick kangaroo court trial, three of the Raiders were beheaded and their bodies disemboweled by a Nipponese officer wielding the traditional samurai sword. Others were placed in Japanese prison camps, where they languished for three years. They were rescued a few days before V-J Day. On October 6, 1943, some eighteen months after the event, the *New York Times* reported the executions of the three Raiders and public hatred against the Japanese boiled over. Hollywood was now ready to produce what, unquestionably, became the best propaganda film of World War II: Twentieth Century-Fox's *The Purple Heart.*

Directed by Academy Award winner Lewis Milestone and starring an all-male cast that included Dana Andrews, Richard Conte, Farley Granger and Richard Loo, *The Purple Heart* was Hollywood's roman-à-clef, depicting the misfortunes of eight crewmen from the Doolittle raid who crash-landed on the China coast and, subsequently, were executed by the Japanese. As a propaganda film, *The Purple Heart* reshaped the events that, historically, befell these pilots and its message became incendiary. Probably no other motion picture stoked up such hatred towards the Oriental enemy; the storyline—from start to finish— emphasized the savagery of life under Japanese captivity.

Unlike other films that depicted brief scenes of Japanese horror, *The Purple Heart* left nothing to the imagination. Under no circumstances, the storyline insisted, should an American serviceman be taken prisoner by the Japanese. Other films had already issued that dire warning: *Bombardier, Flying Tigers, Marine Raiders,* and *Bataan* revealed the consequences of Japanese capture. A few months later, *Objective Burma* lit up the screen with the mutilated corpses of American GIs tortured to death by their enemy.

What made *The Purple Heart* unique? Why was this film chosen as the best propaganda film of the war? What were the cinematic components that transformed this melodrama into such effective super-patriotism that angry audiences would be left cheering its victory-through-death ending? In many ways, the answer to these questions mirrored the broader issue of the War in general. As a nation, the United States was a mixture of ethnic groups, and Hollywood used the country's diversity and heterogeneity in virtually all of its propaganda. It wasn't one type of American fighting the War, the OWI directives explained, it was everyone—all economic classes, all ethnic groups. Only by pulling together, through both good and bad, could victory be achieved; never lose your faith in your country, your God, your President. The War, itself, placed every American on his/her mettle. Such was the theme of *The Purple Heart*—the inward turmoil against adversity during another bleak hour of the Pacific war, as eight doomed fliers struggled hopelessly against a sadistic, crazed Oriental enemy.

From the opening frame, every component of effective propaganda was evident. The lugubrious strains of the American patriotic hymn, "My Country 'tis of Thee," wailing softly in the introductory titles, served as the musical harbinger for the martyrdom that must follow. A few moments later, another martial air, the Air Corps anthem, "Off We Go," played in a languid, funereal tempo, supplied the audio exposition when eight American airmen, appearing confused but healthy, were herded into a Japanese civil courtroom in the capital city of Tokyo. These fliers—the captured crew from the Doolittle bombing raid—represented the OWI policy of ethnic, religious, and economic diversity. Leading the group was Dana Andrews, the downed aircraft's captain, who, along with his charges, was startled to learn they were on trial—in this civil court—for their recent bombing raid, a military operation. Adding to the confusion was the Japanese-appointed lawyer, a smug Oriental who bragged that he graduated from Princeton, Class of '31.

This wasn't the first motion picture that depicted a Japanese national who had studied in the United States and then returned to his homeland to apply the value and content of that education against the people of America. Tom Neal, a Japanese military fanatic in *Behind the Rising Sun,* received his baccalaureate from

Cornell University. The propaganda message was the same: the Japanese dirty everything they touch; even their undergraduate work was rank and obscene. Here, in *The Purple Heart*, the Japanese lawyer, an unctuous and apathetic caricature of the legal system, made light of the airmen's entreaty that no civil court in the world had jurisdiction over military prisoners. Ruefully, the fliers realized that they were victims in a kangaroo court, presided over by sadistic, bucktoothed, rodent-faced judges, whose hatred of everything American oozed out in every frame.

The mockery of a trial continued and as the American flyers listened stoically, one witness after another described the "atrocities" committed by the Doolittle Raiders: a hospital was bombed, school children were machine-gunned in their play yard, religious temples were strafed indiscriminately. A Chinese quisling recounted the boastful manner of the crew, claiming that the Americans had openly bragged about the death and destruction they inflicted on the innocent women and children on the streets of Tokyo. Then a short movie, prepared by the Japanese general staff, flickered on the courtroom screen, visually highlighting the wanton bombing attack. Emotions ran high as some Japanese spectators, wailing for revenge, demanded death to the foreign invaders. The commentary to this badly-doctored, phony film was narrated by the senior Japanese army officer, a glabrous military bureaucrat portrayed by the Hawaiian-American character actor, Richard Loo.

Probably no other performer served the Hollywood propaganda machine as effectively, routinely, and stereotypically as Richard Loo. Consistent as the fanatical, treacherous Japanese soldier, ready to die unhesitatingly for the emperor, Richard Loo appeared in twelve films. These titles riled up American audiences against the trickery, cunning, and double-dealing that he adroitly portrayed: *Wake Island, Bombs over Burma, Across the Pacific, China, Behind the Rising Sun, Jack London, Flight for Freedom, The Story of Dr. Wassell, God Is My Co-Pilot, Betrayal from the East,* and *China Sky.* Clearly, *The Purple Heart* was his best performance. From the moment he faced the Doolittle Flyers, a dismal mood of stealth and apprehension permeated the courtroom. Both ruthless and unctuous with his American captives, the Japanese general embodied those traits that reiterated every scintilla of persuasive propaganda. Here was the real enemy that

Americans were fighting; brutal, vicious, sneaky, and dangerous. Here was the reptile that Americans must eradicate.

Generally, every melodrama contained a subplot to sustain interest as well as provide the needed dramatic counterpoint. In *The Purple Heart,* the main theme was the ordeal of the captured airmen, while a secondary plot depicted the irrational power struggle being waged between the Japanese army and its nemesis, the admiralty. For the American flyers, this political conflict within the Japanese war hierarchy only fostered the sadistic consequences. Having been convicted in the courtroom by the bogus films, the pilots were kept in a small cell, where they were offered a choice. The Army general would spare their lives if the airmen revealed their original embarkation point. Just admit that they flew off the deck of a carrier, the general stated, and the crew would be detained in a comfortable prisoner-of-war camp. For the Doolittle Raiders, jammed inside their cramped cell, this became a moral as well as a patriotic issue.

At first, Richard Loo employed subtlety during his interrogation of Dana Andrews. Here was the classic propaganda scene: the American pilot, clean-cut, wholesome, nonbelligerent, faced off with the Japanese fanatic, a slimy, warmongering, draconian murderer, a man who addressed his superiors as "excellency." Initially, they bantered over mundane matters but the Japanese general was neither casual nor cordial. Resorting to sarcastic braggadocio, he revealed that as a fisherman, working off the California coast, he charted every inch of water from San Diego to Seattle. Soon he became livid with Japanese plans for world conquests: "*. . . No, Captain, Japan is united in this war through emperor worship and hate—hate for all foreigners, White or otherwise. The Japanese will win—he wears wood fiber clothes, cardboard shoes, he cheerfully eats one-third of his usual diet, he works fourteen hours a day, seven days a week. And our soldiers—ask your troops at Bataan—we do not leave any place that we want, you must kill us! We will win this war because we are willing to sacrifice ten million lives. How many lives is the White man willing to sacrifice?*" Swaggering mannerisms accompanied this rhetorical question. Here was a tangible example of Japanese expansionism and Richard Loo's patronizing reference to the Caucasian was simply another demonstration of the racial nature of the War as elaborated by Hollywood propaganda. The facts were simple: the Oriental enemy were crazed subhumans.

Certainly, this was a unique scene. While dozens of Hollywood films depicted the war against Japan in two-dimensional terms, exploiting the physical nature of the enemy—an inept runt, wearing Coke bottle eyeglasses, running up the hill, waving the samurai sword and screaming "banzai"—*The Purple Heart* was the only movie where the two antagonists sat down and discussed the merits of their systems. On the one hand, Dana Andrews represented the best of America; calm but determined, intelligent but casual, he restated the basic principles of democracy to his captor. As for Richard Loo, his performance was a cinematic *tour de force;* also cerebral, but opportunist, each word he uttered manifested his vileness and contempt for the Four Freedoms. The scene was the classic cat-and-mouse confrontation, the Japanese insisting on classified military information, the American remaining obdurate. The propaganda value was superb—regardless of the future consequences, American righteousness would prevail, while the Japanese, frustrated in his attempts to intimidate this valiant Yankee, resorted to fanatical, verbal outbursts.

Naturally, the Japanese tormentor took the interrogation further, and this time the methods were physical, not cerebral. For Richard Loo the situation was critical—he had publicly stated that he would apologize with his life if he failed to obtain the American military information. Again, here was another demonstration of the crazed nature of the enemy: the Yamato suicidal ritual of hara-kiri another example of Japanese derangement. The captured airmen knew that their doom was sealed. Three hapless flyers were methodically tortured but each man refused to talk. From a propaganda standpoint, these horrific scenes riled up American audiences more than any previous film had. One flyer had his tongue cut out; another, his fingers damaged beyond repair, while a third was beaten into incoherence. No other motion picture so graphically depicted the wantonness of the Japanese brutality as *The Purple Heart,* no other title conjured up a more determined call for revenge and retribution.

But the Doolittle Raiders were steadfast. In a passionate courtroom scene, the flyers stated they would not divulge the classified information even though, as an eleventh-hour ploy, the

Japanese promised the dismissal of all charges if the airmen confessed. This defiant closure was the perfect summary. Throughout *The Purple Heart* one underlying theme permeated the storyline: loyalty to your friends, your country, your principles. Even in their darkest moments, Dana Andrews called for a democratic vote to determine the flyers' fate. The roll call was unanimous: do not tell the Japanese they came from the carrier *Hornet*. Let them patrol the Russian borders, make them guard the Chinese perimeters, let them scour the high skies, wear down their defenses, make them watch every approach. For Dana Andrews, this vote became a testimony to the American fighting spirit and in this moment of triumph his dire warning seemed prophetic: *". . . they'll blacken your skies and burn your cities to the ground and make you get down on your knees and beg for mercy."*

But how crazed were the Japanese? How far would they go to reveal their alien and sinister nature? For Richard Loo, the disgraced Japanese general—he had failed his emperor—the answer was a quick, self-inflicted bullet into his stomach, causing instant death. This was a variation of the practice of hara-kiri, the accepted method of suicide by disembowelment, a method of atonement used by other Japanese in similar propaganda films. Peter Lorre, for example, in *Invisible Agent* ended his life this way, as did Imperial Secret Police officer Jack Sergel in *Blood on the Sun*. Both had failed Hirohito. Likewise, a group of Japanese officers trapped in their caves, in *Guadalcanal Diary*, resorted to hara-kiri rather than the shame of surrender to the advancing U.S. Marines. One Japanese agent, however, Sydney Greenstreet, in *Across the Pacific*, began the ritualistic Bushido preparation for his death, but could not culminate the act.

These scenes only reiterated the propaganda message of Japanese fanaticism. For the flyers in *The Purple Heart*, there was no justice, only judgment. When the execution verdict was announced, the airmen slowly left the courtroom and limped down the hallway, while the muted strains of the Air Corps hymn— heard earlier in the opening titles—wailed indistinctively, restating the lugubrious mood. Then the tempo picked up and, with it, the flyers moved faster. When the melody reached crescendo, the men marched in cadence, proud, defiant, heels clicking, eyes straight ahead. Their message was clear: this war was far from over. One of these days the Japanese would be paid back in full—just wait and see.

As propaganda, this closing scene said it all: here were eight airmen, captured after a military bombing raid, tried in a Japanese civil court, enduring brutal and sadistic torture, and, finally, condemned to execution by a subhuman enemy. But through all this travail, the Americans maintained their dignity and composure. No other motion picture produced during the Second World War depicted the Japanese war machine in such pejorative terms. Richard Loo's characterization of the slimy, fanatical Japanese officer represented the worst of the Yamato empire, while Dana Andrews' role as the simple but loyal flyer, determined to safeguard classified information, served as the perfect foil to his tormentors.

Dozens of other Hollywood films depicted the Japanese in warmongering roles, but virtually every one caricatured the Oriental, turning him into some two-dimensional monster, incapable of feeling or thought. *The Purple Heart* pitted Japanese against Japanese (the army versus the navy) and the two adversaries were ruthless to each other. Here was a film exposing the behind-the-scenes life of the Japanese high command, an environment replete with treachery, mendacity, and vileness. And, finally, what made *The Purple Heart* so inflammatory were the American newspaper stories that already had reported three of the Doolittle flyers beheaded by the Japanese after a mock trial had pronounced them guilty of war crimes.

Other motion pictures continued their rage against the Japanese, in one way or another portraying the Orientals as bestial and inhuman. Warner Brothers' *God Is My Co-Pilot* placed Dennis Morgan and Raymond Massey in war-torn China, leading many aerial sorties against Japanese air ace, Richard Loo; once again, Loo died for his emperor. *Objective Burma* assigned Errol Flynn to the jungles of Southeast Asia in a muddled version of American achievements in this war zone. No reference was made to any British victories in this one-sided, controversial film. RKO's *Behind the Rising Sun* took two American film stars, Tom Neal and J. Carrol Naish, and turned them into zealous Japanese nationals, demanding death to all foreigners. MGM's *A Guy Named Joe,* starring Spencer Tracy and Irene Dunne, began in the spiritual world of Valhalla and ended with a distaff civilian pilot destroying an important Japanese installation. Another non-militant aviatrix, Rosalind Russell, succumbed to Japanese treachery in RKO's *Flight for Freedom*. In *Bombardier*, two aviators, Pat O'Brien and Randolph Scott, put aside their personal differences to lead a bombing raid over Japan. Later, Pat O'Brien patched up his strife with Robert Ryan to rout the Japanese out of their jungle lair in RKO's *Marine Raiders.*

American nurses did not survive as well—they were captured, killed or defiled in Paramount's *So Proudly We Hail* and MGM's *Cry Havoc.* However, one Navy doctor, Gary Cooper, had better luck: after a dangerous odyssey, he evacuated his patients to the safety of Australia, barely escaping the Japanese attack on the South Sea island of Java in Paramount's *The Story of Dr. Wassell.* These three titles glamorized the work of the medical personnel caught behind the enemy lines after Pearl Harbor and emphasized the hardships that American doctors and nurses routinely endured.

Over in the Chinese theater, Hollywood depicted the travail associated with the Japanese invasion, and once more showed how American help liberated another hapless nation. Paramount's *China* placed Alan Ladd and William Bendix in the thick of battle, using the important oil supply as the backdrop. Twentieth Century-Fox's *China Girl* was modeled closely after Republic's *Flying Tigers,* two films that glorified the exploits of Pappy Boyington's ill-disciplined air corps volunteers. Unlike John Wayne, the good-looking, smooth-talking George Montgomery pursued romance when not blasting Japanese Zeroes from the sky. In RKO's *China Sky,* Randolph Scott and Anthony Quinn fought the Japanese using an old-fashioned cavalry charge, complete with small arms fired from the hip. Directed by Ray Enright, a filmmaker noted for his many Western adventures, *China Sky* basically resembled another title in the cowboy genre. On a more somber note, MGM's *Dragon Seed* revealed the horror of the Japanese occupation for the Chinese peasantry. With the help of Walter Huston and Turhan Bey, however, the Chinese thwarted their enemies at every turn.

Other films highlighted Japanese treachery and perfidy. In Warner Brothers' *Destination Tokyo,* a Japanese pilot killed an American sailor who was foolish enough to rescue his enemy from the cold ocean waters after the man's plane had been shot down. The film's premise—the groundwork necessary for the Doolittle Raid—reiterated that the famous thirty seconds over Tokyo was a joint operation, involving both the Army and Navy. At another location, the Panama Canal, Humphrey Bogart thwarted the Japanese sabotage of that strategic waterway in Warner Brothers' *Across the Pacific,* while back in Tokyo an American newspaperman, James Cagney, managed to break up a spy ring, write his story, and return to America just a few days before the Japanese unleashed their December 7th attack in United Artists' *Blood on the Sun.*

From an individual point of view, two words could accurately sum up the Pacific war against the Japanese—John Wayne. As a popular Western star, John Wayne had no equal; here was the tough, genial, tight-lipped hero, a champion as American as apple pie. When he fought the Japanese in *Flying Tigers,* he demonstrated Yankee intransigence. This prowess would continue in RKO's *Back to Bataan* and Republic's *The Fighting Seabees.* As propaganda, these two John Wayne pictures were solid. *Back To Bataan* highlighted the dramatic return of Douglas MacArthur to liberate the Philippines. Using actual survivors rescued from the Bataan POW camp, the film glorified the guerrilla forces that helped free these luckless Americans from their inhumane captivity. Likewise, in *The Fighting Seabees* it was John Wayne, alone, who created this specialized Navy unit responsible for constructing the important runways on captured Japanese islands, and no job was too tough for these wiry, heavy-machinery workers. When the enemy attacked, these civilians-turned-sailors fought back with rifles and grenades and, in one case, transformed a bulldozer into a twentieth-century battering ram.

And so it continued. Hollywood churned out dozens of films, one title after another vilifying the Japanese, depicting the enemy in two-dimensional, caricatured terms. Many of the roles were racist in nature, but it was a propaganda tenet to show the enemy as shallow and empty, never to inject empathy, never to allow the enemy to think for himself—to portray him as a blind follower, ready to die for his fanatical cause. Occasionally, a subtle touch was needed to remind audiences that the Japanese belonged to another race, an inferior group bent on destroying the Occidental's serene world of truth, justice, and the American way. In such cases the Japanese were vulnerable to the variety of ethnic slurs that dominated many of these propaganda dramas, and the effects worked well. American audiences quickly identified with innumerable pejorative attitudes against the Japanese. Unquestionably, a great deal of hate and rancor was achieved by these Hollywood productions.

Realistically, the Japanese were a scapegoat for the film industry because the European adversaries, who committed similar atrocities, were spared such racist portrayals. The Italians, for example, came off as a fun-loving, vivacious and, frequently, pro-Allied enemy, while the Nazis (not the German people) bore the brunt of the Hollywood propaganda machine. It was Hitler and his National Socialist Party that threatened America, not the high-minded, Beethoven-loving Caucasians that comprised the Teutonic nation. But over in the Pacific, it was a different matter: every Japanese, by virtue of his birth, was a menace to America. And Hollywood, caught up in the zealous throes of those victory-at-any-price days, accurately caught the fervor of those precarious times. As propaganda, no other group of motion pictures ever attained the effectiveness as the anti-Japanese films produced during the Second World War.

CHAPTER FOUR

THE ASSAULT ON THE FATHERLAND

". . . well, there are certain sections of New York, Major, that I wouldn't advise you to try to invade"—Humphrey Bogart, to Nazi officer Conrad Veidt, in Warner Brothers' *Casablanca.*

For many Americans, watching the events unfold in Europe during the shaky 1940 Battle of Britain days, war with Germany seemed inevitable. The Wehrmacht, employing its blitzkrieg strategy, occupied most of Europe and, in concert with the Italian dictator Benito Mussolini, Adolf Hitler planned new conquests. In 1941, the Axis attacked the Soviet Union, hoping for a quick summer victory. Without question, this eastern assault became the proverbial straw that broke the camel's back. If Russia capitulated, the American public wondered, who would halt Hitler from further aggression?

While politicians debated these ominous issues in the halls of Congress, the Hollywood film industry was hard at work producing one antifascist picture after another, revealing the horror of life in the New Order. Given this outpouring, together with the many newsreels shown at each theater, the American people could not fail to realize that a full-scale war against Hitlerism was close at hand. But how close? When would this confrontation start? Would the Nazis attack American ships? Would they bomb U.S. installations? Would they attempt an invasion on American soil? Where would Germany strike first?

But it was the Japanese who plunged the Americans into the hostilities with the Pearl Harbor raid, and within days the formal declarations were announced. Germany, Italy, and Japan, plus a host of satellite nations, were at war with the United States and its

Allies. And while the nation quickly mobilized its military might, the Hollywood film industry, probably feeling smug with its I-told-you-so attitude, geared up as well. For more than three years, the moguls had produced numerous titles warning of the Nazi menace—now their dire prophecies were front-page news stories. Next time, the directors lamented, listen to us, pay attention to our photoplays.

Initially, the Japanese were the leadoff target for the studios' lenses. First, the Orientals were easy to caricature because of their size, appearance, and pigmentation, and, secondly, Hollywood had been remiss about the Greater East Asia Co-Prosperity Plan. Not one motion picture remotely suggested that Japan would start the War. Germany, the directors had prognosticated, would force America's entry into the world conflict. And, lastly, a clamoring, chauvinistic American public, outraged by the sneak attack, demanded revenge and retribution against Japan, the emperor and his people. Soon after this hysteria died down, Hollywood produced new propaganda films that depicted Nazi aggression and life in the European theater. Once again, Hitler and his cronies were portrayed in unflattering terms and their expansionist policies vilified. Hollywood became the first combat unit to set foot on European soil.

Within a few weeks, a standardized pattern emerged which defined the image of the European enemy. The Nazi villain appeared as a buffoon, a gangster, or a heel-clicking martinet, while down in sunny Italy, *Il Duce*'s soldiers sang nineteenth-century arias and refrained from military combat completely. Hollywood produced dozens of anti-Nazi propaganda films during the war years, but not one title vaguely hinted that Italy, a leading member of the Axis pact, was in the same league as Hitler with his brutal takeover of small European nations. While President Roosevelt reminded the American people that Italy struck the dagger into the back of its neighbor, France, the Hollywood version of such perfidy was personified by the Italian captain in Warner Brothers' *Casablanca*. His comical demeanor and white uniform suggested fun and gaiety, not death and destruction.

At the same time, members of the Third Reich were caricatured as strutting clowns in a manner that seemed both callous and macabre. In United Artists' *To Be or Not to Be*, the famous comedian Jack Benny was paired with Carole Lombard; they were a married couple—both members of a theater troupe—in another version of the cuckold husband farce. Directed by Ernst Lubitsch, this slapstick used the bombing of Warsaw, the arrest of the Jewish population, and the capitulation of Poland as the backdrop to some behind-the-scenes hanky-panky involving husband and wife. While the pulchritudinous Carole Lombard tiptoed around with different admirers, the stoic Jack Benny impersonated a high-ranking Gestapo official, and much of this ruse—which carried the Lubitsch imprimatur—was funny. Jack Benny, of course, was an accomplished raconteur, a performer without equal, and his deadpan role produced numerous laughs.

The denouement in *To Be or Not to Be,* while admittedly humorous, appeared tasteless. One of the actors impersonated Adolf Hitler. The "Fuehrer," on a routine inspection, returned to the airfield, where he and Benny's cohorts climbed inside a waiting airplane. Once airborne, the Nazi "leader" instructed the two pilots to jump out the opened door, without any parachutes. The men made the Heil Hitler salute and immediately complied. Then the aircraft headed toward England. This final scene, depicting the German airmen blindly leaping out of their plane, reaffirmed the basic theme of this film: the inane stupidity of the Nazi soldier. Throughout *To Be or Not to Be* Gestapo members were caricatured as inept buffoons, men who could not punch their way out of a paper bag. While the real Adolf Hitler was ordering the bombing of numerous cities, resulting in untold civilian deaths, and his henchmen were implementing the logistics for the horrific Final Solution, Hollywood's appraisal of the Nazi menace in this 1942 film seemed a cinematic *reductio ad absurdum.*

Another film which employed the same kind of slapstick as *To Be or Not to Be* was Universal's *Invisible Agent,* a low-key science-fiction melodrama that downplayed the Nazi soldier as childish and ineffectual. The star of this B-picture, Jon Hall, portrayed the grandson of the famous scientist who perfected a secret formula that, injected into the blood stream, rendered a person invisible. This was the plot of the original motion picture produced in 1933, *The Invisible Man.* Now a member of Uncle Sam's Army, the good-looking Hall, turned invisible by his grandfather's serum, parachuted into the Fatherland and wreaked havoc on the German war machine, disrupting a romantic dinner between a Nazi officer and an

American spy, stealing an important code book, and destroying numerous Nazi aircraft that were preparing for a massive bombing raid on New York City. He also won the heart of the pretty American agent and escaped back to England.

As a propaganda film, *Invisible Agent* employed the elements of buffoonery. During the dinner scene, the Axis officer's behavior bordered on foppery: he kissed the agent's hand at every whim, behaved obsequiously, and clicked his heels at the mere mention of Hitler's name. This vain and pompous Nazi couldn't perceive the woman's subtle mockery of his rank and position. This was a common appraisal of the German officer, seen in many other films. In *To Be or Not to Be,* Henry Victor portrayed the Nazi captain who snapped his heels together every time Hitler's name was pronounced. Helmut Dantine, in *Hotel Berlin,* practiced impersonating a Gestapo officer for espionage purposes. Dantine's teacher, the pretty Andrea King, gave the necessary instructions about Nazi behavior: "*. . . now leave me as a German officer would: click your heels and kiss my hand.*"

Other scenes stretched the plausibility of the propaganda in *Invisible Agent.* The noted English actor Sir Cedric Hardwicke, whose distinctive British accent and service to the Allied cause were featured in such films as *The Moon Is Down, The Cross of Lorraine, Commandoes Strike at Dawn, Wing and a Prayer,* and *The Keys of the Kingdom,* was ludicrous as a Nazi officer feuding with a Japanese agent, the Hungarian-born Peter Lorre, who, true to stereotype, committed hara-kiri after his valuable code book was taken. Also, it was a science-fiction leap to suggest that in 1942, the Luftwaffe could plan a nonstop bombing raid on New York City—a distance of almost 4,000 miles—using the aircraft available at that time. No airplane, either Allied or Axis, had such a range.

On the other hand, the British bombing raids were shown as much more successful. The RAF flew across the dangerous North Sea barrier and occupied Germany and destroyed important military targets. This was the theme of Warner Brothers' comic-strip adventure, *Desperate Journey,* another film that depicted Nazi officers as incompetent buffoons. Starring the Australian-born leading man, Errol Flynn, and directed by Raoul Walsh, *Desperate Journey* highlighted the fast-moving escapades of an RAF bomber crew, who boldly flew deep into the Fatherland to attack a strategic railway bridge. After crash-landing in enemy territory, the British airmen experienced many close calls as they trekked westward to safety. Modeled after the classical Western genre, *Desperate Journey* employed the stereotypical cowboy-versus-Indian motif (British versus German), including numerous chase scenes and highlighting Nazi ineptitude at every turn.

As a wartime film, *Desperate Journey* exhibited a troublesome ambiguity. One of the basics of effective propaganda was enemy recognition. Above all, be consistent in the portrayal, use the same actor or character in similar roles, allow the audience to know immediately when hostile forces appear on the screen. However, in *Desperate Journey,* the portrayal of the Nazi officer by the distinguished Canadian-born actor, Raymond Massey, here responsible for prisoner interrogation, seemed implausible. American audiences were puzzled by this role. On which side of the fence did Raymond Massey belong? Was it possible that an Academy Award winner, who starred as Abraham Lincoln a few years earlier, could be an Axis dupe? How could the leading man who portrayed a Canadian soldier on leave in the British film, *The Invaders,* a merchant captain in *Action on the North Atlantic,* and the impenetrable General Claire Chennault in *God Is My Co-Pilot,* convince anyone that he was now a Nazi?

Adding to the propaganda dilemma was Massey's characterization as an incompetent simpleton. When the captured airmen refused to divulge specific military information, he offered one of the flyers a deal: explain some of the technical data of a new American aircraft in exchange for some special privileges. The crewman, played by Ronald Reagan, "agreed" and proceeded to spout a barrage of unintelligible gibberish which Raymond Massey, looking nonplussed, pretended to understand. Finally, overwhelmed by this verbal gobbledygook, the Nazi, confused, frustrated, and perplexed, ordered the prisoner out of the room. This scene, in particular, punctuated the levity in *Desperate Journey* and underlined the premise that the German army, as a fighting unit, was ineffective because most of the officers were nincompoops. Included in this entourage, as though to emphasize this theme, was the character actor, Sig Rumann.

Except for Richard Loo, no other Hollywood player put in as much mileage in the propaganda films as Sig Rumann. Usually portrayed as the comical, inept, explosive, heel-clicking, arm-saluting Nazi, Sig Rumann appeared in fourteen motion pictures:

Confessions of a Nazi Spy, Four Sons, Comrade X, So Ends Our Night, World Premier, To Be or Not to Be, Remember Pearl Harbor, Enemy Agents Meet Ellery Queen, Berlin Correspondent, Desperate Journey, China Girl, Tarzan Triumphs, They Came to Blow up America, and *The Hitler Gang.* In the stereotypical Falstaffian role of a rabid Hitler devotee, Sig Rumann usually ended up with egg on his face in his farcical routines. His appearance in *Desperate Journey* reinforced the cartoon-like format of this major Warner Brothers' production.

Other examples enhanced the caricature quality of the Nazi officer in *Desperate Journey.* Not only did Raymond Massey exude aristocratic haughtiness, he arrogantly displayed the official Hollywood symbol of villainy—the monocle. Throughout his interrogation of the captured airmen, he childishly fingered this glass in a way that suggested the eyepiece was a security blanket. Later, when the monocle fell to the ground, he became enraged. Other motion pictures included similar scenes: *Hotel Berlin, Man Hunt, Five Graves to Cairo, Hitler's Children, Escape,* and *Counter-Attack* all depicted Nazi officers and their infantile need for such a corrective lens. The propaganda value was obvious: the American fighting man's uniform always included a small Bible tucked into his shirt pocket; the Nazi officer's accoutrement featured suede gloves and a polished monocle.

Another foppish member of the master race, Walter Slezak, likewise spent time in front of a mirror admiring his sartorial appearance in RKO's *This Land Is Mine.* Portraying a senior Nazi officer in charge of the occupation of a small French town, the portly Slezak looked ludicrous as the military official whose function was to punish resistance fighters. Here was another overweight Nazi buffoon, and his pathetic attempt to woo pretty Maureen O'Hara, a local schoolteacher, seemed comical. The propaganda function of such caricature was obvious. Another film, RKO's *Once Upon a Honeymoon,* depicted Slezak as a pompous boor who underestimated American strength and prowess. In this screwball comedy, the Nazi officer was outwitted by suave, good-looking Cary Grant, a knight in shining armor who rescued comely Ginger Rogers from a life of internment.

Later, Slezak's roles took on new identities. In RKO's *The Fallen Sparrow,* he became a Nazi agent stalking a former Lincoln Brigade member, John Garfield, and in Twentieth Century-Fox's *Lifeboat* his role was deadly. Portraying a German U-boat commander, now adrift with an odd collection of American survivors aboard a lifeboat in mid-Atlantic, the Machiavellian Slezak oozed Nazi treachery in every frame of this controversial motion picture. In these films he was no longer the stereotypical comical windbag, but a tangible Nazi threat. However, these titles had limited propaganda value. *The Fallen Sparrow,* an apologetic tract for the Spanish Civil War, required a thorough knowledge of that conflict for the storyline to unfold, while *Lifeboat* contained a moral ambiguity because the Nazi captain, now in charge of this small boat, perished at the hands of an American lynch mob.

Occasionally, the Nazi officer was more dangerous than comical. In Warner Brothers' *Casablanca*—probably the most popular World War II Hollywood film—Conrad Veidt's portrayal of the Axis commandant, Major Strasser, was another example of a swaggering, heel-clicking martinet who demanded obedience from his subordinates as he attempted to outwit his American foil, Humphrey Bogart. Resorting to Third Reich braggadocio, the impeccably dressed Conrad Veidt imposed draconian policies in the pro-Vichy port city of Casablanca, including routine arrests and executions, and depicted Nazi occupation at its worst. On the other hand, confronted with Bogart's tough, laconic banter, the German officer, unable to handle the American's sardonic ripostes, sat stolidly, in quiet arrogance. During one of their informal interrogation scenes, the serious-minded Veidt, questioning Bogart about his political life in North Africa, was rebuffed by the boniface's terse reply. When asked to identify his nationality, Bogart blurted out, *"I'm an alcoholic."*

But Humphrey Bogart wasn't the only individual ridiculing the Nazi major. Claude Rains, perfectly cast as the womanizing French prefect, downplayed the German's authority on numerous occasions with his equivocal language and sleight-of-hand gestures, while minor characters, jammed into the backdrop, also poked fun at the military command. *Casablanca,* of course, was not a comedy but a serious drama involving international intrigue, patriotism, and lost love. However, elements of humor, even slapstick, were frequently used to depict the Germans as dupes, silly-looking men dressed as soldiers. What was the propaganda value of such characterization? Why the comical stereotyping of Italian and German officers?

One of the tenets of effective film propaganda is clarity. Since audiences must discern between the forces of good and evil, no ambiguity can appear in the photodrama. Simplicity became the cardinal rule: identify the villains early in the plot, embroider them with the necessary trappings of malevolence. *Casablanca,* however, deviated from this rule. Initially, the storyline followed a traditional propaganda format. A huge spinning globe slowly came to rest at the Moroccan port of Casablanca—now part of unoccupied France, a haven for numerous refugees. However, since German and French troops, plus British and American civilians, mingled in a quasi-friendly way, the "real" enemy became obfuscated. If Germany and France were belligerents, why were they fraternizing over mixed drinks at Bogart's Café Américain bar?

This amity was a result of the capitulation settlement between France and Germany, which created certain neutral areas. This strange arrangement permitted fugitives from Nazi Germany, plus numerous refugees from conquered nations, to remain publicly at large, all hoping to obtain exit visas, necessary for a quick air trip to Portugal, another nonaligned nation. Adding to the complexities of this plot were esoteric references to the Spanish Civil War, the 1935 Italian invasion of Ethiopia, and the imprudence of drinking bottled Vichy water. As propaganda, *Casablanca* stood on shaky ground because this convoluted storyline required, as a prerequisite, a primer on recent political history.

But 1942 movie audiences understood the gaiety that existed in Bogart's international bar as play-it-again Sam serenaded the evening crowd while gambling flourished in a large back room. Certainly, it was funny to watch Bogart deny admittance to a haughty German and laugh as the door was slammed in the man's face. A few days later, more humor was provided with the arrival of the Axis entourage at the local airport. Emerging from a small, unimpressive aircraft, the Nazi officer, Conrad Veidt, was flanked by two nondescript assistants who resembled Laurel and Hardy. Adding to the levity was an Italian attaché whose effervescent personality and handwaving gesticulations rendered him militarily impotent.

For the next two hours, *Casablanca* contained other droll episodes in which Nazi personnel were often disparaged by fast-talking adversaries. In one classic scene—a tribute to the

French national anthem, *La Marseillaise*—a group of German rowdies was drowned out as they attempted to sing a popular nationalist melody. Eventually, the comedy turned macabre when Conrad Veidt confronted Bogart, Henreid, and Bergman in the most famous finale in film annals. Here, at the Casablanca airdrome, the uxorial Miss Bergman remained steadfast to her marriage vows and departed with her husband; a few moments later, the antifascist Bogart, in a typical Western showdown, killed the Nazi officer, rather than allow him to thwart the escape plan. Veidt's death scene was really another caricature of Nazi ineptitude and its offbeat handling reaffirmed a propaganda staple: the Third Reich's incompetence was its fatal flaw. Certainly, in the case of Conrad Veidt, the Nazi major was portrayed as menacing and ruthless; but he was also silly and foolhardy. And, as with other German officers, in dozens of similar roles, his fate was predictable. Comical Nazis were ineffectual.

But why should Hollywood stop with high-ranking military personnel? If Nazi officers and bureaucrats—including Goering and Goebbels—were lampooned, why not go all the way to the top? Why not portray the Fuehrer as the typical Sig Rumann bumpkin, a stereotypical prattling fool, lacking any practical skills or basic competency? If Chaplin could poke fun at Hitler before the War, why not elaborate on this theme now that hostilities were under way? Certainly, such an approach followed another dictum of propaganda—show the enemy leadership, as well as his underlings, in inept and vainglorious roles; disparage the adversary, make him look impotent. If possible, make the enemy crawl for mercy, while begging for his life.

Not surprisingly, then, Adolf Hitler was caricatured in three motion pictures, which showed the Fuehrer as nothing more than a Sunday morning newspaper cartoon figure, and each time the character actor Bobby Watson played the title role. United Artists' *The Devil with Hitler* and *That Nazty Nuisance,* plus PRC's *Hitler—Dead or Alive,* reduced the Nazi leader to a fumbling incompetent, incapable of leading a huge war machine on a worldwide conquest. While all three films were routine B-productions, they still served a propaganda need. In *The Devil with Hitler,* a slight allegorical twist gave this low-key slapstick its storyline. From the depths of Hades came an emissary of the potentate, Satan, with a mission for Hitler: perform one good deed. The threesome of Hitler, Mussolini and a Japanese official named Suki Yaki could not comply with the devil's request. Later, this same trio, in *That Nazty Nuisance,* landed on a desert island, hoping to solidify a treaty with the natives. The Axis, however, were outwitted by a shipwrecked American sailor. Both times, these bunglesome leaders quarreled with each other, suggesting mutual distrust and hostility.

While these two titles poked fun at the Fuehrer, *Hitler—Dead or Alive* went one step further, claiming that the Nazi leader was killed by a German firing squad. As propaganda, however, this film stretched all limits of credibility by suggesting that in 1942, an American industrialist posted a million dollar bounty on the Fuehrer, dead or alive. Soon, this offer was accepted by three former inmates from Alcatraz. Eventually the trio, headed by cowboy star Ward Bond, arrived in the Fatherland and, after a series of comic-strip adventures, the Fuehrer was kidnapped. Alone with the Nazi leader in a cellar hideaway, the Americans shaved off his trademark moustache and cropped his hair short. When the Gestapo arrived, they quickly arrested the Americans and some underground friends but did not recognize their leader because of his changed appearance. When Hitler professed his identity, he was ridiculed by the Nazi officers and then quickly executed along with the others. As a postscript, the American tycoon who financed this bizarre operation explained that the man called Hitler, now leading the German nation, was an impostor, and one day this "Fuehrer" would be eliminated.

In retrospect, *Hitler—Dead or Alive* seemed a tasteless way to depict the horror of Germany's lebensraum policy ravaging much of Europe. But the film only restated the production codes of the Second World War, which trivialized the Nazis by emphasizing the comical nature of its military leadership and suggested that Hitler was nothing more than a bag of wind. Earlier, in the Jack Benny movie *To Be or Not to Be,* Hitler was caricatured as a raving lunatic, ordering his pilots to jump out of their aircraft without a parachute. This small scene was typical of Hollywood's oversimplification of the Nazi leader and did little to acknowledge the wanton destruction caused by the blitzkrieg attack against Poland. Another inappropriate film, Universal's *The Strange Death of Adolf Hitler,* offered the same theme. Here, Ludwig Donath, via some plastic surgery, assumed the role of the Fuehrer and, because of another mix-up, was killed by his wife. One year later, in Paramount's *The Hitler Gang,* a film that traced the rise of the Third Reich, Bobby Watson portrayed a somber Fuehrer intent on conquering the world and eliminating the Jewish population. To create a serious mood, Paramount, in its billing, changed the name of its main actor: Bobby Watson was listed as Robert Watson.

But not all Germans were lighthearted fools; some were depicted as gangsters and their roles seemed reminiscent of the American felons that appeared time and time again in the crime film genre of the 1930s. Instead of speeding around corners in fast-moving cars, firing machine-gun bullets at some rival gang, the Nazis were portrayed as unconscionable thugs, men skilled at torture, extortion, and brutality. In lieu of wearing a tight-fitting fedora that covered half his face as he mumbled some indiscernible epithets, the German gangster wore a uniform replete with military decorations and polished belt buckles, while his guttural diction was exaggerated with mispronounced "v's" and "w's". And as in the popular Hollywood crime films—featuring the good versus evil theme—the Nazi thug always came to a bad end, thwarted by the unremitting righteousness of the Allied cause.

A good example of Nazi gangsters imposing their will on subjugated people was Warner Brothers' *Edge of Darkness,* a film describing life in a small, occupied Norwegian town. Starring Errol Flynn and Ann Sheridan, *Edge of Darkness* was both an indictment of Axis rule and a paean to Norwegian resistance. Here, in their small fishing village, the townspeople stood by helplessly as German officers controlled their daily activities: routine arrests, torture, rape, and executions created a mood of hopelessness. Finally, the populace, inspired by a Lutheran pastor wielding a submachine gun, rebelled, and a classic end-of-the-movie shootout brought the film to a dramatic denouement similar to that of an earlier Errol Flynn extravaganza, *They Died with Their Boots On.* In this 1941 Western, Flynn portrayed General George Armstrong Custer, the cavalry officer whose entire command was killed at the battle of Little Big Horn. In *Edge of Darkness* all the Norwegians perished in an elaborate finale that also claimed the lives of every German, including a ritualistic suicide by the commander, who feared Nazi reprisals for allowing this civilian uprising.

As propaganda, *Edge of Darkness* contained two discrete elements. On one level, the Nazi gangsters, in the form of the occupying forces, were disparaged as one swaggering officer after another brought misery to the villagers with their iron-fisted rule. In one poignant scene, the townspeople stood in fear as a seventy-year-old retired school teacher was manhandled in the public square and his possessions burned. On the other hand, the film solidified the friendship between the Americans and Norwegians, two allies united against Germany. President Roosevelt's famous "Look-to-Norway" speech, broadcast in the closing moments of this picture to the melodic strains of the Lutheran hymn, "A Mighty Fortress Is Our God," served as a reminder that both the Deity and the American people were on the side of this Scandinavian country.

This wasn't the only title that featured Norwegian intransigence against their German foe. Warner Brothers produced *The Moon Is Down,* another motion picture depicting Nazi gangsters/officers terrorizing the local populace, while Columbia released two titles lauding Scandinavian resistance. *Commandos Strike at Dawn* highlighted the efforts of Norwegian guerrillas mounting a surprise attack against the Nazi invaders, while *First Comes Courage* placed a pretty spy in Nazi headquarters via a bogus marriage. PRC's *They Raid by Night* glorified another commando landing on Scandinavian soil. Each time, the propaganda message was the same: the Allied forces would not abandon their commitment to Norway or their fight against the quislings, those local residents who collaborated with the Axis conquerors.

But other occupied nations endured the ordeal of Nazi occupation. In RKO's *This Land Is Mine,* veteran French film director Jean Renoir, who resided in the United States, depicted the hardships of his native people as they struggled to maintain a modicum of dignity under the New Order. Using a small, nondescript, unnamed village as the backdrop, *This Land Is Mine* reiterated a constant propaganda theme—the French people would fight oppression and subjugation, no matter what reprisals awaited them. Even though the local residents were governed by stern decrees, including the death penalty for an array of minor infractions, a small resistance movement was active. While some Frenchmen sabotaged enemy installations, though, others were passive. The local schoolteacher, played by Charles Laughton, initially lacked the physical courage to openly defy the Third Reich, but later would rise to a heroic occasion. His martyr's death, by a German firing squad, restated Gallic intransigence.

This was a common theme in other films that glorified the Maquisard. In MGM's *The Cross of Lorraine,* a large contingency of French prisoners of war struggled to eke out a precarious living from the meager rations their German guards doled out to them. However, a battalion priest, Sir Cedric Hardwicke, reassured his men that with faith in God, the final victory belonged to France. Soon two prisoners—Jean-Pierre Aumont and Gene Kelly— escaped and eventually reached the safety of a small town, announcing that they also bore the cross of Lorraine. Here, they organized the farmers into a strong civilian army that, in the final minutes of this film, routed the German forces, burned their own village, and fled into the nearby hills to continue the fight, while the powerful strains of the heroic national anthem, *La Marseillaise,* proclaimed the righteousness of this cause.

If music could enhance the propaganda value of a motion picture, so could allegory. Warner Brothers' *Uncertain Glory,* starring Errol Flynn, lauded French heroism in a roundabout way somewhat reminiscent of Charles Dickens' *A Tale of Two Cities.* A convicted murderer agreed to switch places with a condemned patriot in exchange for three more days of life. During these seventy-two hours, the criminal (Errol Flynn) displayed an ethereal composure that reaffirmed the promise of a free France. His heroic death, in the closing sequence, suggested a heavenly reward for his unselfish act. This same idea—a felon spared death from the guillotine—was the plot of Universal's *The Impostor.* Here, Jean Gabin joined the French Army, was decorated for gallantry, and died while protecting his battalion. Likewise, in RKO's *The Pied Piper,* a similar allegorical theme denounced the Nazi invasion of France. This time, an English traveler, Monty Woolley, escorted a group of children to safety during the early blitzkrieg days. Thwarted by air attacks and German patrols, this contemporary version of the Pied Piper of Hamelin outwitted his foes with the help of simple peasants.

Sometimes aid was provided in a more sophisticated fashion. In MGM's *Reunion in France,* pretty, haute couture socialite Joan Crawford masterminded an elaborate escape route for a downed RAF pilot, John Wayne, that included his impersonating a chauffeur. Her handsome industrialist boyfriend, Philip Dorn, meanwhile, manufactured defective parts for the German war machine. RKO's melodrama, *Joan of Paris*, starred pretty Michelle Morgan who, with her parish priest, Thomas Mitchell, helped some British airmen escape from the Gestapo. When captured by the *Schutzstaffel*, the intransigent Miss Morgan refused to reveal military information and her martyr's death fueled more hatred against the Germans. While the locale for both *Reunion in France* and *Joan of Paris* was the capital, the same message from the countryside prevailed: as a nation, the French people would resist their occupiers at every turn.

Propaganda, like most intangibles, had certain limitations and a screen director had to be careful that these boundaries were not overstepped. While these motion pictures glorified the Gaullist spirit, they seemed to caricature the French people. American audiences, certainly, must have thought that the celebrated British actor, Charles Laughton, was a strange choice for a docile French school teacher. Likewise, who would believe that Hollywood stars Sir Cedric Hardwicke and Thomas Mitchell—two actors with notable Anglo accents—would sound credible as French priests? The same held true for the Australian-born Errol Flynn in his role as a martyred Frenchman. Michelle Morgan, certainly, was perfectly cast and her native accent added credibility to her portrayal of a simple, neighborhood girl working for the underground, but Joan Crawford—another American actress with a distinct speech pattern—sounded incongruous as a French fashion model. Probably, these films did a better job of vilifying the Nazis than of glorifying the Gaullist cause. But who can say? How effective were their portrayals? How could one accurately determine the influence of propaganda in seemingly ambiguous circumstances?

Hollywood's treatment of Czechoslovakia, however, was devoid of such cinematic equivocation. In MGM's *Hitler's Madman,* the German occupiers were depicted as cold-blooded murderers, carrying out their execution orders with such sangfroid that American audiences had no problem in comprehending the propaganda message. Loosely based on historical reports, *Hitler's Madman* explained the events that caused the destruction of Lidice, a small Czech farming village, as a reprisal for the assassination of the Nazi protector, Reinhard Heydrich. In this poignant film, the Nazi death squad shot every male over the age of sixteen and then burned the town to the ground, literally removing Lidice from the map. The women and children fared almost as badly: they were deported to concentration camps.

In recreating these horrific events, director Douglas Sirk assigned John Carradine the title role of Reinhard Heydrich and his performance as the draconian leader was convincing, especially his sadistic treatment of the Czech women he routinely compromised. Likewise, his henchmen were stereotypically brutal and arrogant, two traits that stated Hollywood's image of the Nazi/gangster conqueror. To complement the propaganda value of *Hitler's Madman,* a great deal of religious material was used: prayers and hymnals attested to the Czech's strong belief in the Deity, while a quiet but dignified reading of Edna St. Vincent Millay's heroic poem, "The Murder of Lidice," summarized the tragedy of that June 1942 massacre.

Hitler's Madman wasn't the only film depicting the Lidice tragedy. One month earlier, the emigré director Fritz Lang recreated a fictional account of Heydrich's assassination in United Artists' *Hangmen Also Die.* Starring Brian Donlevy as a patriot-turned-killer, *Hangmen Also Die* concentrated more on the efforts of the Gestapo—whose delineated hierarchy resembled an American gangster organization rather than an elite Nazi military group as they searched endlessly for the Czech fugitive. Aided at every turn by his friends, the fate of the quick-thinking Donlevy eventually became a matter of speculation. Many of his countrymen, however, perished in the ensuing reign of terror. Adding to the propaganda value, the storyline included an ironic subplot about a Czech quisling, a man adamantly loyal to the Third Reich. Later, this collaborator was summarily executed by the Gestapo, not for any malfeasance but simply to placate some high-ranking Nazi officials.

From a propaganda viewpoint, both films worked effectively. On one level, the Czech people were sympathetically portrayed as innocent victims of Hitlerism. Happy, carefree, and religious, the Czech nationals, when pushed to extremes, retaliated against their tormentors in a dramatic fashion. The propaganda message was clear: the Nazi occupation was anathema. In contrast, the German brutes were typical small town bullies, military louts who derived sadistic pleasure from hurting smaller, indefensible people. With-

out question, these films aroused American audiences against the
Third Reich to a degree resembling the existing hatred of the
Japanese. The monstrous deeds of the Nazis, in both pictures, had
the same emotional impact as the Japanese atrocities in such titles
as *Bataan* or *Wake Island*. Here, nothing was left to the imagination; the mass execution scene, for example, in the closing
moments of *Hitler's Madman* summarized Nazi brutality at its
worst. Later, another film—Paramount's *Hostages*—repeated this
same format. An innocent group of twenty-six Czechs was slated
for execution because a Nazi officer accidentally drowned.

But Hollywood did not stop with the occupied countries. If life
was deplorable under the New Order for the Czechs, French and
Norwegians, how did the Germans fare themselves? Were the
Nazis able to taste the sweetness of their conquests in their own
land or did the German people find themselves in the same boat as
the subjugated nations? Were Hitler's followers confident that the
Third Reich would endure for the promised one thousand years or
were the seeds of disloyalty, mistrust, and rebellion emerging?
These questions the film propagandists exploited to maximum
advantage.

An important tenet of effective propaganda was to portray
unrest in the enemy camp. Whenever possible, show disunity
between the Japanese, Germans and Italians. Create a mood that
suggested this Axis bloc would collapse under the weight of the
internal strife prevalent in their shaky alliance. Show conflict even
within the ranks of each power. This was the theme of RKO's
anti-Nazi production, *Hitler's Children*. Directed by Edward
Dmytryk, *Hitler's Children* paired popular American cowboy star
Tim Holt and pretty Bonita Granville as two young German
students living in Berlin who, eventually, were executed for their
anti-Nazi beliefs. Their tragic ending only reaffirmed what American audiences knew—that children growing up under National
Socialism reached a bad end.

But the plot of *Hitler's Children* was more complicated than a
sweeping generalization. In 1933 Berlin two students became
good friends. Bonita Granville, an American born on German soil,
attended the school for U.S. citizens, while her German admirer,
Tim Holt, bragged incessantly about his pure Aryan background.
While their political bantering seemed sophomoric, the two
youngsters were miles apart when discussing Hitler and his

grandiose New Order. Eventually, Tim Holt became an army lieutenant, mouthing off the typical Nazi shibboleths he embraced with blind obedience. As for Miss Granville, the comely blonde was stripped of her American citizenship and thrown into a women's detention camp.

Later, the two met and quarreled. Offended that his old girl friend repudiated Hitlerism, the Nazi officer arrested her as a "traitor." As punishment, the healthy American was sent to a medical institution, a place where women were forced to bear babies for the New Order. Such a predicament, of course, kept the propaganda ball rolling, but director Dmytryk saved the best for last. After a short-lived escape—that included sanctuary in a local church—Bonita Granville was returned to the center, labeled a recalcitrant, and tied to a whipping post. Here, she was to receive ten lashes on her bare back. After two strokes, a Hollywood "miracle" occurred. Young Tim Holt, realizing the errors of National Socialism, emerged from the crowd and, after a show of bravado, stopped the punishment. He professed his love for the girl and openly renounced the Third Reich. Soon the twosome were brought before a kangaroo court and were publicly executed after attempting to broadcast a repudiation over the radio station covering their trial.

This closing scene, with Bonita Granville's pretty hands tied to the lashing post, was, perhaps, the most famous image Hollywood created in its war films. Here was the essence of Axis brutality. If women could be punished for refusing involuntary impregnation, then everyone was in danger unless Nazism was eradicated. Fortunately, Tim Holt, a red-blooded American cowboy star, saw the light and came to the rescue, preventing most of the flogging. For most Americans, sitting securely in their neighborhood picture show, it became a matter of priorities. Many things were tolerated and charged off as the ravages of war. But one thing was axiomatic: Americans would never forgive an enemy who tied a young women to a post and lashed her bare back with a long black whip.

Some other films were just as inflammatory as *Hitler's Children* in their depiction of life in autarchic Germany. A number of pictures portrayed an intricate Allied spy network that routinely disrupted the Axis war machine. In Columbia's *Appointment in Berlin,* the suave film actor George Sanders starred as a "cashiered" RAF officer working surreptitiously for the Crown. After being recruited by the Fatherland to broadcast anti-British propaganda, Sanders—now a famous Axis radio commentator modeled after Lord Haw Haw—roamed around military head-quarters, where he gleaned important tactical information. Using an intricate linguistic code system, Sanders aired secret informa-tion to his superiors in London. Among other things, *Appointment in Berlin* claimed that the Third Reich's counterintelligence network was an ineffective organization.

This same idea—the radio announcer as a spy—was also the theme of Twentieth Century-Fox's *Berlin Correspondent*. This time an American journalist, Dana Andrews, stationed in the German capital prior to December 7th, routinely dispatched intelligence reports over his nightly program. When war was declared, Andrews experienced many harrowing adventures, on one occasion donning a Nazi uniform in order to elude the Gestapo. As in *Appointment in Berlin,* the Nazi officers were either fools or thugs, two traits commonly found in the typical cops-versus-robbers genre. Both films showed life for the German people, under the New Order, as austere and dictatorial.

This was, of course, a typical propaganda component: divide the portrayal of the enemy into separate parts. While the military waged war, its members lived high on the hog. Gestapo members, for example, enjoyed lavish meals in the company of well-dressed, attractive women in plush, well-heated apartments, while the general populace waited stoically in line for scarce, rationed items, afraid to utter one word of dissent. While the New Order promised every German a better life, the reality of the War for the civilians included hardship and doubt. In MGM's *Above Suspi-cion,* Fred MacMurray and Joan Crawford, posing as honeymoon-ers vacationing in the Fatherland during the uneasy pre-war days, noticed fear and anguish on every civilian's face, while young children, members of Nazi youth groups, spouted hateful slurs or chauvinistic slogans. Childhood, Miss Crawford averred, had vanished from Germany.

Marital bliss, likewise, no longer existed under National Social-ism. In RKO's *Once Upon a Honeymoon,* Ginger Rogers, a former New York City ecdysiast, married a Nazi official in pre-war Vienna. Unable to tolerate her husband's devotion to the Fuehrer, the frustrated bride, cajoled by good-looking, fast-talking Cary Grant, abandoned her spouse and, after a series of high jinks and adventures, returned to her homeland. While basically a screwball comedy, *Once Upon a Honeymoon's* minimal propaganda message was clear—misery and frustration were the chief components in any conjugal relationship between a German and an American.

But were all Germans evil? Could the race of people that produced Goethe, Beethoven, and Schiller be that uncaring? Were there any nationals who found Hitlerism repugnant and reprehensible? This became a legitimate question for the film propagandist, because if every German was fiendish, wouldn't the message become trivial from overkill? Occasionally a "good" German must appear to balance the constant anti-Nazi propaganda. In Twentieth Century-Fox's *The Pied Piper*, a Nazi officer, Otto Preminger, admitted to a vacationing Englishman, Monty Woolley, that anti-Semitism was a basic principle under the New Order. Soon, the Gestapo major orchestrated an elaborate escape plan for a young Jewish girl and eventually the child reached England. Also, in Warner Brothers' *Desperate Journey*, Errol Flynn and his flying crew were aided by a pretty German woman, Nancy Coleman, a member of a secret underground movement that helped downed airmen.

But the film that glorified the untainted German was MGM's *The Seventh Cross*, a picture that downplayed the evils of Nazism while elaborating on the innate goodness found within most people regardless of national origin. Directed by Fred Zinnemann, a refugee from Germany, *The Seventh Cross* described the peripatetic adventures of a hapless German who, in 1936, escaped from the Westhofen Concentration Camp and finally reached safety at the Dutch border. With the redoubtable Spencer Tracy in the starring role, *The Seventh Cross* carried the propaganda message that the United States was not at war with the German people, only with the Nazi leaders. In scene after scene, Tracy came into contact with fellow nationals who secretly aided his escape, despite the ever-present danger of capture.

Released on July 24, 1944, *The Seventh Cross* demonstrated an obvious naiveté regarding the concentration camps located in Germany. According to MGM, most inmates seemed reasonably well-fed and healthy, and the living conditions were generally tolerable. Some eight months later—in April 1945—the U.S.

Army liberated these death camps and their gruesome conditions were revealed on the front page of every newspaper. This important discrepancy aside, *The Seventh Cross* became the first motion picture that exonerated the German people from the crimes committed by the Nazi officials. In fact, the image of the "good" German, as depicted in this film, was a glamorous one: these nationals helped downed airmen escape, hid fugitives from the Gestapo, and arranged passage to neutral nations.

But Hollywood was never noted for its consistency and its image of a "good" German, like so many other themes, was ephemeral. Some eight months later, on March 2, 1945, Warner Brothers released *Hotel Berlin*, a routine melodrama depicting the frustrations of defeat that Nazi officials—ensconced in a palatial hotel—endured, as overhead Allied bombers put into operation the Götterdämmerung of the Master Race. Starring Raymond Massey, Peter Lorre and Alan Hale, *Hotel Berlin* praised the strength of airpower as the chief component responsible for bringing the Nazis to their knees. As a liberal German professor, just released from Dachau, Peter Lorre's pithy observations vitiated the notion that a "good" German existed: "*. . . a good German, ha, ha, ha. Have you not read the Bible? God would have forgiven Gomorrah if He could have found ten righteous men there. Ten, only ten. But He did not find them and He destroyed Gomorrah. There are not ten good Germans left and He shall destroy Germany. It shall be wiped off the face of the earth.*" In contrast to some of the homilies Spencer Tracy uttered in *The Seventh Cross*, these words were a strong indictment against the German people for their role in World War II. However, *Hotel Berlin* ended on an optimistic note. President Roosevelt's radio address, as read by Peter Lorre, offered succor to a nation that now was, literally, aflame in ruins: "*. . . we bring no charge against the German race for we cannot believe that God has eternally condemned any race of humanity.*"

While the Hollywood propaganda team wrestled with its conscience, debating the thorny issue of whether or not there was a good German roaming around Europe, the beleaguered Londoners could supply an immediate and succinct answer. Each night, the Nazi terror bombing raids pulverized their capital, inflicting enormous civilian casualties. As far as the British were concerned, there was no "good" German. While the Battle of Britain would later become the country's Finest Hour, the daily toll in "blood, sweat, and tears" was staggering. Since the United Kingdom and the United States shared so much in common, this stoic determinism—in the face of overwhelming odds—became a feature of many motion pictures.

Another component of effective propaganda emphasized the innocent victims of war: the children, the elderly, the ill, or any other group of noncombatants. As Nazi aircraft dropped tons of incendiaries on London, their targets were not strategic military installations but the British people themselves. If Goering thought he would frighten the populace into submission and capitulation, he grossly miscalculated the cohesive power that bonded the nation during these dark days. This was the theme of MGM's homage to the British spirit, *Journey for Margaret,* a film that showed that the fight being waged on English streets was, indeed, the people's war.

With Robert Young and Laraine Day in the leading roles, *Journey for Margaret* was a poignant drama describing the travail endured by an American couple seeking to bring a five-year-old British orphan, a victim of the nightly attacks, to the United States. After a few bureaucratic setbacks, the travelers finally reached New York, where a safe home and a life without fear of Axis bombs awaited the young girl. But on a propaganda level, *Journey for Margaret* highlighted the alliance that fused the Allied powers in the global war. In one isolated scene, the Japanese ambassador, stationed in London, made a hasty exit from the capital, bragging to reporters that his government required his presence in Tokyo by early December.

But it was an MGM blockbuster, *Mrs. Miniver,* that told an elaborate story about the bombing raids and the new hardships they created for the beleaguered English people. Directed by William Wyler and starring Greer Garson (in the title role), Walter Pidgeon and Theresa Wright, *Mrs. Miniver* received five academy awards—best picture, best direction, best actress, best supporting actress, and best screenplay—for its stereotypical portrayal of an upper-middle class British family living in the London countryside, caught up in the throes of the war. Initially, the problems seemed innocuous as Greer Garson oversaw the duties of the household servant, while Walter Pidgeon tinkered with his expensive sports car. But soon the Battle of Britain changed everything and now the couple, along with the entire nation, banded together in their fight against the Axis, putting aside, at least temporarily, former class distinctions.

But a caste system could not vanish overnight and while *Mrs. Miniver*—with its numerous soap opera subplots—succeeded as a melodrama, its propaganda value seemed dubious. While the Nazi bombs fell incessantly on the British capital, some fifty kilometers away, the indomitable Miss Garson suffered stoically in a Sydney Guilaroff coiffure. Other counterplots hinted at some of the social ills prevalent in England prior to the War: an ongoing feud between the town's matriarch and the stationmaster created numerous problems; a romance between the Miniver's maid and a British tommy had its private ups and downs; a marriage involving the Miniver son and the granddaughter of a prominent family ended tragically; and the attack on the local parish church, by Nazi bombers, restated the dignity of Protestant England.

Overall, *Mrs. Miniver* glamorized the quiet heroism of the British people during their Finest Hour in a manner that seemed refined, but polarized. On one level could be found the vestiges of the aristocracy, men who gallantly sailed their private boats into the dangerous waters off Dunkirk to rescue the remnants of the retreating Allied forces, while back in the countryside their women argued incessantly over which bloom would win first prize at an annual flower-growing contest. But off in the distance, the lower classes—huddled in the damp London underground stations for long hours at a stretch—endured the nightly hardships caused by the Luftwaffe's attacks. Even with Theresa Wright's untimely death Britain would survive, the film averred, and this small message certainly increased the warmth that American audiences felt toward their number one ally. If nothing else, the propaganda value of *Mrs. Miniver* rested in the premise that while American moviegoers could empathize with British suffering, the Nazi air raids, witnessed daily on their local screens, were far away in distant England. Invincible America, separated by that large ocean, was safe from any Axis bombings.

Occasionally, the Nazis managed a foothold on North American shores, but quick-thinking governmental organizations or high-ranking military officials routed these Axis before any damage ensued. In Warner Brothers' *Northern Pursuit*, Errol Flynn, now a member of an elite Canadian Mounted Police unit,

traveled many cold miles until he finally captured a fifth columnist network intent on wrecking the Allied war effort. Directed by
Raoul Walsh, *Northern Pursuit* highlighted the efficacy of this
crack unit as Errol Flynn, wearing an elaborate fur coat for
comfort against the frigid northern wilderness, tracked down his
Nazi nemesis, Helmut Dantine. *Northern Pursuit* brought the
propaganda message home in vivid terms. While Britain was
struggling under the weight of repeated German attacks in such
films as *Mrs. Miniver, Journey for Margaret* or *This Above All,*
the United States and Canada, two nations strong in their alliance
against Hitlerism, could thwart any Axis invasion on their territory, because both countries prided themselves on their vigilance.
No foreign foe would breach their elaborate security system.

But some enemy warships were sighted off the Canadian
shores. In Universal's *Corvette K-225,* Navy officer Randolph
Scott endured many adventures before he wreaked havoc on a
Nazi submarine that was terrorizing the large vessels sailing the
dangerous England and Canadian shipping lanes. In Warner
Brothers' *Action in the North Atlantic,* tough merchant marine
Captain Humphrey Bogart finally sailed his crippled cargo vessel
into the Russian port of Murmansk after an elaborate game of
hide-and-seek with an Axis U-boat. Sometimes, the American
Navy manned the submarines that chased the Nazis and launched
surprise raids against German refueling installations. Against a
lighthearted rivalry between submarines and PT boats, good-
looking Tyrone Power destroyed an important Nazi operations
base in Twentieth Century-Fox's *Crash Dive.* All three of these
titles contained the standard propaganda message: the Allied
forces controlled the North Atlantic Ocean.

Other Allied victories reinforced the Hollywood message by
reminding audiences of the global nature of the War. In the North
African campaign, the Nazi juggernaut and the heat of the desert
served as the backdrop for two films depicting the El Alamein
battle. In Paramount's *Five Graves to Cairo,* Franchot Tone
portrayed a lone British corporal, separated from his unit, who
finally stumbled into a small, dilapidated town away from the
conflict. Aided by the local innkeeper, he quickly regained his
strength. Then German tanks entered the town, and soon the
British tommy convinced a Nazi lieutenant that he was an Axis
spy working undercover in the village. The Nazi officer, played by

Peter Van Eyck, naively accepted this story. Once more, a German jackboot was hoodwinked by an Allied soldier. The propaganda message was obvious: junior officers of the Third Reich lacked common sense and military acumen. But what about their leaders? Could their field marshals be duped?

Certainly, if Hollywood had successfully caricatured Hitler, Mussolini, Tojo, and Goebbels, this treatment could be extended to Field Marshal Erwin Rommel, the leader of the famed Afrika Korps. If *Five Graves to Cairo* depicted a foolish Nazi subordinate accepting the cockamamie story proffered by Franchot Tone, why not try the fabrication on the Axis leader in charge of the North African campaign? To portray the aristocratic Field Marshal Rommel, director Billy Wilder selected the former Austrian actor, Erich von Stroheim, whose triumphant arrival in the small town was heralded with much fanfare as Nazi officers posted their orders regarding the new military occupation. When brought before the Axis commander, Franchot Tone's prevarication fooled everyone, and soon the British corporal learned about the hidden oil reserves—the five graves—buried deep in the Egyptian desert.

Eventually, the field marshal dispatched his new-found "spy" to another location but Franchot Tone returned instead to the British lines, where he supplied the necessary information for an attack. Soon the Axis forces were routed and Franchot Tone, now wearing a clean military uniform, entered the small village, this time as a conquering hero. Rommel's defeat, according to Columbia Pictures, was engineered by one lone Englishman, whose skill and cunning brought the German war machine to a dead halt in the hot desert sun. As a fictional account of the North African campaign, *Five Graves to Cairo* stretched all limits of plausibility. According to the storyline, a German scientific expedition team, in 1937, anticipating a protracted land war, secretly buried a large cache of refined oil in the desert for retrieval by the Third Reich. However, this plan was thwarted by a leading Hollywood star whose good looks and lean appearance made him the ideal foil against the stereotypical Nazi officer, the imperious Erich von Stroheim.

If a handsome movie star could wreck the Nazi war machine in the North African desert, so could a motley team drawn from several Allied nations and headed by a tough, unshaven American tank sergeant. This was the theme of Columbia's *Sahara,* a propaganda film closely akin in style and format to other pictures that highlighted the group concept as a salient ingredient for victory—*Bataan, Air Force, Wake Island,* and *Guadalcanal Diary.* Directed by Zoltan Korda, *Sahara* starred the indomitable Humphrey Bogart—in another of his loner roles—as the leader of ten soldiers, cut off from their unit behind enemy lines in the torrid, waterless Sahara. Fleeing from a successful Axis frontal attack, this small team jumped aboard Bogart's Sherman tank—appropriately dubbed *Lulu Belle*—and headed for the nearest oasis, some 160 kilometers away. En route the crew picked up an Italian prisoner of war, J. Carrol Naish, and captured a Nazi Messerschmitt pilot, Kurt Krueger. Eventually, they reached the watering hole, but their expectations received a dramatic setback: the well was empty.

Now what? Should Bogart push on, hoping eventually to find his front lines, or should he attempt a rear guard defense? Should he run from the Nazi Wehrmacht or stand and fight in the abandoned oasis? For Bogart, the choice was easy: dig in and fight—slow the enemy down, become a thorn in his side, allow the Allied forces time to regroup. But this small crew, stranded in the middle of a desert, without food or water, was still a democracy and Bogart's plan required a plebiscite. As a propaganda device, following the OWI's directives, the group vote was always an effective scene, reiterating every wholesome trait found in the Allied forces' credo. Democracy was not fascism, the OWI echoed, every man had his say.

Bogart's arguments were ecumenical, heaping praise on numerous countries: *". . . why did your little [English] boats take the men off the beaches at Dunkirk? Why did the Russians make a stand at Moscow? Why did the Chinese move whole cities thousands of miles inland? Why Bataan, why Corregidor? . . . They delayed the enemy!"* Now it was settled. A small force of Allied soldiers—a South African, an Irishman, a Frenchman, two Englishmen, a Sudanese, and two Americans—agreed to defend the dried-up watering hole against a large convoy of Nazi troops heading their way, while another American volunteered to drive a captured Nazi truck into the desert, hoping to find reinforcements.

To a large degree, the action in *Sahara* evoked scenes from the stereotypical Hollywood Western. Here was a group of civilians-turned-soldiers (the settlers) waiting inside an abandoned oasis (the fort) while the Nazi enemy (the Indians) slowly advanced, as a lone GI (the scout) sneaked away to locate his unit (the cavalry). When the Nazis/Indians attacked the stronghold, they were repelled by the defenders. Casualties were heavy on the Axis side, as many died under the incessant fire power of Bogart's men. However, the Germans fought back, and one by one the Allied soldiers were killed by sharpshooters or explosives. Finally, two survivors—Bogart and the British tommy—stood defiantly against a large contingent of dehydrated Afrika Korps soldiers slowly meandering towards the water hole, their hands in the air, muttering *"wasser."* The remnants of the Nazi battalion finally capitulated and Bogart collected dozens of prisoners. When the British reinforcements (the cavalry) arrived, the officers cheered Bogart as he stood victoriously atop *Lulu Belle,* marching his beleaguered captives to the Allied lines.

As propaganda, this closing scene in *Sahara* borrowed heavily from an identical ending in Warner Brothers' 1941 Academy Award winner, *Sergeant York.* In this earlier motion picture, Gary Cooper portrayed the Tennessee hayseed who became a World War I Medal of Honor winner by capturing over a hundred German prisoners—at the battle of the Argonne in October 1918—and marching them straight to his own headquarters. Both films stressed the prowess of the U.S. fighting man and reiterated the theme that overwhelming odds were not an impediment in wartime. The American hero relied on his fortitude and conviction when confronted by the German foe. The German fighting forces were no match for the American heroes who flickered across the silver screen at hundreds of shows across the land. With Humphrey Bogart in the driver's seat of his M-3 air-cooled tank, not even the Sahara was a formidable obstacle.

If the German Army—weaned by a rigid Prussian military discipline system—capitulated every time they ran into stiff Yankee determinism, what threat could the Italian soldier offer against the Allied cause? If the Nazi fighting man avowed to fight to the end for his Fuehrer, would the Italians sacrifice as much for *Il Duce?* Could a nation of carefree souls—one that seemed more interested in pursuing good food, happy music, pretty women, and robust wine—pose a serious threat? For Hollywood, the answer was simple: portray the Japanese as sewer rats, the Germans as brutes and the Italians as fun-loving simpletons. Let the Japanese and Germans fight to the death; the Italians would include a generous glass of *vino* in their surrender pact.

In Billy Wilder's *Five Graves to Cairo,* the Italian officer (Fortunio Bonanova) attached to Erwin Rommel's retinue bemoaned the field marshal's militarist attitude after he was rebuked for singing popular arias in his hotel room, while over in humid North Africa, the French prefect, Claude Rains, poked fun at the Italian attaché's loquacious speaking style and noticeable gesticulations in Michael Curtiz' *Casablanca.* Similarly, in Zoltan Korda's *Sahara,* the Italian prisoner of war, J. Carrol Naish, delivered a passionate antifascist tirade against Mussolini and his Axis followers, claiming that the Italian people were frightened into accepting the bellicose expansionist policies that *Il Duce* decreed. Later, this harmless Italian was murdered by a Nazi officer in a scene that reaffirmed Hollywood's premise that the Germans, not the Italians, were the warmongering nation.

As propaganda, these three films simplified the real issue of America's fight with Italy. It was Mussolini, not the Italian people, the Hollywood directors averred, who forced the nation into an unholy alliance with Hitler. The real enemy was fascism, and for most Italians, sitting in their outdoor cafes, sipping their morning espresso, this political concept was over their heads. However, by autumn of 1943, the tide shifted dramatically with the successful Allied invasion of southern Europe. On September 8, 1943, the Italians quietly surrendered to the advancing American forces. A few weeks later, a dramatic political volte-face changed everything. A provisional government ousted Mussolini and his followers. On October 13, Italy declared war against Germany.

Now that Italy was an ally instead of a belligerent, Hollywood fattened up the propaganda value of America's new-found friend. In United Artists' *The Story of GI Joe,* director William Wellman produced a wonderful encomium to the American war correspondent Ernie Pyle, who traveled throughout Italy writing poignant stories about the GIs marching northward. When confronted by the sixth-century Monte Cassino Abbey—now used by Germans as a strategic observation tower—the Allies attacked the religious shrine rather than allow American soldiers to perish, and justified the bombing raid on moral rather than military grounds. The Italian people, the film stated, were unwilling pawns in a complex struggle between Hitler and Mussolini.

In its own maudlin style, *The Story of GI Joe* produced a significant propaganda message that erased any reference to Italy's allegiance to Hitler. As the GIs advanced toward Rome, they confronted the Germans, not Italian forces, who were making their last ditch effort. After the Nazis retreated to the Fatherland, this southern campaign was over and the victorious Allies, determined to expunge all facets of the former fascist rule, established a reconstructive government charged with bringing normalcy back to the Italian people. This was the theme of Twentieth Century-Fox's *A Bell for Adano,* the last propaganda film made during the Second World War about the Italian theater.

With John Hodiak and William Bendix in the starring roles, *A Bell for Adano* sugarcoated every aspect of Italy's role in the Axis pact and suggested that Mussolini, not the Italian people, caused all the misery associated with the War. Directed by Henry King, *A Bell for Adano* depicted the amity that developed between a handful of American soldiers and some friendly rustics living in the small southern town of Adano in the fall of 1943. Initially, the Americans established an orderly transition of government but soon the Army commander, John Hodiak, became enmeshed in the everyday problems of a happy group of people who only wanted their old way of life returned. A chief concern was a new bell for their church, a needed symbol that would signify the restoration of the village.

Any religious icon, of course, provided a strong dose of propaganda and this needed church bell restated the theme of this film. For the Italian peasants living in a small town, their church—located prominently in the village square—became the focal point of their existence: births, baptisms, marriages, and funerals were ritualistic moments of everyday life. Without the bell to call forth the faithful, a significant part of these ceremonies was lost. To frustrate matters, the Italians argued, it was the Nazis who removed the original bell and melted it down to make bullets for the Fuehrer's war. Would the U.S. Army, the villagers asked, return pride and dignity to their town by locating a bell for Adano?

With the help of an old Navy buddy, John Hodiak requisitioned an obsolete ship's bell, and its delivery to Adano elicited spontaneous jubilation. Townspeople rushed out, marveling at the sight, while old women literally kissed the hand of John Hodiak, imploring the blessings of various saints to show appreciation for this gift. As a final gesture, a portrait of Hodiak was placed in the lobby of the municipal building, a tangible reminder of the kindness of the American occupying forces. For the Army major, this moment of triumph served as a reminder of the friendship that existed between these two nations.

As a propaganda film, *A Bell for Adano* did much to erase the historical fact that Italy and the United States were legally at war for two years. Unlike the Nazis, who were vilified in dozens of motion pictures, the Italians were transformed into noble innocents caught up in the vortex of a conflict they did not want. While the Germans, *per se,* were militaristic, determined to expand their boundaries under their vicious lebensraum policy, the Italians only wanted peace, happiness, and sunshine. In many ways, *A Bell for Adano* defined the true nature of wartime propaganda. Here, an obvious enemy, scorned by the Americans back on the Home Front, was transmogrified into an unfortunate victim of regrettable circumstances.

For Hollywood, the war in Europe really meant the fight against Germany, and all other members of the Axis pact were simply whitewashed out of existence. Italy was a nonbelligerent nation, while Austria, Bulgaria, Finland, Hungary, and Rumania were never mentioned. This technique, of course, restated a basic tenet of propaganda—simplicity. The rules for audience persuasion required that only one enemy at a time could be featured; complex issues or alliances were taboo. Using these parameters, Hollywood's salvo against Germany was more than complete or detailed—it was also efficacious.

CHAPTER FIVE

WE'RE ALL IN THIS TOGETHER: AMERICA'S RUSSIAN AND CHINESE ALLIES

Clark Gable: *". . . how is the old Kremlin?"*

Eve Arden: *". . . same old rattrap; full of stuffed shirts, double-crossing the masses. Someday, the people are gonna get wise and take it apart brick-by-brick."*

—Clark Gable and Eve Arden, as two American journalists discussing current Russian politics in King Vidor's 1940 anti-Soviet film, *Comrade X.*

Walter Huston: *". . . Russia will never stop fighting its fascist foes. They will defend their cities; they will fight in the streets."*

—Walter Huston, as Ambassador Joseph E. Davies, praising Soviet intransigence, in Warner Brother's 1943 pro-Russian tract, *Mission to Moscow.*

When the United States went to war in December 1941, the Hollywood motion picture industry found itself in an embarrassing quandary over its newest ally, the Soviet Union. For more than twenty years—as far back as 1919—American audiences were regularly warned about the expansionist policies of communist Russia and its goal of world domination. In one film after another, Soviet leaders were portrayed as godless Bolsheviks, intent on destroying the American free enterprise system.

Some of the titles—United Artist's *Red Salute* (1935) and Columbia's *He Stayed for Breakfast* (1940)—chipped away at Leninist ideology, while others—Paramount's *Spawn of the*

North (1938) and Warner Brothers' *Tovarich* (1937)—revealed the inherent baseness of Russian opportunism. Other films, likewise, reiterated this basic theme: don't believe the Russians, beware of the Red menace.

In 1939, MGM released *Ninotchka,* a typical screwball comedy that lampooned the Soviet system in every frame. Directed by Ernst Lubitsch and starring Greta Garbo, *Ninotchka* told the easygoing story of a stony-faced Russian bureaucrat (Garbo) who was ordered to Paris as an official communist emissary to negotiate the sale of some seized royal jewelry. Captivated by the splendors of western capitalism and the smooth-tongued charms of handsome Melvyn Douglas, the comely party official capitulated to moonlight love and French perfume, while denouncing the evils of the modern communist state. A few months later—following the same tone—a second MGM comedy lambasting the Soviet Union appeared just in time for the 1940 Christmas season: King Vidor's *Comrade X.*

Using the typical MGM all-star cast, *Comrade X* launched a devastating attack on the 1939 Soviet government as seen through the picaresque eyes of an American journalist, Clark Gable, posted in Moscow, who dispatched his news stories under the pseudonym, Comrade X. Eventually, the reporter became enamored of a pretty Russian streetcar conductor, Hedy Lamarr, and after some slapstick adventures, escaped across the western border to the freedom of Brooklyn's famed Flatbush section.

Historically, this film was ill-timed because six months later— on June 21, 1941—Hitler unleashed Operation Barbarossa against the Soviet Union and, within a few days, communist Russia became an ally of the United States. For Hollywood, this meant another change of policy toward its old antagonist. MGM, of course, was reluctant to shelve *Comrade X* because it had already reaped substantial revenue. Within days, the producers added an introductory trailer to the film, insisting that its caricaturing of the Russians was intended solely for public entertainment. In reality, this ten-second tag stated, *Comrade X* was merely good-natured humor between old buddies. Now the motion picture industry began to crank up its typewriters because the one-time dastardly communists, vilified for so many years in American theaters, needed immediate cosmetic, cinematic surgery.

Once the floodgates opened, an array of pro-Soviet films told stories of the venturesome Russians fighting the Axis scourge. Always outnumbered and lacking proper equipment, the Slavs relied on their prowess and mettle to rout the Nazis at every turn. The first title to reach the silver screen was Lothar Mendes' *Miss V. from Moscow,* a B-production from Producers Releasing Corporation. Starring Lola Lane, *Miss V. from Moscow,* in its sixty-minute format, recounted the heroism of a female Russian spy hiding in Paris and sending important intelligence information to the Allied command. When confronted by the Gestapo, she chose death rather than betray her cause.

Martyrdom, of course, reiterated a basic propaganda tenet: if Miss V. sacrificed herself, so could other Soviet nationals. After all, according to Hollywood's dictum, wasn't suffering part of the Russian psyche, its roots going all the way back to Dostoevsky? In MGM's *The North Star,* a small village in the Ukraine was overrun by the Nazi juggernaut and every peasant responded valiantly, implementing the Stalinist scorched earth policy. Willing to burn their wheat fields rather than allow the grain to fall into Nazi hands, the freshly-scrubbed rustics, led by Dana Andrews and Walter Huston, endured numerous deprivations, including the draining of blood from small children, before routing the Wehrmacht.

As a propaganda film, Lewis Milestone's *The North Star* certainly waved the hammer and sickle alongside Old Glory, but this pro-Soviet tract contained some subtle but obviously contradictory messages. On one hand the film depicted the Soviet peasants as devoted to Stalin, willing to sacrifice everything for the Motherland. In an aerial scene, Comrade bomber-pilot Dana Andrews plunged his crippled aircraft into a row of Nazi tanks to thwart an impending assault against his village. His death reaffirmed the Hollywood maxim that Soviet heroics were routine occurrences along the eastern front. However, while the storyline of *The North Star* took place in an unnamed, fictitious Ukrainian village, there was no remote indication that the inhabitants were Ukrainians, not Russians. This ethnic group—the Ukrainians—was delicately expunged from the plot.

Why was this? Didn't Hollywood know that referring to a Ukrainian as a Russian was the same as calling a New Yorker a Texan? Weren't the Tinseltown moguls aware that the Ukraine

and Russia had been at odds with each other over the centuries and
that their many historical conflicts had left a great deal of bad
blood as an unwanted legacy? When Hitler's troops first invaded
the Ukraine, some nationals went over to the Axis side, joining the
numerous liberation battalions that the Nazis organized to fight
against Russia. Like other ethnic groups hostile to Stalin's
dictatorial rule, these Ukrainians viewed the Wehrmacht more as
a deliverer than a conqueror. But in many American eyes, the
large assortment of nationalities living in the Soviet Union were
conveniently grouped together under the appellation "Russian."
It didn't matter in what part of the Union anyone lived—they were
all Russians. Uzbekistans, Armenians, Georgians—their birth-
right made little difference to Hollywood

Other titles heaped praise upon Uncle Sam's new friend. In
Columbia's *The Boy from Stalingrad* a group of youths stole
German weapons and fought their adversaries behind the Axis
lines. Warner Brothers continued the attack with *Background to
Danger,* a spy-versus-spy melodrama that paired U.S. agent
George Raft and Russian operative Brenda Marshall as allies who
wrecked an Axis fifth column ring working in neutral Turkey.
Directed by Raoul Walsh, *Background to Danger* exaggerated the
cooperation that existed between American and Soviet intelli-
gence agencies. Another Warner production, *Action in the North
Atlantic,* almost deified the U.S. Merchant Marine sailing its
"floating firecrackers" across the submarine-laden waters of the
North Atlantic, heading for the Russian port of Murmansk with
needed supplies for the Red Army. Under Jerry Wald's direction,
Action in the North Atlantic featured Humphrey Bogart and
Raymond Massey as two seamen responsible for delivering the
ship's vital cargo to the Soviet people.

The adulation continued as other motion pictures glorified
Comrade Ivan's struggle against fascism. MGM's *Song of Russia*
starred Robert Taylor as an American symphony orchestra conductor on tour in the Soviet Union when Operation Barbarossa
was unleashed. Directed by Gregory Ratoff, *Song of Russia*
pumped up the volume of the Tchaikovsky piano concerto while
highlighting the Red Army's efficiency as it mobilized against
Hitler's invading forces. At the same time, Russian partisans
fought from their hideaways in RKO's *Days of Glory,* in which
Gregory Peck, under Jacques Tourneur's cinematic tutelage, led

many nighttime sorties against the Wehrmacht. Over in Leningrad, American test pilot Kent Smith aided the Russian Air Force in United Artists' *Three Russian Girls,* a B-film directed by Fedor Ozep.

Some ideas were unusual. In Universal's zany B-production, *Invisible Agent,* Jon Hall portrayed the grandson of the famous Invisible Man, now working for the U.S. intelligence forces with the secret formula perfected by his grandfather. Assigned to parachute into Nazi Germany, the American spy received his final instructions from a Russian officer moments before starting his science-fiction adventure. While the premise of Edwin Martin's *Invisible Agent* was pure hokum, this briefing scene was significant because it glamorized the harmonious Russo-American relationship. A similar storyline showed up in Columbia's *Counter-Attack,* starring Paul Muni and directed by Zoltan Korda. In this bizarre plot, the Russian Army secretly built an underwater bridge a mere six inches from the surface in a strategic German-controlled river. Later, this engineering feat enabled the Soviets to launch their offensive. Adding to the hyperbole of *Counter-Attack* were the humanlike qualities of the soldiers' mascot, a quick-thinking dog with an esoteric barking system that literally saved the day for some trapped Russian commandos.

One film, however, topped them all. Warner Brothers' *Mission to Moscow* became the most outspoken motion picture film of the War and is often called the greatest propaganda film ever made. Directed by Michael Curtiz, starring Walter Huston in the title role of Ambassador Joseph E. Davies, and featuring an impressive array of well-known character actors, *Mission to Moscow* was overblown and full of historical inaccuracies, subtle prevarications, and pious oversimplifications that rationalized every Soviet misdeed committed in the previous twenty years. Both Stalin and Kalinin appeared as sanitized, benevolent leaders who only wanted to help their new friend, the United States, defeat the Axis pact, while the happy Russian peasants stoically endured any hardship necessary to achieve victory.

Released in April 1943, *Mission to Moscow* took on a pseudo-documentary air. Various world leaders—Molotov, Stalin, Kalinin, von Ribbentrop, Churchill, Hull, and Roosevelt—were convincingly portrayed by character actors. The ''real'' Joseph E. Davies, the former U.S. ambassador to Russia, appeared in an opening trailer to introduce the film version of his book, by the same title, which revealed why the American people needed to know the "truth" about their new ally. According to Davies, the Soviet Union recognized the Nazi threat long before other western nations, entrenched in their own isolationism, finally understood the seriousness of lebensraum. In one passionate speech, Walter Huston (as Davies) argued with some pro-American skeptics that the Russians were holding the ramparts of civilization by repelling Hitler's advances.

Similar claptrap emphasized the propaganda aspects of *Mission to Moscow*. In 1936, the film explained, President Roosevelt hand-picked Davies to serve as the U.S. representative to the Soviet Union. FDR's instructions were blunt: find out Russia's true intentions. For the next two years, this former trial lawyer, with a sharp eye for detail, traveled throughout Europe, meeting national leaders, visiting collective farms, and attending the purge trials. Finally, he returned to Washington with his report. The Russians, Davies declared, were our best friends.

After talking with Roosevelt, the former ambassador embarked on an elaborate speaking tour to reeducate the American people and counteract the Russian horror stories that had been reported in the national press. The Moscow trials, according to Davies, revealed that the accused Russian officers were conspirators in a plot engineered by Trotsky, Germany, and Japan to undermine the Soviet military. Likewise, the invasion of Finland was necessary because that nation's expansionist policies, implemented by Hitler's friend Mannerheim, represented a threat at the Russian border. The same logic prevailed regarding the Russo-Germany nonaggression pact. This agreement was a cleverly orchestrated stall tactic, devised by Stalin himself, to give the Red Army needed time to strengthen its defensive positions.

Other groups were lambasted by the ambassador: Britain's Chamberlain government, with its policy of appeasement, could not understand Stalin's regime, while the French and Polish envoys were stewing in their own anti-Soviet bias. As for the isolationists in Congress, they were shortsighted men, living in the past, unable to comprehend the ever-changing nature of international politics.

No other propaganda film of the War contained as much misinformation as *Mission to Moscow* and no other title stirred up such diversified critical reaction. The Left saw the picture as a fitting tribute to a gallant ally, while the Right denounced the storyline as mere whitewash. However, most American moviegoers seemed convinced by Walter Huston's skillful oratory in explaining recent Russian history. Adding to the Bible-quoting ambassador's claims was a pious, religious ending, complete with rhapsodic, angelic music, that asked an important Old Testament question: "Am I my brother's keeper?"

The answer, of course, was yes. As propaganda, *Mission to Moscow* contained every element needed for mass persuasion and American audiences accepted this premise, hook, line, and sinker. Why not? Famous world leaders consistently praised the Soviet cause, and the Russians, themselves, prostrated their appreciative bodies before the tenets of Jeffersonian democracy. What else could this Slavic nation do to prove its worth to the alliance? If Walter Huston, who had already portrayed two American icons— Abraham Lincoln and Uncle Sam—in Hollywood films, accepted the Soviet Union, who could argue differently? In one glowing scene, the Soviet President (Vladimir Sokoloff) called FDR a great man with a deep sympathy for mankind. Not to be outdone, Joseph Stalin (Manart Kippen) added that his government's friendship toward the U.S.A. exceeded that of any other country.

Another rule for effective wartime propaganda was to show the conflict solely from the viewpoint of one side, by using selective material and half-truths. This axiom clearly applied to *Mission to Moscow.* How much "friendship" did the Soviets demonstrate in April 1942 when they interned a crew of the Doolittle Raiders after the five airmen were forced to make an emergency landing on a Siberian runway hours after their famous Tokyo bombing attack? After a one-year ordeal on various Russian military bases, the flyers managed to bribe some border guards and slipped into neighboring Iran.

These events, of course, did not appear in Hollywood propaganda films. Instead, the Soviets' struggle against fascism and the heroic fighting of the Russian soldier became the motif of every storyline. While Russian leaders sat in cushioned chairs, balancing small trays of beluga caviar on their laps, discussing realpolitik with Walter Huston, other nationals did not fare as well. In *Days of Glory,* a group of partisans worked behind enemy lines, sabotaging the Wehrmacht at every turn. Headed by Gregory Peck (in his screen debut), the Russian group was a composite of various ages and temperaments, living in a crude but efficient underground cave, determined to rid the scourge from their land.

Each nightly sortie contained its own frustration as members perished or reports from other partisans revealed Nazi advances. In one harrowing scene a captured sixteen-year-old boy was brutally hanged because he would not reveal the location of the guerrillas' camp. This execution—emphasizing the victim's youth and innocence—was gruesome but its cinematic purpose was to highlight the wantonness of Nazi aggression. His death, however, provided the instant martyrdom necessary for propaganda and his final tirade reiterated the mission of every Russian: *"You cannot hang a nation—death to the German invaders. Kill them, kill them!"*

Naturally, as partisans, the Motherland's peasants were portrayed as superior fighters, able to live off the land, while occasionally returning to their forest lair for needed supplies. When they were ordered to counterattack, the finale was always the same—victory. In *Days of Glory,* the Nazis were routed in a glamorous version of the cavalry-to-the-rescue, as Gregory Peck and his Slavic guerrillas emerged from their hiding places to decimate the German forces. This same worn-out motif—the John Wayne hero leading the cavalry charge—also appeared in *The North Star.* Here a group of Ukrainian peasants, mounted on their village horses, galloped into a Nazi camp to rescue some captive children. This equestrian attack was reminiscent of any B-Western. Firing from the hip, with outdated rifles, the Ukrainians only lacked some yellow ribbon around their necks to complete the stereotype. Transformed to the wheatlands of western Ukraine, with Nazi soldiers instead of American Indians as an adversary, the entire scene, anachronistic to the core, maintained the necessary propaganda message: good always triumphs over evil.

Since the Red Army fought alone on the eastern front, these Hollywood films portrayed the individual soldier or partisan as an agile, wiry patriot, adept at scampering over the snow-covered fields. This was an important part of the propaganda message—show continuity. If American GIs attacked their Axis enemies on faraway jungle islands or in hot, desert wastelands, the Russian soldier's portrayal must have a similar consistency, including the milieu. As a member of the Allied forces, the Soviets, like their American counterparts, had to demonstrate initiative and win battles. Tough, brawny, victorious and apolitical: this was the image of Mother Russia.

It was an entirely different story with the Chinese. The Russians, of course, were depicted as a Caucasian ally with many traits, features, and mores in common with their American allies. But with the Chinese, their 1930s image—emblazoned in the minds of most American moviegoers—was always a combination of docility, servility, and Confucianism. Occasionally, an Oriental character showed promise—Charlie Chan, for example—but for the most part, no Chinese national could function competently without American help, guidance, or authority. For depression-ridden America, Hollywood created a needed stereotype—the Chinese as a placid, inscrutable people lacking both leadership and initiative.

Not much changed after the Pearl Harbor attack. On the silver screen, China was still a beleaguered nation, a country with a pitiful military, ill-equipped to stop the advancing Nipponese Army. Soon American forces arrived, first as a volunteer group and then as a specialized unit created especially for this theater by President Roosevelt. The Fourteenth Air Force was commanded by a man who epitomized every component of World War II propaganda films—John Wayne.

When Hollywood's toughest fighter pilot, John Wayne, climbed into the cramped cockpit of his Curtiss P-40 aircraft, cranked over its engine and headed off into the wild blue yonder, in Republic Pictures' *Flying Tigers,* one thing was certain—the Chinese people would sleep securely that night because the Japanese Air Force was heading toward extinction. With John Carroll and Paul Kelly in supporting roles, *Flying Tigers* dramatized the exploits of General Claire Chennault's airmen. While the Chinese peasants washed dishes, swept floors, or functioned as obedient servants, American pilots—with their mastery of western technology—saved their Oriental ally from capitulation.

John Wayne wasn't the only American flyer keeping the wolf from China's door. In Warner Brothers' *God Is My Co-Pilot,* Dennis Morgan, another member of Chennault's air warriors, became a double ace, knocking down ten Japanese Zeroes; his docile Chinese maintenance workers helped by checking the aircraft's oil and cleaning the windshield. Twentieth Century-Fox also used this Flying Tiger theme in Henry Hathaway's *China Girl*. Here, George Montgomery, a former vaudeville actor, took on the Japanese Air Force, while Chinese waiters served Tom Collins to the thirsty volunteers who, during their idle hours, gathered in local bars bragging about their airborne exploits.

Sometimes, the Chinese performed as valuable assistants. In RKO's *China Sky*, cowboy-star Randolph Scott worked long hours as an American doctor, caring for the sick and wounded in a remote village dispensary. Helping the good-looking practitioner were capable but obedient Chinese nurses, carefully patting their physician's sweaty brow as the American performed delicate surgery. But once in a while there were subtle deviations from this stock role. Occasionally, a Chinese professional—educated in the United States—reciprocated by aiding Americans who were in a precarious situation. In MGM's *Thirty Seconds Over Tokyo*, bomber pilot Van Johnson—one of the Doolittle Raiders— required immediate medical attention for his gangrenous leg. A Chinese doctor performed the lifesaving amputation. Later, the clean-cut airman lauded his surgeon's skill and heaped praise upon the Chinese people for their fight against the Japanese.

As a propaganda film, *Thirty Seconds Over Tokyo* stressed many positive images of the Chinese peasants as they carried the wounded crew members over rough terrain to eventual safety. Another picture, Twentieth Century-Fox's *The Purple Heart*, depicted a similar rescue mission as Chinese villagers hid the downed fliers in their small huts. Later, a Chinese youth, Benson Fong, publicly assassinated his father to atone for the shame of the elder's collaboration with the Japanese. The propaganda message was clear: the Chinese people were devoted to the American cause. Any traitor, regardless of propinquity, was to be severely punished.

Other titles, however, were not as laudatory. In Paramount's *China*, blond-haired Alan Ladd portrayed an American opportunist peddling oil to the Japanese invaders, while a ragtag Chinese army offered feeble rear-guard resistance. After a series of convoluted experiences, including the Pearl Harbor attack, the renegade entrepreneur finally saw the light and turned against his Nipponese customers. Soon, he organized the Chinese into an effective guerrilla force. However, in the final reel, it was Alan

Ladd, not the Chinese fighters, who lured the Japanese into a narrow mountainous pass. Here, the converted Sinophile sacrificed his life to dynamite a Japanese convoy. His martyrdom reaffirmed the doctrine that only American skill could save China from its enemies.

Alan Ladd wasn't the only American working with subordinate Chinese guerrillas, diminutive men wearing rope-soled sandals who were quick to obey any command uttered by a Caucasian. Producers Releasing Corporation's B-pictures, *Bombs Over Burma* and *Lady from Chungking,* both featured Anna May Wong in her stereotypical Oriental heroine part, fighting off enemy generals, German agents and a White Russian, while praising the American way of life and lauding President Roosevelt. Other B-potboilers likewise emphasized the importance of American leadership and Chinese obsequiousness. In MGM's *A Yank on the Burma Road,* Paramount's *Night Plane from Chungking,* Universal's *Escape from Hong Kong,* and Monogram's *China's Little Devils* all depicted Oriental servility under the tutelage of an American leader.

One film, however, downplayed the American influence and suggested that the Chinese people, employing their own ingenuity, were capable of fighting off their Japanese invaders. MGM's *Dragon Seed* told the poignant story of some Chinese peasants whose lives were shattered when their eastern enemy occupied their small village. Based on the novel by Pearl S. Buck and directed by both Jack Conway and Harold Bucquet, *Dragon Seed* starred an array of Occidental actors in the leading roles: Katharine Hepburn, Walter Huston, Akim Tamiroff, Turhan Bey, and Agnes Moorehead all wore exaggerated makeup to create a Hollywood, oblique-eyed image.

These characterizations were ludicrous. Playing the wife of a Chinese farmer, Katharine Hepburn's Bryn Mawr accent and her tailored silk pajamas rendered her unfit for duty in the rice paddies, while her Confucius-quoting father-in-law, Walter Huston, sounded like a New England official running for local office. The other Occidentals were just as unconvincing. For the most part, their portrayals echoed D. W. Griffith's 1915 silent Civil War epic, *The Birth of a Nation.* In this film, the roles of the emancipated Black slaves, now under the control of Northern carpetbaggers, were played by Caucasian actors who smeared their faces with greasepaint.

Even with the performers' funny-looking appearances, *Dragon Seed* kept the propaganda ball rolling as the Chinese peasants repeatedly thwarted the Japanese invaders. In one elaborate scene, the deft Miss Hepburn skillfully poisoned the food of an entire Japanese regiment, an event that temporarily brought the conqueror's war machine to a halt. Later, she convinced the villagers to burn their homes and fields to slow down the Japanese advances. Finally, she joined the guerrilla forces operating from the interior. The propaganda value of such scenes was obvious; like their American ally, the Chinese people fought for the most intangible of ideals—freedom—and, if necessary, sacrificed their homes, their well-being, even their lives.

Hollywood, for the time being, basked in the warm cinematic sun for producing these many films depicting the strong alliance between both Russia and China and the United States. Throughout the war, these motion pictures proved invaluable in shaping public opinion about these two faraway countries. For most Americans back on the Home Front, sitting in their sparse kitchens and saving cooking oil from the daily meals, a political complacency was fostered by the motion picture industry. In its own funny way, it was comforting to know that Chinese and Russian soldiers, like their American counterparts, were fighting for FDR's dictum: unconditional surrender.

Later, it became an entirely different matter. In less than five years after the jubilant V-J Day celebration, both China and Russia became the United States' chief adversaries and a new conflict—the Cold War—was in full swing, with millions of Americans being warned about the dangers of communism and the evils of Uncle Joe and Chairman Mao. In the blink of an eye Hollywood called up its cameramen and, by 1950, a new array of anti-Soviet and anti-Chinese films flickered on the silver screen. Like the sinister-looking man walking away from the airplane crash in Peter Arno's classic cartoon, it was time for the Hollywood propagandists to go back to the drawing board.

CHAPTER SIX

SINCE WE'RE ALL AWAY: THE FOLKS LEFT BEHIND

"You know, folks, this Home Front is mighty important. Maybe we can't all turn in scrap, but we can get in it. One way is to buy from honest dealers and put black-market men like Corbin out of business."

—Western B-actor Denny Moore, to his sidekick Alibi Terhune, reminding audiences that the battle on the Home Front against unscrupulous retailers requires everyone's diligence, in Monogram's *Black Market Rustlers.*

While the American GI was off fighting the Axis foes in those faraway places with strange-sounding names, the civilians back home soon found their normal way of life completely altered. First, the American family confronted numerous consumer goods shortages as routine supply routes were no longer available. Rubber became an early victim of Japanese aggression in the Far East and crude oil was next as Nazi submarines torpedoed tankers in the North Atlantic. Sugar, coffee, butter and meat, likewise, were scarce and by early 1942, President Roosevelt, realizing the enormity of the problem, instituted formal rationing.

Now people carried their war ration books to the stores and stamp-sized points were torn out for each purchase. Clothing and shoes joined the list as well as canned foods, prompting the resourceful to learn sewing or tend a victory garden. Blackouts and air raid tests kept everyone on their toes and anxious Americans, worried about possible attacks, gathered around over-sized Atwater-Kent radios to hear Gabriel Heatter, a popular social commentator, proclaim "there's good news tonight" or some similar message to sustain morale.

Soon, another wartime term—the Home Front—entered routine conversation and its everyday usage redefined the nation at large. Franklin Delano Roosevelt, using his new sobriquet "Doctor-Win-the-War," constantly reminded radio audiences that the battles fought on some remote Pacific island were first won in the hot steel mills of Pittsburgh. The Home Front, the President averred, required numerous sacrifices and inconveniences, all necessitated by the global conflict. All citizens, he continued, must do their part, from saving bacon fat and collecting newspapers and scrap metal, to rolling bandages and standing air raid watches.

Hollywood, of course, was an integral part of the Home Front and many of its stars engaged in publicity tours to sell war bonds or served coffee at USO clubs—the stage door canteens. Over in the production departments, it was a similar story: the film moguls, encouraged by an OWI directive advocating that motion pictures highlight the common folks making their small sacrifices for victory, released numerous titles describing the everyday adventures of an eclectic America, standing steadfast to its President's proclamation concerning defense of the Home Front.

The motion picture directors could choose from an array of subjects related to this timely topic. One of the first was the glorification of the American factory worker, praising his hard work and extolling his patriotism. In MGM's *Joe Smith, American,* Robert Young embodied a clean-cut assembly worker, putting together a classified bombing sight for the Air Corps. During his free time, the good-looking civilian offered homiletic lectures to his small son and reminded his wife about wartime frugality. When captured and tortured by German agents, the flag-waving Young refused their questions. After escaping from their hideaway, he retained enough composure to lead law officers back to the Axis lair. Acclaimed a hero, the easygoing Young reminded everyone that all Americans must safeguard their country against Nazi agents.

As a propaganda film, *Joe Smith, American* lauded the everyday virtues of an ordinary factory worker, whose loyalty and vigilance thwarted the Nazi foe. This became a standard storyline for Home Front movies. Universal's *Saboteur* pitted another factory mechanic, Robert Cummings, against fifth columnists in southern California who were blowing up important installations.

After an elaborate cross-country chase, the assembler-turned-pursuer confronted his Axis nemesis on top of New York's fabled Statue of Liberty, where, after some slippery footwork, the German fell to his death. With the saboteur threat removed and Robert Cummings back at his lathe, wartime production resumed.

But new problems confronted the assembly line as most industries switched over to twenty-four-hour operations. War material technology, in every format, needed improvement and employees' suggestions were important. This was the theme of Universal Pictures' tribute to the steel worker, *Pittsburgh*. Directed by Lewis Seiler and featuring two high-powered stars—John Wayne and Randolph Scott—*Pittsburgh* told the simple story of a pair of good friends who became industrial magnates in the rough-and-tumble Pennsylvania mining town. When an unscrupulous woman married John Wayne the partnership turned acrimonious, and the two men squared off in an elaborate fight scene, symbolically in a mine shaft.

Like so many other propaganda films, *Pittsburgh* employed the renegade-turned-believer motif. After the men severed their business arrangement, John Wayne fell into economic ruin and ostracism, while Randolph Scott, a skillful entrepreneur, gained new prosperity and respect. After Pearl Harbor, the penniless John Wayne recognized the errors of his selfish ways and resolved to make amends. Soon, he found work at his old friend's steel mill and, using a *nom de guerre,* implemented several important technical changes. When news of his dramatic quota upswing reached Randolph Scott, the two men confronted each other and with the American flag waving in the backdrop, quickly reconciled their differences. In a stereotypical finale, the steel workers gathered at a patriotic rally to hear an elaborate pep talk about their contribution to the war effort. Moments later, the men returned to their jobs, determined to set new production records.

But there was another side to the Home Front that Hollywood needed to praise: the distaff workers—the Rosie-the-Riveters—could not be ignored, since a large number of women routinely exceeded their production quotas in the wartime industry. RKO's *Tender Comrade* dramatized the daily existence of five working women, sharing joy, sorrow, shortages, and loneliness in a rented old house, while their men were away dealing with the business of war. Directed by Edward Dmytryk and written by Dalton Trumbo,

Tender Comrade starred Ginger Rogers and Robert Ryan in the principal roles of husband and wife.

For the pregnant Miss Rogers, separated from her GI spouse, each day became an exercise in wartime frugality as she and her friends adapted to their new roles in the V-for-Victory effort. When the ladies discovered a black-market butcher in their neighborhood, they become enraged; later, after one of their own members bragged about her hoarding skills, the woman was lambasted by the vitriolic expecting mother. Both scenes, of course, were laden with strong doses of propaganda because, in reality, these two social ills were creating frustrations for many people. The message of *Tender Comrade* was clear: black market-eers and hoarders took their orders from Berlin.

A few months later the comely Miss Rogers gave birth, but the joy of her new son was short-lived when news of her husband's death reached the household. Initially saddened, the stoic widow cuddled her infant, reaffirming that his father's sacrifice had helped protect the freedom that all Americans enjoy. In this film's last sequence, the five women again comforted each other as another wartime crisis needed resolving. This closing scene also revealed the deft hand of the propagandist. Combat casualties could not be ignored; if Ginger Rogers was strengthened by her husband's death, could other American women react differently?

There were also frivolous moments on the Home Front. Bob Hope's gags provided much merriment in some lighthearted comedies. Paramount's *My Favorite Blonde* and RKO's *They Got Me Covered* involved the topical theme of Axis spies hoping to wreck the American defense industry. When confronted by the master jokester, the guttural-sounding agents were quickly dis-combobulated and soon found themselves in the hands of FBI agents. Two other titles from Paramount—*Let's Face It* and *Star Spangled Rhythm*—allowed America's favorite comic to show off some of his song and dance routines while making a pitch for the Red, White, and Blue.

Like other low-budget films released by major studios, those featuring Bob Hope's comical antics provided escapism for a moviegoing audience that wanted some diversion from the war news that permeated every hour of their life. A good laugh was always better than a woeful cry and the Hollywood directors—mindful of that wonderful scene in Paramount's *Sullivan's Trav-*

els depicting the small moments of happiness some Georgia road gang inmates found while watching a Mickey Mouse cartoon—worked hard to keep America chuckling. Warner Brothers' *The Doughgirls* and Columbia's *The More the Merrier* poked fun at the housing shortage in crowded Washington, D.C. with thousands of new employees arriving in the nation's capital and finding they had no place to sleep. Even the serious theme of draft-dodging was downplayed into comedy in RKO's *Mr. Lucky.* Here Cary Grant delivered many gags as he portrayed a slick gambler who finally saw the light and bet on Uncle Sam.

Farce, slapstick, and screwball comedy brought needed levity to the Home Front and one director, Preston Sturges, said it all in films that painted the wacky behavior of simple Americans floundering as they tried to deal with wartime life. Paramount's *The Miracle of Morgan's Creek* and *Hail the Conquering Hero* became two of the funniest movies ever made and the storylines oozed that special Sturges charm and warmth in every frame. Each featured the antics of an enlisted man and the madness that ensued when the best laid plans of soldiers, Marines, and civilians went awry.

In *The Miracle of Morgan's Creek*—a tale of small-town Norman Rockwell America—a young, naive, and shy Eddie Bracken bemoaned the high blood pressure that caused him to be classified unfit for military service. When his next door neighbor, Betty Hutton, committed a sexual peccadillo with some smooth-talking GI, the 4-F Bracken, always a gentleman, agreed to marry the girl of his dreams and, nine months later, the bride was rushed to the hospital. There, she delivered sextuplets, prompting a proud governor to declare an official holiday; he called the birth of the six boys a "miracle." As friends and relatives cheered the couple's achievement, headlines all over the world heralded the fourth estate's own felicitations.

As a Home Front film, *Morgan's Creek* accentuated every wholesome quality associated with the new spartan life style that most Americans were beginning to accept. Neighbors discussed shortages and rationing in jocular terms, and when some GIs came to town for a short furlough they received the royal treatment. Even the town's constable—character actor William Demarest—extended the red carpet to the young soldiers, a scene reminiscent of his own World War I days as a doughboy in France. With such adulation heaped upon the Army men, no wonder Eddie Bracken felt frustrated when his repeated attempts to enlist were turned down.

But the world is always a comedy for those who think: if Eddie Bracken were eligible for induction, Preston Sturges could not tell a funny story about a typical, lovesick hayseed pining to wear a uniform, and the many misadventures that befell him in Hicksville, America. Parenthood, patriotism, and marriage were lampooned in the typical screwball comedy format, culminating with the usual upbeat, risible ending. If Hollywood had a Jonathan Swift in its studios, his name was Preston Sturges.

In *Hail the Conquering Hero,* Sturges took a swipe at both jingoism and hero-worship. Eddie Bracken portrayed a shy Marine recruit, who was discharged after a few months of training because of a chronic hay fever problem. Feeling lonely and rejected, the former jarhead—his name was Woodrow Lafayette Pershing Truesmith—accidentally ran into some combat-decorated Marines in a California bar. After a few cozy drinks, the top sergeant concocted a wild plan to bolster the spirits of his new found friend: they would all return to Private Bracken's home town and proclaim the youngster a combat hero.

To his astonishment, Eddie Bracken's return to rural America became an elaborate ceremony as countless friends, relatives, and officials rejoiced in the news that a favorite son was now a war hero. He received the key to the city, the affections of an old girl friend, and a guarantee for the next mayoralty position. Unable to keep the charade going, the shy leatherneck-turned-civilian finally admitted everything, but before he could sneak away he was quickly forgiven and raised to an even higher level in the townspeople's eyes.

A fast-paced comedy, *Hail the Conquering Hero* poked fun at America's obsession with hero adulation and the fraternal organizations that promulgated such needs. Loud bands, patriotic music, windbag speeches, nationalistic platitudes, and cheering school children were all lampooned in the quick, caustic language of the screwball comedy, and the results were hilarious. Movie audiences placed the grim war news on hold for two hours and took time out to laugh at their own foibles. But what about the propaganda value of satire? Would Preston Sturges' picture help win the War?

Of course it would. *Conquering Hero* became a salient soft propaganda production because many persuasive elements were present that highlighted noble sentiments. The American Marines, while somewhat misguided, were clean-cut and proud and the civilians saw them only as role models. Sturges' movie mocked jingoism but, on the other hand, advocated patriotism. When the Marines boarded their train, leaving Eddie Bracken behind with his new-found fame, there was no question about the leathernecks' next destination. They would return to the South Pacific, then on to Tokyo.

But not every film focused on rural America with its motley collection of rubes, bumpkins, pollyannas, rustics and horse-drawn milk deliveries. The upper-middle class milieu had its own share of frustrations and one motion picture paid homage to those families who owned expensive, suburban homes, employed live-in maids and drove fancy cars. United Artists' *Since You Went Away,* produced and written by the Hollywood mogul David O. Selznick, and directed by John Cromwell, provided 171 saccharine minutes of the tedious, prayerful, and maudlin life style a Midwestern wife must endure after her husband has left to join the commissioned ranks of the U.S. Army.

As a major motion picture, *Since You Went Away* included many famous stars—Claudette Colbert, Joseph Cotten, Jennifer Jones, Shirley Temple, Robert Walker, and Monty Woolley—in an overblown storyline that David O. Selznick dedicated to the unconquerable fortress—the American Home, 1943. Replete with homilies and pseudo-brotherhood slogans, the film offered its own version of a Home Front that included domestic frugality, adolescent infatuation, gasoline rationing, innocent flirtation, and an eccentric boarder. While millions of American workers were jammed into cold-water flats and riding crowded buses to defense plants, *Since You Went Away* depicted the delicate Miss Colbert stipulating that she would only rent her spare bedroom to a military officer, and browbeating her obsequious maid, Hattie McDaniel, into accepting lower wages for household work.

Similar problems abounded in this film. A retired military officer resented his grandson because the lad had flunked out of West Point and their many conversations become acerbic. Later, the youth would die during the Salerno invasion and as penance, the grandfather volunteered for some war work. Snob appeal and racism appeared everywhere and the treatment of the Black maid reflected an honest look at the thorny subject of class separation. In Miss Colbert's genteel world there was little tolerance for blue-collar mores, foreign-sounding names or, as Monty Woolley exclaimed, "houses that smell of cabbage." Later, her younger daughter was admonished for showing romantic interest in an enlisted man.

But eventually Miss Colbert saw the light. When a telegram announced that her husband was missing in action, she took a job in a local factory and soon came into contact with the common people. In one poignant scene, a refugee bragged about the advantages of living in America, and, in her best broken accent, praised the inscription on the famed Statue of Liberty. Completely transformed, Miss Colbert—as wholesome as apple pie—permitted her older daughter to volunteer as a nurse's aide in the town's hospital.

What a break for the Home Front's medical facilities! While thousands of high school students spent their study hall time rolling bandages or packing Red Cross boxes for the war effort, a concerned mother, fearful that her daughter would rub elbows with the "wrong" element, finally capitulated and allowed the youngster to change a few bedpans. With Jennifer Jones now in the fray, victory for the Allies seemed certain.

Only one more scene was needed to cap *Since You Went Away*. As an experienced filmmaker, David O. Selznick knew precisely how to bring off the perfect Currier and Ives ending: gather the family around the holiday tree on Christmas day. With friends and neighbors jammed into her elaborate living room, Miss Colbert's languid mood contrasted the joy of the yuletide season. A single question persisted: where was her husband? While her guests freely enjoyed the lavish food and drinks that adorned the dining room table, the lugubrious Miss Colbert could only ponder: was her spouse alive?

Now what? After watching *Since You Went Away* for over 160 minutes, would American audiences "allow" an Army officer's fate to remain undisclosed on the most festive of days? With holiday presents and toasts of goodwill filling the air, would United Artists deny a faithful, upper-middle class wife her one Christmas wish? Family wholesomeness, of course, was at the core of film propaganda, and this closing scene left nothing to the imagination: truth, goodness, friends, the flag, children, even the pet dog's tail wagging testified to the fidelity of the American hearth.

Apparently, Selznick ran out of steam with his cliché ending. In the midst of this Christmas cheer, the telephone rang and its message, hot off the Western Union wires, proclaimed the husband's safety and announced that he was coming home. While the entire gathering praised the Deity in this elaborate fade-out sequence, the heavenly voices of angels sang the popular carol, "Joy to the World." As a finale, this jubilant scene reaffirmed a basic American principle—American GIs, with the help of the Almighty, would return to their loved ones.

By most standards, *Since You Went Away* was a dreadful film, employing in one form or another racism, snobbery, and Wasp America as preponderant themes. As an "average" housewife bemoaning her fate in the safety of the Home Front, Claudette Colbert's role would elicit little sympathy from the millions of workers who were unable to enjoy any of the upper-middle class comforts depicted. Consequently, this motion picture did not provide the propaganda message the director had originally planned. Instead of cheering the troops on to victory, the audience-turned-voyeur, empathizing with some of the problems of conjugal life, found only escapism in this 1944-style American soap opera.

Since You Went Away wasn't the only melodrama that recreated life in the upper-middle class stratum. Other motion pictures depicted the problems of solid American families who found themselves involved in serious problems with fifth columnists. Warner Brothers' *Watch on the Rhine* starred Paul Lukas and Bette Davis as two German resistance fighters, who returned to their stately Washington, D.C. home, only to find a Nazi traitor operating within their close circle of friends. After some suspenseful cat-and-mouse dialogue, the Axis spy eventually admitted his allegiance to the Fatherland and perished in a classic end-of-the-movie shoot-out scene.

As propaganda, *Watch on the Rhine* restated the need for vigilance at every turn. Anyone could be a spy, traitor or fifth columnist, the film averred. America's enemies do not wear badges or insignias while operating on the Home Front. Sometimes they were twins. Such was the theme of MGM's *Nazi Agent,*

On trial in a Tokyo civil court for "crimes against humanity," Lieutenant Richard Conte—a captured American flyer—threatens General Richard Loo, his Japanese nemesis in Lewis Milestone's *The Purple Heart*. (Museum of Modern Art; courtesy of Twentieth Century-Fox.)

In Frank Ryan and William Hamilton's *Call Out the Marines*, top sergeant Victor McLaglen—his chest emblazoned with medals earned during the Great War—explains to Edward Lowe some of the subtleties of amatory pursuits. (Museum of Modern Art; courtesy of RKO Radio Pictures.)

Suave American journalist George Sanders questions the sincerity of pretty Virginia Bruce, while Robert Armstrong looks on intently, in Leonide Moguy's B-adventure yarn, *Action in Arabia*. (Museum of Modern Art; courtesy of RKO Radio Pictures.)

Even during wartime, two newspaper reporters—Clark Gable and Lana
Turner—find time for some old-fashioned bill and coo romance in Wesley
Ruggles' glorification of the fourth estate, *Somewhere I'll Find You*. (Museum of
Modern Art; courtesy of MGM.)

Looking grim and determined, Colonel Randolph Scott studies the hostile jungle terrain before ordering his tight-knit Marine raiders into combat against the Japanese in Ray Enright's *Gung Ho*. (Museum of Modern Art; courtesy of Universal Studio.)

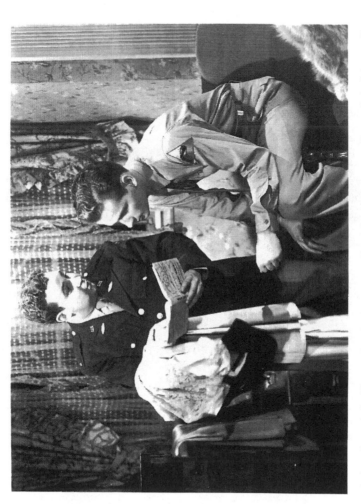

Two newly commissioned married officers—Stanley Prager and Frank Latimore—try to forget their tight, sardine can quarters and, instead, concentrate on basic child care in Otto Preminger's *In the Meantime, Darling*. (Museum of Modern Art; courtesy of Twentieth Century-Fox.)

Flying Tiger pilot George Montgomery swears vengeance for the death of his Eurasian girlfriend, Gene Tierney, in Henry Hathaway's *China Girl.* (Museum of Modern Art; courtesy of Twentieth Century-Fox.)

Bomber crew members George Tobias and Harry Carey discuss flying rudiments while John Garfield—the stereotypical loner—feigns disinterest in Howard Hawk's paean to the B-17, *Air Force*. (Museum of Modern Art; courtesy of Warner Brothers.)

Squadron Leader Dana Andrews and his fellow aircraf. carrier pilots learn of their new attack mission—the upcoming Battle of the Coral Sea—in Henry Hathaway's *Wing and a Prayer*. (Museum of Modern Art; courtesy of Twentieth Century-Fox.)

In Jacques Tourneur's *Days of Glory*, Comrade Gregory Peck—making his screen debut—orders an elaborate counterattack against the Nazi war machine that invaded his Russian village. (Museum of Modern Art; courtesy of RKO Radio Pictures.)

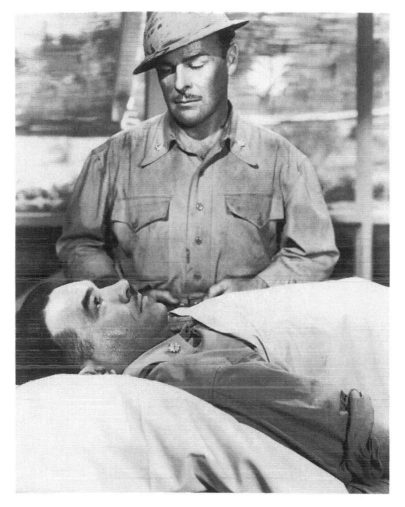

In John Farrow's *Wake Island,* Marine Major Brian Donlevy comforts fellow officer Walter Abel as Japanese troops creep closer and closer to their military stronghold. (Museum of Modern Art; courtesy of Paramount Pictures.)

Appearing tired but stony-faced, Army tank sergeant Humphrey Bogart confers with British officer Richard Nugent as they plan their trek across the hot North African desert in Zoltan Korda's *Sahara*. (Museum of Modern Art; courtesy of Columbia Pictures.)

Two Home Front volunteers—Victor Moore and Betty Hutton—plan a gala variety show for a shipload of tars in George Marshall's *Star Spangled Rhythm*. (Museum of Modern Art; courtesy of Paramount Pictures.)

On a battle-scarred South Pacific island, two gyrenes—William Bendix and
Richard Jaeckel—enjoy an idle respite from their foxhole drudgery, taunting
each other with news about certain stateside female admirers in Lewis Seiler's
Guadalcanal Diary. (Museum of Modern Art; courtesy of Twentieth Century-
Fox.)

Chaplain Alan Hale and Colonel Dennis Morgan ponder the spiritual nature of
aerodynamics in Robert Florey's tribute to the Flying Tigers, *God is My
Co-Pilot*. (Museum of Modern Art; courtesy of Warner Brothers.)

Fighter pilots John Wayne and John Carroll—dressed to the nines—enjoy an afternoon away from their volant responsibilities in David Miller's *Flying Tigers*. (Museum of Modern Art; courtesy of Republic Pictures.)

Hoping for the best, wide-eyed Betty Hutton and shy Eddie Bracken (wearing a hand-me-down World War I doughboy's uniform) try to arrange a quickie marriage in Preston Sturges' Home Front spoof, *The Miracle of Morgan's Creek*. (Museum of Modern Art; courtesy of Paramount Pictures.)

In Alfred Green's *Mr. Winkle Goes to War,* the subject of the overage recruit received full treatment as a 44-year-old bank clerk, Edward G. Robinson, proved maturity was no barrier to military service. (Museum of Modern Art; courtesy of Columbia Pictures.)

General Spencer Tracy offers his hospitalized flying officer, Captain Van Johnson another opportunity to serve in his air corps command in Mervyn LeRoy's elaborate testimony to the legendary Doolittle bombing raid, *Thirty Seconds over Tokyo.* (Museum of Modern Art; courtesy of MGM.)

In Sam Wood's portrayal of the Ernest Hemingway novel *For Whom the Bell Tolls,* Ingrid Bergman and Gary Cooper plan an attack against a fascist installation while Akim Tamiroff offers minimal encouragement. (Museum of Modern Art; courtesy of Paramount Pictures.)

another title that warned against Third Reich espionage, operating just blocks from the White House. Starring Conrad Veidt in the double role, *Nazi Agent* told the convoluted story of two brothers with different loyalties: one embraced Hitlerism, his twin gloried in his American citizenship. A fatal gunshot accident changed the direction of the storyline and eventually, with the American assuming his dead brother's fascist role, a Nazi espionage ring was uncovered by the FBI.

There were other problems on the Home Front. In United Artists' *Tomorrow the World,* a twelve-year-old German orphan finally reached the safety of a small, average American town and was placed in his uncle's care. Directed by Leslie Fenton, *Tomorrow the World* starred Fredric March as a university professor who became the guardian of his German-born nephew, played by Skip Homeier. The youth, however, could not shake off his Nazi upbringing and soon found fault with his new surroundings. In a matter of days, the youngster bragged about the Third Reich, uttered numerous ethnic and racist slurs, and rejected most acts of kindness proffered by his uncle and friends.

This was a new twist in propaganda films. There were no spies or fifth column cells in *Tomorrow the World;* no enemy agents were spotted writing cryptic messages on matchbox covers. Instead, a misguided boy, whose formative years were spent under National Socialism, needed help to adjust to basic American ideals and principles. Success was slow, but eventually the youth succumbed to his new lifestyle. Patience, guidance, and education—plus some clean sheets and home-cooked food—changed the boy from an ardent Nazi devotee to a flag-waving patriot.

As propaganda, *Tomorrow the World* contained a strong message about the German people and their Nazi ideology. When the War is finally over, the film suggested, all vestiges of the New Order must be eradicated. At the same time, Americans needed to be wary of resurgent neo-Nazi organizations that could spring up anywhere. Such warnings were already trumpeted in *Hotel Berlin* and *The Master Race,* two titles that touched upon fleeing Nazi officers who had been ordered to create unrest and dissension in selected Allied countries. In a similar mood, MGM's *Keeper of the Flame* promulgated domestic vigilance, reminding moviegoers that demagoguery and mind control were not restricted to fascist countries.

Axis agents on American soil was a common theme. In RKO's
The Fallen Sparrow, a former Abraham Lincoln Brigade member,
John Garfield, became enmeshed with some Nazi espionage and
murder traced back to a New York City apartment. An intricate
plot—emphasizing the complexities of the Spanish Civil War—
vitiated much of the propaganda value of this film. Nevertheless,
John Garfield, with the help of some local officialdom, routed the
spy ring while winning the heart of pretty Maureen O'Hara.

This was not the first time a World War II movie was hard to
follow because of a storyline that required knowledge of current
affairs. Both *Casablanca* and *Mission to Moscow* were excellent
propaganda films that sometimes became bogged down in their
own tendentiousness. How many viewers understood the subtle
references to Spain, Ethiopia, or Vichy water in *Casablanca?*
How many moviegoers recognized Kalinin, Mannerheim, and
Trotsky in *Mission to Moscow?* The same held true for Warner
Brothers' *The Desert Song* and Paramount's *For Whom the Bell
Tolls,* two titles about the Spanish Civil War.

There were some lighthearted moments on the Home Front
when large groups of Americans gathered to sing popular tunes
and exhibit fancy dance steps while making derogatory remarks
about Hitler, Mussolini, or Tojo. As always, the Hollywood
musical provided needed escapism from the uncertainty associated with a war that was being fought on numerous fronts,
thousands of miles from anywhere, in all sorts of climates and
terrains. However, Hollywood made sure that the boys in uniform
were not neglected. Both United Artists' *Stage Door Canteen* and
Warner Brothers' *Hollywood Canteen* highlighted the frivolity
found in these off-hours service clubs where many motion picture
stars served coffee and donuts to the thousand of GIs who came
through the doors. Both studios used so many top stars crooning
their famous theme songs that no marquee was large enough for a
listing. In Paramount's *Star Spangled Rhythm* numerous parodies
of well-known actresses added to the fun, while vocalist Betty
Hutton's double-entendre rendition of "I'm Doing It for Defense" evoked a few smiles.

Other pictures that provided needed enjoyment included
RKO's *Up in Arms, Four Jills in a Jeep, The Sky's the Limit* and
Seven Days Ashore, all featuring big-band music and lively
dancing. And Paramount's *Holiday Inn, Here Come the Waves*

and *The Fleet's In* and MGM's *Anchors Aweigh* produced enough songs, tap dancing, standup comedy, pratfalling, and chauvinism to entertain movie audiences everywhere. How prevalent were these war musicals? By V-J Day, over seventy-five of these song-and-dance films had been released. As a separate category, the war musical outflanked all others—it became the dominant film genre during the Second World War.

Some of these titles were fine-tuned by the propagandists. Universal's *Follow the Boys* paid elaborate homage to the USO entertainers who traveled to battle zones all over the world. Directed by Eddie Sutherland, *Follow the Boys* starred George Raft, the dancer-turned-gangster, as a hard-working impresario, putting in long hours to organize shows for the GIs. Another film that featured a USO troupe organizing a variety show for servicemen was Warner Brothers' *This Is the Army*, a picture that became the top wartime musical with its extravagant stage sets, Irving Berlin score, and famous Hollywood stars, including the songstress Kate Smith, whose unique rendition of "God Bless America" literally brought American audiences to their feet in chest-beating admiration for their country.

Warner Brothers' *Yankee Doodle Dandy* went one step further by writing President Roosevelt into the script. Here the Chief Executive presented song writer George M. Cohan with a congressional medal for his wartime services to the American people. Directed by Michael Curtiz, *Yankee Doodle Dandy* was an elaborate diorama of American patriotism. In one set, the heroes of the American Revolution marched by with fife and drum. Then, Abraham Lincoln issued his Emancipation Proclamation; later, both the Spanish American War and World War I veterans were honored. Walter Huston appeared, dressed as Uncle Sam, while Rosemary de Camp, attired as the Statue of Liberty, stood nearby. As a finale, the patriotic notes of Cohan's World War I classic, "Over There," called every American to arms.

But there was also poignancy, self-sacrifice, and hardship on the Home Front. In United Artists' *I'll Be Seeing You*, a shell-shocked GI, Joseph Cotten, slowly learned to adjust to his new stateside surroundings after his release from an Army mental hospital. Soon, he savored those items denied to him in the combat zone good food, pleasant family company, and a warm hug from Ginger Rogers. As a Home Front film, *I'll Be Seeing*

You emphasized the strong values of the American family. The storyline downplayed the heroics of battle, reminding audiences that final victory will be accompanied by tears and sorrow.

Other films reiterated the quiet heroism of combat. Warner Brothers' *Pride of the Marines,* starring John Garfield, recreated the real-life story of Al Schmid, a Marine hero who was blinded at Guadalcanal, and his long road to recovery back in Philadelphia. Paramount's *A Medal for Benny* portrayed the small-town virtues of a southern California community, when a local soldier received a posthumous Medal of Honor. As the father of the deceased GI, J. Carrol Naish restated the stoic dignity found in Main Street America. Fox's *Captain Eddie* heralded the exploits of the aviation legend, Eddie Rickenbacker, culminating with his nineteen-day ordeal on a raft in the Pacific. Fred MacMurray low-keyed the flamboyance of the World War I ace, elaborating, instead, on the airman's faith in God and country. His dramatic rescue—a tangible propaganda symbol—reconfirmed America's commitment to its serviceman.

Naturally, the War brought many casualties and every family on the Home Front knew those houses where a small gold star emblem was placed in a front room window, a poignant reminder that a son had died in battle. Once in a while, there might be two gold stars, this double tragedy only reaffirming the high cost of the War in terms of the young lives lost in battle. But in August 1942, a loss occurred that virtually no one on the Home Front could comprehend or ever forget: an American mother, living in Waterloo, Iowa, learned that her five Navy sons had perished in a single day during a Japanese attack off the coast of Guadalcanal. The boys were Al, Frank, George, Matt, and Joe—the five Sullivan brothers.

When Twentieth Century-Fox revved up its motion picture cameras to make the life story of the Sullivan brothers a year later, the studio selected five unknown actors to portray the young men who grew up in America's heartland, began careers, and—in one case—a family. Soon after the Pearl Harbor attack, they all enlisted in the U.S. Navy. Later, the five sailors hoodwinked some naval officials into assigning them the same berth aboard the U.S.S. *Juneau,* which eventually was attacked and all five sons died. For Hollywood, this became a special motion picture, a film replete with joy, sorrow, empathy, and victory-through-death.

Inadvertently, *The Fighting Sullivans,* a 1940s tearjerker depicting life through rose-colored glasses, became one of the best propaganda films of the War.

With Lloyd Bacon as the director, *The Fighting Sullivans* starred Thomas Mitchell and Selena Royle as the hard-working, ever-caring parents of the five brothers and their one sister, from their Roman Catholic baptism to their tragic deaths in the South Pacific. During this twenty-year-plus maturation period, the boys were as American as apple pie: they spent their idle days fishing with homemade poles, hanging around the railroad tracks, chopping wood, caring for the dog, and—in one comical scene—trying their hands at home improvement. Their entire household spilled over with love, warmth, kindness, sharing, frugality, and comfort. As the sole breadwinner, Thomas Mitchell, working as a freight conductor for the Illinois Central Railroad, provided stability and leadership, while in the kitchen, Selena Royle heaped plenty of home cooking on all eight plates. Nowhere in this Norman Rockwell picture-perfect childhood were there any signs of the approaching tragedy.

But their idyllic *Our Gang* world couldn't last forever and soon the boys were grown men, already part of the working force in rural America, with 1930s interests and aspirations. But they still retained the cohesiveness that kept them so closely knitted as kids. When Al became interested in a girlfriend, pretty Anne Baxter, his older brothers almost wrecked the romance with their wisenheimer behavior, but after their wholesome fraternal apology, the couple soon married and their first son was born.

Pearl Harbor changed everything. Minutes after the news was flashed the Sullivans decided to join the Navy. At first, military regulations forbade five brothers to serve together, but a letter from the War Department permitted an exception. Soon, all five bluejackets were assigned aboard the U.S.S. *Juneau* and eventually they were sent to the Solomon Islands. During a Japanese air attack, the ship was destroyed and the five Sullivan brothers were killed in action.

Now what? How would Hollywood deal with such a tragic event? A tenet of film propaganda required that audiences "feel" for the characters on the screen, rather than "think" about the reasons for the actors' behavior. Moviegoers should display their emotion rather than rationalize the events in the storyline. How would parents, seated in the comfort of their local theaters, "feel" if their five sons were lost to the War? Would they hold up as well as Mr. and Mrs. Sullivan?

Probably not. In the closing minutes of *The Fighting Sullivans,* character actor Ward Bond simply stole the show with his wonderful, poignant role as the Navy commander who informed the family of their sons' death. No other scene in World War II films produced such deep emotion over the loss of American servicemen, while in a subtle, unobtrusive way, provoking such hatred for the enemy. After hearing the officer's words, both mother and father went about their business with quiet resolution. The price of liberty, they implied, did not come cheap in America.

Certainly, there were no dry eyes during the last scene: the father returned to his caboose to keep the railroad schedule operational, while the mother prepared some coffee for the Navy commander. Later, as a quick epilogue, a Navy destroyer, the U.S.S. *Sullivan,* was commissioned and the proud parents watched the ship's maiden voyage. To add to the patriotic mood, the Sullivans' daughter enlisted in the Navy.

What made this motion picture so touching? Probably the hometown feelings that permeated much of *The Fighting Sullivans* reflected the simple joys so common to American kids growing up in a rural setting. Here was a film that emphasized the wholesomeness of American life, with young boys slowly emerging as grown men, looking for their own dream at the end of the rainbow. But December 7th shattered their tranquil lives and now they acted together, heeding their country's call. The Japanese treachery, they averred, would be avenged. *"Those Japs will be sorry they were born,"* they vowed, *"we'll lick them, but it'll take plenty of time."*

As propaganda, this film contained the necessary persuasive elements because it aimed at an audience that already shared the values of the five brothers. Here was a picture that pitted the forces of good and evil and the results were discernible. Appealing to the common emotion of indignation, *The Fighting Sullivans* told the story of the loss of innocence, a loss that cried out for revenge. Everyone left the theater in a retributive mood. With the strains of "Anchors Away" in the background, it was time to join the Navy and get into the fight.

Five other Home Front movies highlighted the wholesomeness of youth: Paramount's *I Love a Soldier,* MGM's *The Clock,* RKO's *The Enchanted Cottage* and Twentieth Century Fox's *Sunday Dinner for a Soldier* plus *Happy Land.* These titles pushed the war into the background, concentrating instead on simple virtues: transforming a barren attic into a family apartment, running a race against the bureaucracy to marry a new-found girl friend, helping a disfigured airman adjust to his convalescence, providing a home-cooked meal for a GI, and commiserating with a family when their only son became a wartime fatality. Occasionally, the Home Front was threatened. In Warner Brothers' *Escape in the Desert* the townspeople banded together to capture some Nazi POW's. This picture again reinforced the versatility of small-town American folks. When their country needed help, loyal people mobilized.

Overall, the Home Front motion pictures appealed to a sense of duty by reminding audiences that shortages, rationing, and casualties were here to stay as long as the War continued. While the troops were overseas battling the Axis, the people back home would save their bacon fat, till their victory gardens and denounce the black marketeers. Pride and patriotism were the salient themes of these propaganda films. As long as there were families like the Sullivans, there would always be America.

CHAPTER SEVEN

THE B'S FINEST HOUR:
OUR SIXTY-MINUTE UNSUNG HEROES

". . . please don't applaud. Applause won't keep this flag flying or keep our boys fighting. Use those hands to dig down deep in your pockets for those last hidden dollars. Protect your right to freedom. Insure your share of American victory. Before you leave here today, buy war bonds and stamps."

—B-actress Evelyn Finley, making a direct appeal to the audience in the concluding minutes of Monogram's 1943 B-Western, *Cowboy Commandos.*

During the early Depression years, between 1930 and 1933, movie attendance began to drop significantly as the worsening economy created a belt-tightening lifestyle for most American families. The Hollywood moguls, aware of the dismal statistics for this period—ticket sales had dropped from 100 million down to 60 million—realized it was time for a new gimmick, some novel approach to lure audiences back into the theaters. These film capitalists hit upon a new idea: they would show two movies for the price of one. The double feature was born.

By 1935, more than seventy-five per cent of America's cinemas ran a double bill, consisting of the major feature—supplemented with shorts, newsreels, and cartoons—plus a low-grade supporting film, a little more than sixty minutes long, using fresh actors and directors, and known simply as the B. What did the letter B represent? To the wags, it meant bread-and-butter or bottom-of-the-bill. But for the studio accountants, B was for budget. Any title that was hacked out quickly and effortlessly, requiring little capital and about seven days of shooting time, wore the B imprimatur.

Every major studio had its own B-section churning out dozens of these inexpensive films and some companies developed their own recognizable genre. Later, small, independent studios entered the selling market and production names such as Monogram, Republic, and Producers Releasing Corporation became well known to moviegoers. By 1936, FDR's New Deal created consumer confidence in the national economy and audiences flocked back to their movie houses. Why wouldn't they? For the wage-earning public, the shows provided the best entertainment for the least amount of money. And now an evening at the movies included some new B-film, another sixty or seventy minutes of escapism.

By 1941, hundreds of B-movies flickered on the screen and their series' titles adorned marquees everywhere. Charlie Chan, Mr. Wong, Michael Shayne, the East Side Kids, Mr. Moto, the Cisco Kid, Tailspin Tommy, the Three Mesquiteers, Johnny Mack Brown, Blondie, Nancy Drew, Dr. Kildare, Dick Tracy, the Saint, Andy Hardy, and Philo Vance were just a handful of the popular characters shown alongside the major titles. For many future stars—John Wayne and Ronald Reagan, for examples—the B-picture became the stepping stone to fame and fortune. Other actors, of course, went nowhere. Their careers started and ended on the backlots of small independent B-companies.

When Pearl Harbor shook the American people from their complacency, the B-industry went immediately to a war footing and, using some stereotypical themes from other genres, quickly turned out one title after another which touched upon the national emergency. No subject, issue, person, or location was omitted. Unlike the major studios, when the B-films went off to war they covered every facet, no matter how implausible, *in toto*. No bizarre or incredulous storyline was discarded if it remotely resembled anything germane to the global conflict.

For example, in Monogram's *Revenge of the Zombies,* a mad scientist, John Carradine, tried to create an incorporeal army for the Fuehrer in the bayous of Louisiana. He was routed by officialdom. Warner Brothers' *The Gorilla Man* featured two depraved doctors using their medical skills for the Nazis; they, too, suffered defeat—this time by a British commando. What was the propaganda value of such off-beat science-fiction titles? Very little, except to remind audiences that the Axis could be anywhere and to provide the needed escapism that could be found in darkened movie houses. A little harmless fun provided some relief from the problems of wartime, and this popular genre, with its dark, creepy staircases, jolts of electrical current, and bodies that slowly regenerated, livened up the evening for moviegoers. Who could resist the antics of a fiendish ghoul experimenting with some cadaver on his operating table?

For the best in vicarious thrills, nothing could top the B-Westerns—the oaters—especially since the traditional rustlers, the men in black, now wore swastikas and had trouble pronouncing their ''v's'' and ''w's.'' No longer did the villains steal cattle from the range; the new enemy wanted to undermine defense work or destroy some important land mineral needed for the war effort. In Monogram's *Cowboy Commandoes,* a gang of German-American Nazis attempted to steal shipments of magnesite. The three Range Busters—Crash Corrigan, Denny Moore, and Alibi Terhune—moved in fast, with their six-shooters drawn, to wreck this Axis spy ring.

Later, these three found themselves in the midst of an old-fashioned open-range problem. In Monogram's *Black Market Rustlers* huge quantities of beef were siphoned from the military by unscrupulous vendors. Their acts uncovered by the Range Busters, the meat dealers wound up in the calaboose. To capitalize on this important theme, the cowboys made another one of those patriotic pitches directly to the audience: in a closing trailer the men in white delivered a strong exhortation: don't buy black-market meat.

Other cowboy features battled the Axis powers. Monogram's *Texas to Bataan* put the Range Busters to work delivering needed horses to a U.S. outpost in the Philippines, and they uncovered a spy network back on their Texas ranch. Columbia's *Riders of the Northland* pitted the Texas Rangers against Nazi henchmen building a secret runway in the wilds of Alaska, while over in Montana the Three Mesquiteers tracked down three German war prisoners in Republic's *Valley of Hunted Men,* before they stole a secret formula for extracting rubber from an exotic plant.

This trio also saw action against Gestapo agents operating under western skies in another Republic sixty-minute yarn, *The*

Phantom Plainsmen. PRC's *Wild Horse Rustlers* highlighted the adventures of two B-Western stars, Bob Livingston and Fuzzy St. John, as they foiled a Nazi U-boat saboteur team that landed on their Texas ranch. The cowboys, quick on their feet, routed the Germans before they poisoned the horses that were being shipped to Uncle Sam's cavalry. The Royal Canadian Mounted Police battled their Axis foes in Republic's *Yukon Patrol,* a seventy-minute remake of the twelve-part *King of the Royal Mounted* serial. Starring Allen "Rocky" Lane, the film proved, again, that the redcoats always got their man.

Manpower problems plagued the open range. In Columbia's *Cowboy Canteen* a troupe of vaudeville performers filled in for some drafted cowhands and opened a needed USO office for the soldiers stationed at a nearby camp. Tex Ritter, Jane Frazee, and the Mills Brothers provided wholesome entertainment. Women, likewise, volunteered their skills. In Republic's *Raiders of Sunset Pass* equestrian artist Jennifer Holt, with the help of cowboy clown Smiley Burnette, organized the distaff faction into the paramilitary Women's Army of the Plains— the WAPS—to fight off some modern-day cattle rustlers.

Sometimes the cowpunchers learned new skills. In Columbia's *Sundown Valley,* B-icon Charles Starrett honed his cattle workers into an assembly team to manufacture strategic gunsights for the Army, while fighting off some unsavory gamblers and war opportunists. Republic's *Corpus Christi Bandits* placed cowboy hero Allan "Rocky" Lane in the dual role of a World War II veteran and, in a flashback, a Civil War hero. Both men faced similar problems after returning home and the two storylines provided a good analogy. Columbia's *Cowboy in the Clouds* served as a recruitment pitch for the Civilian Air Patrol, glamorizing the heroic deeds of the men who patrolled the skies over the open range. Charles Starrett sat in the cockpit, and Dub Taylor provided his usual high jinks in this fifty-five-minute title.

Western music strummed regularly on the Republic sound track: Roy Rogers, along with the Sons of the Pioneers, sang many popular ballads in *King of the Cowboys,* while routing some factory saboteurs. Not to be outdone, Gene Autry's last oater, before he enlisted in the Air Corps, staged a Red, White, and Blue finale at Madison Square Garden in *Bells of Capistrano.* PRC also provided a few guitar tunes. In *Rolling Down the Great Divide,*

Bill "Cowboy Rambler" Boyd's mellifluous voice—combined
with some cryptic lyrics—enabled government agents to smash a
cattle-rustling ring.

As both fantasy and adventure, these B-Western films contributed their share of war propaganda. For millions of theatergoers,
sitting in their neighborhood shows, one truth was obvious: when
Roy Rogers, Gene Autry, or Crash Corrigan hitched up his saddle
and galloped off into the sunset, the American frontier was secure.
Once in a while, some low-down German spy or Japanese
saboteur lurked on the ranch, but, in less than sixty minutes, these
enemies were exposed, captured, and imprisoned by the men who
wore ten-gallon hats, clipped spurs on their boots, and pulled their
gun belts tightly around their waists.

More heroes emerged to safeguard America's defense away
from the prairie, uncovering the crime and espionage operating in
the big cities. In Columbia's *Enemy Agents Meet Ellery Queen* the
famous private investigator broke up a Nazi network which was
attempting to steal some valuable Dutch diamonds. James Hogan
portrayed the popular gumshoe. Republic's *Secrets of the Underground* featured lawman John Hubbard as the district attorney
who smashed a counterfeiting ring. MGM's *Eyes in the Night*
pitted a blind detective, Edward Arnold, against some Axis agents
led by Katherine Emery. They were after an Allied secret formula,
but with the help of the seeing-eye dog Friday, the police wrecked
their scheme.

Another title, Twentieth Century-Fox's *Quiet Please, Murder,*
offered a soupçon of murder, forgery, bibliopoly, and espionage in
its urban tale. B-actor Richard Denning caught the culprits, while
pretty Lynne Roberts supplied the romance. Columbia's *Sabotage
Squad* revealed the perseverance of a hard-working patriot, Bruce
Bennett, in tracking down Nazi agents who dynamited a power
plant, while his girl friend, Kay Harris, proffered an occasional
patriotic homily. Monogram's *Spy Train* put Richard Travis and
Catherine Craig aboard a fast-moving streamliner in which Axis
agents sat in every compartment, hoping to steal an important
traveling bag that always disappeared. Eventually, the Nazis
grabbed this satchel, but discovered it contained only sticks of
dynamite. Seconds later, the villains suffered a fitting demise
blown to bits by this unsuspecting trap. Columbia's *Secret
Command* made Pat O'Brien a naval intelligence agent who

ferreted out Nazi rats plotting to blow up a new flattop moored in a large shipyard. As a happy ending to his travail, Carole Landis agreed to a nuptial union.

Other B-movies offered similar yarns. United Artists' *Fall In* paired two Army sergeants, Joe Sawyer and William Tracy, squaring off against a spy ring operating near their base. To simplify matters, the Axis leader named himself Arnold Benedict. Another Army enlisted man—Buck Private Lee Tracy—worked clandestinely for military intelligence to infiltrate a Japanese fifth column group operating near the Panama Canal in RKO's *Betrayal from the East*. After some implausible adventures, the Nipponese sabotage network was uncovered, but both Lee Tracy and his girl friend, Nancy Kelly, became fatalities for the cause of *e pluribus unum*. Over in Portugal, Richard Arlen prevented two heavies—Erich von Stroheim and Otto Kruger—from snatching some important microfilm from an unsuspecting journalist in Republic's *Storm Over Lisbon*. Helping out the fourth estate was Vera Ralston.

Sometimes the action created old-fashioned pathos. In Columbia's *Flight Lieutenant* an over-the-hill aviator, Pat O'Brien, worked long hours to develop an experimental Army aircraft; meanwhile, his good-looking son, Glenn Ford, earned his wings. When the prototype airplane was tested, a structural flaw caused the death of Pat O'Brien. Now his Air Corps son would continue his work. In RKO's *Army Surgeon* a military nurse—Jane Wyatt—recalled her service during the Great War as she prepared to embark for overseas duty against the Axis. Together with James Ellison, she and this medical unit would serve again in the Second World War.

Warner Brothers kept the pot boiling by churning out one B-suspense after another. In *Busses Roar* handsome Marine sergeant Richard Travis wooed a fellow passenger, pretty Julie Bishop, aboard an overnight California bus, and prevented a bomb explosion that was designed to signal an enemy submarine off the coast. In *Secret Enemies* Craig Stevens and Faye Emerson worked hand in glove to uncover an espionage ring. PRC's *Nazi Spy Ring* pitted American chemist Michael Whalen and his girl friend, Anne Nagel, against some guttural-speaking agents who were trying to steal a hybrid gasoline formula in this sixty-three-minute meller.

Sometimes, the storyline seemed remote from the audience. In Twentieth Century-Fox's *Careful, Soft Shoulders,* B-actress Virginia Bruce played a vapid socialite living among the upper crust of Washington, D.C. society. Bored by the war news enveloping much of the capital, the comely Miss Bruce, looking for diversionary excitement, haphazardly offered to work as a spy. Her adventures vacillated between slapstick and suspense until her boyfriend, James Ellison, stepped in and routed an enemy espionage ring. As propaganda, this B-movie operated on shaky ground because it depicted the members of the wealthy class as frivolous about the war effort and the President's call for mobilization.

Other plots were more down-to-earth. The ominous problem of the black market was the theme of Monogram's *Rubber Racketeers,* starring Ricardo Cortez as a petty hoodlum trafficking in tires. The film predictably ended with the breakup of this illegal operation and a short pitch to the audience about the need to conserve rubber. A similar title—Columbia's *The Racket Man*—featured Tom Neal as a minor hood drafted into the Army. After mixing with other conscripts, the good-looking Neal renounced his unsavory ways and, after some quick adventures, broke up his old black-market ring. His hero's death, an expiation for all his former misdeeds, added a patriotic coda to this sixty-minute potboiler. Another Columbia B-melodrama, *Underground Agent,* lauded the Four Freedoms. Here, Bruce Bennett wrecked an Axis espionage ring that taped important telephone connections in strategic defense plants.

Enemy agents seemed ubiquitous. Universal's *Madame Spy* starred Constance Bennett as a counterintelligence officer who broke up a New York fifth columnist organization, while her war correspondent husband, Don Porter, provided masculine succor. Over on the West Coast, clean-cut John Shelton snuffed out some Nazi operatives who were seeking the plans for a Hollywood searchlight filter, while his girlfriend chanteuse, Gale Storm, sang "It's Taps for the Japs" in Monogram's *Foreign Agent.* Universal's *Unseen Enemy* placed chubby Andy Devine along the San Francisco waterfront in the midst of Axis agents plotting to destroy American shipping. With the help of comely Irene Hervey and Canadian intelligence officer Don Terry, the enemy organization was effectively quashed.

In Twentieth Century-Fox's *Little Tokyo, U.S.A.,* lawman Preston Foster wrecked a Nipponese hate group, the Black Dragons, operating stealthily in Los Angeles. Another Fox B-quickie, *Ladies of Washington,* paired Trudy Marshall and Anthony Quinn in a minor espionage plot operating in the nation's capital. MGM's *The Bugle Sounds* depicted an aging Army sergeant, gravel-voiced Wallace Beery, as an experienced NCO unable to accept some of the new military format. Always alert, the popular B-actor smashed an Axis spy ring operating outside his base, while his matronly companion, Marjorie Main, smiled approvingly. Metro used this popular duo again in *Rationing,* in the bumbling roles of a butcher and a postmistress, working harmoniously to break up a black-market gang that was siphoning needed meat from Uncle Sam's forces.

Unsavory elements lurked everywhere. In PRC's *Waterfront,* B-stars John Carradine and J. Carrol Naish, paired as Nazi agents, plotted to undermine America's security. They were no match for lawman Martin Lamont. Paramount's *Submarine Alert* showed that a competent radio engineer, Richard Arlen, would foil an Axis spy ring at every turn. Twentieth Century-Fox's *They Came to Blow up America* took its script from current newspaper reports about a Nazi submarine that landed saboteurs on Long Island. Starring George Sanders as a double agent and Ward Bond as the G-man hot on his trail, the movie glorified J. Edgar Hoover's elite corps. Columbia's *The Unwritten Code* told the story of a Nazi posing as an Englishman in small-town America. He was quickly exposed by Army sergeant Tom Neal, with the help of his junior commando pal, young Bobby Larson.

Other sleuths chased down Axis dupes. In Monogram's *Charlie Chan in the Secret Service,* character actor Sidney Toler aided America's exclusive law officers by capturing a Nazi fraulein who was responsible for the murder of an important scientist. Over in London, Basil Rathbone portrayed the pipe-smoking master detective in two anti-Nazi films: *Sherlock Holmes and the Secret Weapon* and *Sherlock Holmes and the Voice of Terror.* With Nigel Bruce as Dr. Watson, the twosome traveled to the States to help the FBI rout some fifth columnists in *Sherlock Holmes in Washington.* With both Charlie Chan and Sherlock Holmes stationed in the capital, what did American audiences have to fear?

There were other themes beside espionage, intrigue, and murder. Many B-titles featured laughter, comedy, and levity while using the War as a distant backdrop to the plot. Paramount's *The Navy Way* made light of basic training at the Great Lakes Training Station as wide-eyed recruits gathered to serve Uncle Sam. B-actors Bill Henry and Jean Parker provided the laughs and a little military romance. The popular comedy team, Alan Carney and Wally Brown, poked fun at military induction in RKO's *Adventures of a Rookie*. Here the twosome ran amuck during boot camp, creating merriment for the clean-cut inductees. Monogram's *She's in the Army* placed pretty Veda Ann Borg in the WACs, where, after mixing with other volunteers, she learned the value of Old Glory, while her good-looking boyfriend, Lyle Talbot, held her military hand.

Columbia's *There's Something about a Soldier* described the wholesome life found in Officer's Training School as Tom Neal and Bruce Bennett learned the Army rudiments; Evelyn Keyes supplied the needed feminine succor. Columbia turned to the comic strips with *Blondie for Victory*, with Penny Singleton organizing the neighborhood women into victory drives, while Dagwood and Mr. Dithers helped with routine matters. Two other titles from Columbia—*Good Luck, Mr. Yates* and *She's a Soldier, Too*—saluted war plant workers who spent long hours in front of their lathes, grinding out every type of wartime materiel.

RKO's B-paean to the factory crowd—*Gangway for Tomorrow*—offered five short vignettes, explaining why a refugee, a racetrack driver, a beauty-contest winner, a prison warden, and a hobo were now working in the defense plant. Robert Ryan, John Carradine, and Margo shared top billing for this picture. MGM's *Swing Shift Maisie* put Ann Sothern on the aircraft factory assembly line until a jealous rival accused her of sabotage. Her boyfriend, handsome James Craig, quickly brought the truth to light.

Life on the Home Front had its own set of problems. Monogram's *Johnny Doesn't Live Here Anymore* joshed the cramped living conditions fostered by a booming wartime economy. Starring Simone Simon, this B-quickie described the comical antics of a defense worker involved in a complicated apartment-sharing lease that involved numerous males, including two sailors, James Ellison and Chick Chandler, who sported their own keys. A similar situation existed in Warner Brothers' *The Doughgirls*. Here, three young women—Ann Sheridan, Alexis Smith, and Jane Wyman—juggled the comings and goings of various war workers, all looking for a place to sleep. Republic's *My Buddy* restated the problems associated with returning veterans whose tour of duty was over. Starring Donald Barry and Lynn Roberts, the film was a strong reminder to a postwar planning committee to provide the men in uniform with needed social services.

Twentieth Century-Fox's *In the Meantime, Darling* poked fun at the housing crunch as comely Jeanne Crain squeezed into a makeshift apartment with her Army husband. Monogram's *GI Honeymoon* placed another field officer, Peter Cookson, and his bride, Gale Storm, in some funny situations as the twosome began their connubial life on a military post. Another Monogram title, *Army Wives*, highlighted the problems that Elyse Knox encountered while trying to marry her conscripted boyfriend, Rick Vallin. Eventually, the nuptial knot was tied. RKO's *Seven Days Leave* put Corporal Victor Mature in the unenviable position of needing a wife to satisfy an inheritance claim. Vivacious Lucille Ball finally accepted his proposal.

In Paramount's *True to the Army*, quick-thinking Judy Canova, a circus high-wire artist, sought refuge in the Army camp where her sweetheart, Jerry Colonna, was stationed. After some slapstick comedy involving a uniform masquerade, the charade unraveled and the couple united. Universal's *Weekend Pass* described the lighthearted adventures of a shipyard worker, Noah Beery, Jr., who won a bonus for his production output and soon found himself entangled in some amusing contretemps with Martha O'Driscoll, a young runaway. Universal managed to squeeze ten new songs into this sixty-three-minute picture.

Almost as many tunes appeared in PRC's *The Underdog*, another soldier-and-dog musical drama. With Barton MacLane and Bobby Larson in the leading roles, this picture oozed kindness to canines in every frame. Three other B-pictures glamorized man's best friend without using any crooning assistance. RKO's *My Pal Wolf* starred young Sharyn Moffett as a small child who hitchhiked to Washington to obtain a military exemption for her pet dog, Wolf. The Secretary of War explained the importance of canines in the Army and, after a change of heart, the youngster returned home and placed a one-star service flag in her window. Columbia's *Sergeant Mike* put another dog—nicknamed Sergeant Mike—on a Pacific island with his trainer, Larry Parks. In less than sixty minutes, the twosome ferreted out a Japanese machine-gun nest, carried messages through enemy lines, and led reinforcements back to the battle area. Monogram's *Pride of the Army* allowed young Billy Lee an opportunity to help Uncle Sam by donating his police dog, Pal, to the Army. Some actual training footage, inserted into the storyline, reminded all Americans about the canine's role in wartime.

As propaganda, the B-musicals stirred up every patriotic urge in the red-blooded American. A song, of course, could be hummed, whistled, or mimicked long after the movie was seen. Universal Studios supplied enough music to last a week. *Private Buckaroo* starred Harry James and the Andrews Sisters in a sixty-three-minute songfest that glorified the young draftees who were now training for the business of war. *When Johnny Comes Marching Home* spotlighted the soporific sounds of Phil Spitalny and his all-girl orchestra, while Yankee war hero Allan Jones remained low-key about his combat achievements.

Republic's *Joan of Ozark* paired the master jokester Joe E. Brown with songstress Judy Canova in the Missouri hills, while Nazi carrier pigeons flew overhead. Along with some unique hog-calling, this duo performed a medley of catchy, patriotic tunes. Columbia's *Hey, Rookie* put together Ann Miller and Larry Parks as a romantic couple producing an Army musical play for the troops at a California camp. Bolstered by numerous vaudeville-type stars, the seventy-one-minute film featured seven modest songs and a ventriloquist. As always, Miss Miller's dancing and cavorting stole the show.

In a similar vein, Monogram churned out two B-musicals for the war effort. *A Wave, A Wac and a Marine* allowed fast-talking Henny Youngman another opportunity to show off his linguistic skills as he directed a musical comedy pitched towards the men in uniform. Elyse Knox and Ann Gillis, working as two understudies in this slapstick adventure, provided the musical entertainment. In *Sweethearts of the U.S.A.* Una Merkel proved, once more, the indispensability of the distaff factory worker, while handsome Donald Novis held her hand. One song, "You Can't Brush Off a Russian," highlighted the Soviet-American alliance.

Probably the best known B-musical was Republic's *Rosie the Riveter*, a film that idealized the distaff factory assemblers who worked long hours—often on swing shifts—turning out military aircraft in noisy defense plants. Jane Frazee starred as the all-American girl who postponed her marriage to Frank Albertson because Uncle Sam needed everyone to pitch in and fight the Axis. Soon, her fiancé wore an army uniform and the apple pie twosome agreed to wed when the last plane left the assembly line. As a closing tribute to Rosie—and all the riveters—a U.S. senator awarded her the prestigious ''E'' certificate, as an all-female chorus sang out its own acclaim: ''There's Something True about Red, White, and Blue.''

This B-title became a catchword on the Home Front and its linguistic application covered a variety of situations. Many women, regardless of their wartime occupations, became known as ''Rosie'' and the new appellation had a sharp patriotic ring to it. While the fighting man was called a ''GI,'' the female workers— the ''Rosies''—kept the factories rolling, producing important supplies. As a propaganda film, *Rosie the Riveter* caught the public's attention because almost every family sent at least one female member to work on the assembly line.

Another morale-boasting B-musical that caught the public's fancy was Columbia's *Reveille with Beverly*, a high-jinks comedy that starred Ann Miller as a switchboard operator who became a popular early morning disc jockey, broadcasting music to the awakening GIs. A 1943 black-and-white version of MTV, Miss Miller's spinning records slowly came to ''life'' as the performers appeared on the screen, complete with background orchestras. Highlighting the film was the appearance of a young, lanky Frank Sinatra, crooning Cole Porter's ''Night and Day,'' with a bevy of female violinists providing the counterpoint. Adding to the musical festivities were songs by Count Basie, Bob Crosby, the Mills Brothers, and Duke Ellington. In a flag-waving finale, the shapely Miss Miller took to the stage floor with another one of her famous pyrotechnic tap-dancing renditions. The tune, ''Thumbs up for V for Victory,'' was a nondescript B-melody.

Sometimes, the B-films shipped the fighting man to faraway locations. In United Artists' *Abroad with Two Yanks*, two gold-bricking Marines, Dennis O'Keefe and William Bendix, basked in the warm Australian sun as their unit practiced endless military maneuvers. Later, the two gyrenes returned to their base and, finally, to the business of war, in this sixty-minute low-grade comedy. Another title spotlighting the touchy topic of goldbricking, Twentieth Century-Fox's *Iceland*, placed the Marines on this strategic island. Here, John Payne and Jack Oakie flirted with girls while Sonja Henie demonstrated her Olympic-winning ice skating skills to the ogling jarheads.

The high seas were the scene of many B-adventures. Columbia's *Atlantic Convoy* starred John Beal as a civilian weatherman who, with comely Virginia Field, cleaned out a Nazi spy nest responsible for sinking Allied ships in the cold Icelandic waters. A similar yarn, this time set off the coast of Brazil, was the storyline of PRC's *Submarine Base*. Here John Litel and Alan Baxter exposed more Axis agents operating in South American ports. In the skies, two American flyers, Richard Greene and Donald Stewart, demonstrated the capabilities of America's own firepower, the B-17, in Warner Brothers' *Flying Fortress*, as they crossed the Atlantic, heading for Berlin. In RKO's *The Navy Comes Through* seamen Pat O'Brien and George Murphy teamed up to sink four Nazi U-boats operating in the dangerous Atlantic war zone. Columbia's *U-Boat Prisoner* concerned an American seaman, Bruce Bennett, who assumed the role of a dead Nazi spy aboard a U-boat. After a series of adventures in sixty-five minutes, the submarine was destroyed and all American prisoners were rescued.

RKO's *Action in Arabia* placed an American newspaperman, George Sanders, in the center of Nazi espionage involving murder and betrayal in this Middle Eastern location. With a little help from Virginia Bruce, the journalist unraveled a spy network. Another newshawk operating in the hot desert sun, Walter Woolf King, smashed a Nazi smuggling ring in PRC's *A Yank in Libya*. In Warner Brothers' *Adventures in Iraq*, B-actor John Loder crash-landed his malfunctioning civilian airplane on the flat sands of this neutral country, only to find himself incarcerated in a pro-Nazi sheik's jail. After a few comic strip adventures, the U.S. Army Corps arrived, rescuing the pilot and routing the Axis leaders. Columbia's *Passport to Suez* featured a popular Hollywood sleuth, the Lone Wolf, played by Warren Williams, in another B-meller. This time, the reclusive detective thwarted the destruction of the Suez Canal by some bumbling Nazi agents.

Over in Egypt, newspaperman Robert Young confronted the Third Reich in MGM's *Cairo*, another low-budget thriller about Nazi espionage. To add a little entertainment to this slow-moving potboiler, operetta star Jeanette MacDonald sang some old-fashioned patriotic tunes, while her American boyfriend chased down the Third Reich villains. On a different note, the African jungle shared in the global conflict. RKO's *Tarzan Triumphs* starred the indomitable Johnny Weissmuller as the Ape Man, living a quiet, arboreous life with Jane, Boy, and Cheeta. When Nazi forces threatened his treetop home, the vine-swinging Weissmuller, with the help of some natives and a few animals, decimated the guttural-speaking invaders. Later, in *Tarzan's Desert Mystery*, the jungle man shared some equestrian adventures while breaking up a Nazi conduit operating in the hot Sahara. PRC's *Jungle Siren* placed swimming star Buster Crabbe in the thick of Nazi intrigue, while animal trainer Frank Buck, famous for "bringing them back alive," jostled the Axis in *Tiger Fangs*. Universal's *Drums of the Congo* put U.S. intelligence officer Don Terry in the midst of Axis intrigue in darkest Africa.

Sometimes France became the backdrop for action stories. Twentieth Century-Fox's *Paris after Dark* heaped praise upon General de Gaulle as two Parisians, George Sanders and Brenda Marshall, distributed clandestine leaflets in their own arrondissement, frustrating the Gauleiters. Another Fox production, *Tonight We Raid Calais*, highlighted English agent John Sutton who gathered important military information with the help of the resistance force—the Maquis. In MGM's *Assignment in Brittany*, the French underground, with a British Agent, destroyed a Nazi submarine base operating in the northern part of France.

Another B-espionage thriller, RKO's *The Master Race*, warned of neo-Nazism emerging in the Low Countries after the Allied D-Day invasion. George Coulouris appeared as a Gestapo officer, posing as a Belgian patriot and hoping to start World War III. The U.S. Army and a Russian doctor wrecked his plans. RKO's *Passport to Destiny* described the adventures of an English charwoman, Elsa Lanchester, who attempted to sneak into Germany to assassinate the Fuehrer. Unable to carry out her plan, the would-be-murderer proffered wartime shibboleths as a patriotic substitute.

Over in the Balkans, the Nazis suffered new defeats. In Yugoslavia, Philip Dorn and his guerrilla army killed many

German soldiers in Twentieth Century-Fox's *Chetniks—the Fighting Guerrillas*, a loud tribute to the controversial royalist, Draja Mikhailovitch. After the War, this B-picture was shelved because its "hero," an acknowledged fascist, was executed for war crimes. Another B-drama, Columbia's *The Black Parachute*, placed handsome Larry Parks in some remote Balkan region, attacking the Third Reich behind their own lines. Jonathan Winters (famous for his Mr. Dithers role in the popular *Blondie* series) played the deposed king of this nameless country.

Monogram took the fight into the Fatherland with three low-powered productions. *I Escaped from the Gestapo*, starring Dean Jagger, depicted the implausible adventures of a forger the Nazis released from prison to counterfeit bonds and currency. After some contrived episodes, the good-looking Jagger turned the tables on his Axis captors. *Enemy of Women* traced the career of the Nazi propagandist Dr. Joseph Goebbels, from his early days as a struggling playwright to his rise as Hitler's number three man. With Paul Andor in the chief role, the film concocted a series of implausible episodes, each one testifying to the brutality of this egomaniacal Prussian soldier. On another issue, *Women in Bondage* took a serious theme—Himmler's eugenic edict that SS officers must impregnate their own wives plus childless women, thirty years or older—and ran it into the ground. Starring Gail Patrick as the wife of a paralyzed Third Reich officer, the B-storyline revealed the misfortunes of German women, including sterilization, forced sexual intercourse, and euthanasia.

Fox's *Bomber's Moon* highlighted the elaborate escape route of two American flyers—George Montgomery and Kent Taylor—downed in the Rhineland. B-heroine Annabella guided the airmen to safety. In Columbia's *The Wife Takes a Flyer*, Franchot Tone, a British flyer hiding from the Gestapo, posed as the husband of a Dutch socialite, Joan Bennett, in order to sneak back to England, while the Nazi officer, Allyn Joslyn, constantly stumbled over his own feet.

The B-war against Japan demonstrated American prowess in every frame. Columbia's *Submarine Raider* starred John Howard as the Navy commander who rescued pretty Marguerite Chapman after her yacht was destroyed by a Nipponese aircraft carrier en route to the December 7th attack. Eventually, the American seaman caught up with the Japanese ship and, after some tricky underwater maneuvering, sank the enemy with a bull's-eye torpedo launch. The same theme—the destruction of a Japanese war vessel—held together the convoluted plot of another Columbia production, *Two-Man Submarine*. With Tom Neal and Lloyd Bridges in the leading roles, this B-sea tale involved some low-grade espionage as the two Americans, stranded on a remote South Sea island, fought off some Axis duplicity.

PRC's *Corregidor* highlighted the B-version of the victory-through-defeat motif found in such important films as *Bataan* and *Wake Island*. Donald Woods and Elissa Landi paired as two medical doctors trapped on the doomed peninsula as enemy troops bombarded this last Army bastion. Using a great deal of stock newsreel footage of explosions, this seventy-five-minute photodrama sanitized the capitulation of this base with mock heroics, including hand-to-hand combat between some tough GIs and inept Japanese soldiers. A similar storyline—Twentieth Century-Fox's *Manila Calling*—featured Lloyd Nolan and Cornel Wilde heading up an ill-supplied bank of guerrillas in the Philippines, fighting a hopeless battle against a strong Japanese force. After sixty minutes of jungle warfare, only three Americans survived and their impending demise was left to speculation. Fox also produced *The Eve of St. Mark*, a poignant story based on the Maxwell Anderson stageplay, about the death of a small group of American defenders on a Philippine island during the early days of the War.

On a positive note, Republic's *Remember Pearl Harbor* spotlighted cowboy star Red Barry (now billed as Donald M. Barry), wearing U.S. Army standard-issue jungle khakis and a Frank Buck hat, wrecking an Axis fifth column ring before it could launch a Japanese invasion of the Philippines. PRC's *Prisoner of Japan* featured Alan Baxter as a captured American astronomer who outwitted some Axis dupes on an unnamed Pacific island. In a similar role, Richard Quine posed as an American "turncoat" in Universal's *We've Never Been Licked*. Later, he would perish when U.S. dive bombers destroyed the Japanese battleship with the American spy on board. Paramount's *Minesweeper* assigned Richard Arlen to a Navy defensive vessel operating in the dangerous Pacific waters. His martyr's death, during an experimental operation, served as a patriotic coda.

Other B-titles methodically hammered away at the Japanese. Republic's stable included *Escape from Hong Kong, Top Ser-*

geant, and *Danger in the Pacific.* All three films starred B-actor
Don Terry in his typical clean-cut American hero roles. Monogram's *Lure of the Islands* put Margie Hart on a tropic isle loaded
with Axis agents. With the arrival of Robert Lowery and Guinn
Williams the enemy disbanded and the "native" girl was rescued.
RKO's *Rookies in Burma* placed the comedy team of Alan Carney
and Wally Brown in the southeast Asia jungle, where the two
dogfaces thoroughly discombobulated a Japanese infantry squad
hiding in the underbrush. MGM's *Salute to the Marines* allowed a
thirty-year leatherneck veteran, Wallace Beery, a chance to see
action against the "mustard-colored monkeys" in the Philippine
underbrush. His battle death enhanced *semper fidelis.*

Universal's *Destination Unknown* found William Gargan and
Irene Hervey in the Chinese interior, hot on the heels of some
valuable jewels needed to purchase munitions for Chiang Kai-
shek's guerrilla army. After traveling by train, ox cart, taxi, and
their own reliable shank's mare, the twosome finally delivered
their important cargo. Monogram's *Wings Over the Pacific*
allowed American hermit Montagu Love fifty-nine minutes of
action against Japanese agents who discovered oil on his reclusive
Pacific isle. With the help of his daughter, pretty Inez Cooper, the
Nipponese—and their Nazi cohorts—found themselves in the
deep six. On a lighter note, United Artists' *Yanks Ahoy* employed
slapstick in the war against the Japanese as two Army sergeants—
William Tracy and Joe Sawyer—captured an enemy submarine,
using a fishing line from the deck of their transport.

MGM offered *Pilot No. 5* as a primer on Jeffersonian democracy. With Franchot Tone and Gene Kelly in the leading roles, this
B-melodrama traced the career of a young lawyer who exposed a
corrupt, fascist-minded southern governor. When war broke out,
the tough-dealing counselor became an Air Corps pursuit pilot,
fighting in the South Pacific. In an elaborate B-finale, the airman
rammed his aircraft onto a Japanese aircraft carrier, rather than let
the ship escape to safer waters.

The overaged hero received double recognition from Co-
lumbia's B-section. *Mr. Winkle Goes to War* glamorized the
adventures of a mild-mannered, forty-four-year-old bank clerk,
Edward G. Robinson, who, despite his age, was drafted into the
Army. Assigned to a combat unit, the infantryman landed on a
South Pacific island where he singlehandedly leveled a Japanese

pillbox. Acclaimed a hero, the soft-spoken Robinson returned home to the accolades of his friends and family, a testimony to the homebred values of America. Later, in *Destroyer*, Chief Petty Officer Edward G. Robinson, stationed aboard a Navy cruiser, crawled into the hole of his ship to make repairs as Japanese planes and a submarine attacked the American vessel. Once more a hero, the elderly Robinson received acclaim from his superiors and crew members.

In their fight against Japan, the B-propaganda films provided the same type of caricature, distortion, and racial epithets as could be found in such major productions as *Guadalcanal Diary, Gung Ho*, or *The Purple Heart*. As always, the Nipponese soldier wore thick eyeglasses and spouted "banzai," while his officers—frail, diminutive men brandishing samurai swords—volunteered their lives to Emperor Hirohito. Frequently, these characterizations seemed ludicrous because so many Occidental actors, wearing exaggerated makeup, portrayed these Japanese heavies with no concern for cultural verisimilitude.

As a cinematic genre, the B-productions played an important part in the overall film propaganda of World War II. By sheer numbers alone, these B-chestnuts consistently hammered home the same old themes, including such bromides as: spies were everywhere, so watch out; Uncle Sam needed workers, do your part, find a job in a defense plant; and, the Axis enemies, when confronted on the foreign battlefield by the American GI, always capitulated to the Red, White, and Blue.

For the millions of moviegoers who watched these second features each week, the message was ever the same, even biblical: the race belonged to the swift. With the support of its allies, the Hollywood B-propaganda proclaimed, the United States, with the help of Red Barry, Lloyd Nolan, and Philip Dorn, would emerge victorious after this Second World War.

CHAPTER EIGHT

DISTORTIONS, PREVARICATIONS, FICTION-AS-FACT: REFLECTIONS ON PROPAGANDA

". . . your boys are not going to be sent into any foreign wars."
—President Franklin Delano Roosevelt, in response to Wendell Willkie's election campaign charge that the New Deal would force the United States into war with Germany by April 1941 (Boston, October 30, 1940).

When the Hollywood directors mobilized right after the December 7th attack, one question troubled everyone: how long would this war last? While a few optimists predicted an early finish, most filmmakers saw the handwriting on the wall—it would take years for complete victory. During that time, the motion picture industry, governed by various federal edicts, played an important part, disseminating information about the conflict through its many propaganda films. Audiences, for the most part, seemed confident, after watching Spencer Tracy bomb Tokyo, that American troops—the best fighting men in the world—would force their Axis foes to their knees.

These propaganda films, of course, satisfied Home Front viewers about various Allied victories and kept civilian and military morale high. What difference would it make if some of the titles skewed the truth? Who cared if the photoplays contained distortions, prevarications and fiction-as-fact? American audiences wanted reassurances that their side was winning. As for the GIs, watching these pictures in PX theaters, weren't they, like everyone else, entitled to a little escapism, a two-hour furlough?

But one unidentified GI, fed up with Hollywood's propaganda, aired his disgruntlement in the pages of a leading magazine. On

148

September 11, 1944, *Time* published (in its letters to the editor section) a blistering 209-word statement by an enlisted man—his name withheld for obvious reasons—about the war films shown on his current overseas base. Calling the movies "idiotic hoopla," the GI derided the screen's marveled "hero," with rouged lips and a do-or-die voice coupled with Pepsodent-perfect molars. With his well-manicured bare hands this "superman" killed 180 Japanese soldiers, thus saving his battalion from annihilation. Along with other complaints, the GI ended by saying that some troops stormed out of the theater before the movies were over, expressing their disgust with one-word expletives.

What happened? What caused this anonymous enlisted man to vent such public frustration at the Hollywood motion picture industry? Was he fed up with the realities he knew as a GI, compared with the anesthetized version of military life portrayed on the screen? While millions of Americans faithfully watched lowly GIs, led by intelligent, fair-minded, higher-paid officers, rout their Axis foes, how many moviegoers knew that such propaganda films were a tenuous veneer, sugarcoating the unpleasant facts of life for the enlisted man. How many film watchers understood the basic hierarchy of the military pecking order? Did audiences realize that most GIs felt they were constantly being screwed, blued, and tattooed by a harsh and unyielding autocratic system? Certainly Private Eddie Slovik knew. So did another enlisted man fighting in the South Pacific, Norman Mailer. Years later, everyone would know.

What films bothered this nameless GI? What movie pushed him over the edge, prompting a letter to *Time* magazine? Perhaps, Columbia's *Mr. Winkle Goes to War* was the culprit. In this picture, a shy forty-four-year-old bank clerk, Edward G. Robinson, received his selective service notice. A few days later, he reported to the draft board, passed a medical examination, and that afternoon was bused to a local military base. Within minutes, along with some younger recruits, he appeared in a perfectly fitted uniform, sitting idly in a well-ordered barracks. Soon the sergeant arrived, welcomed the men, and after some paternal advice they sauntered off to the chow hall.

What army was this? Didn't Columbia Pictures understand what military basic training was all about? What happened to the draft board's omniscient instructions, the "go home and put your affairs in order'' dictum that every recruit heard after the medical officer stamped his imprimatur on his folder? Every GI knew the initiation rite into the service was the two-minute military haircut, where every man's head was reduced to peach fuzz. But in *Mr. Winkle*, Private Robinson and his pals spend their first sixteen weeks in the Army without any tonsorial services. Every GI remembered his first hours in the supply room, where new clothing was thrown around with explicit instructions—press the shirts, shine the shoes, alter the trousers. Yet, Private Robinson— in the Army less than two hours—wore a creased uniform, starched shirt, and a spit-shined shoes. How come? Was valet service part of the deal?

There were more problems. Where did Columbia find that kind, sympathetic, soft-spoken drill sergeant, the noncom who spoke like a village parson, suggesting that the troops stroll over to the dining room before the doors closed? Didn't Alfred E. Green, the film's director, comprehend that most drill sergeants bellowed orders without regard to syntax, enunciation, or civility? Didn't Mr. Green realize that new troops marched to the chow hall three times a day while their noncom screamed cadence at them? No wonder the overseas GI penned his letter to *Time*. As a combat film, *Mr. Winkle Goes to War* could only aggravate American GIs with its Norman Rockwell storyline. As propaganda, however, it was a different matter: *Mr. Winkle* reminded civilian audiences about the wholesomeness of U.S. Army life.

Other propaganda films offered similar distortions and untruths. In RKO's B-yarn, *Call Out the Marines*, two salty leathernecks, Victor McLaglen and Edward Lowe—stationed in sunny California, spent their evening hours in an expensive night club, sipping overpriced cocktails and flirting with well-dressed women. Nearby, a large group of young, handsome PFC Marines—all decked out in their spiffy dress blue uniforms—sat at their darkened tables, billing and cooing with their dates, promising to meet tomorrow evening.

Was this the United States Marine Corps? How did these jarheads manage to obtain base liberty every evening to frolic at an expensive eatery? Who picked up the tab for such an evening on the town? Didn't the film's directors, Frank Ryan and William Hamilton, realize that the bar bill for one night's outing was roughly the equivalent of a serviceman's monthly pay? How

about the women in expensive clothing? Do members of the haut
monde routinely chase after young men holding the rank of
private first class?

No wonder the GI letter writer showed annoyance. As he spent
his off-hours sitting on his bunk bed, cleaning his piece for the
next morning's inspection, Hollywood's version must have
seemed wildly skewed. According to RKO, every evening a group
of smiling Marines and their sergeants relaxed in luxurious
surroundings, eating filet mignon, sipping highballs, while pretty
women squeezed their hands. What a way to win the War!

Another RKO B-story, *My Favorite Spy*, didn't fare much
better with real-life GIs. In this off-beat comedy, a famous band
leader, Kay Kayser, received his draft notice on the afternoon of
his wedding day. Undaunted by this news, the marriage proceeded, followed by an elaborate reception for the bride and
groom. Later, the couple retired to their apartment and, in
accordance with OWI regulations, no conjugal activities were
discussed or implied. End of scene.

Early next morning, Mr. Kay Kayser left his new bride and
reported to the U.S. Army. By 9:00 a.m., Lt. Kayser, hopelessly
inept, was instructing enlisted men about the rudiments of military
life. By late afternoon, the base commander, recognizing the
inexperience of his new officer, issued another directive. Lt.
Kayser became an intelligence agent in an undercover operation
designed to locate Axis spies.

Was this the U.S. Army? Didn't Tay Garnett, the film's
director, understand that most men received more than eighteen
hours notice to report for induction? Where did Lt. Kayser pick up
a uniform in time for a 9:00 roll call his first morning in the
service? Isn't an officer required to fill out numerous forms prior
to receiving an assignment? Doesn't a lieutenant receive some
billeting the first day in the Army? Does the undercover operations team send a man on a spying mission with only eight hours
service time?

Maybe this deprecatory, letter-writing GI was angry at another
director, Edward Dmytryk, for creating similar false scenes.
RKO's *Behind the Rising Sun* purported that the April 1942
Doolittle bombing raid over Tokyo reduced the Japanese capital
to rubble. In this fiction-as-fact account, J. Carrol Naish (as a
Japanese administrator) walked through street after street of

charred debris, pondering the events that turned Tokyo into a city of ashes. Historically, of course, Doolittle's ten American twin-engined B-25s dropped forty 500-pound bombs on the city, causing relatively minor damage. RKO completely ignored that information and turned the raid into an elaborate victory.

In Japan, the attack caused scant concern. The militarists, stunned by the audacity of such a raid, ordered their island defense network strengthened. However, three years later, in 1945, the tide changed dramatically and the U.S. XXI Bomber Command, stationed in the Marianas, under the leadership of cigar-smoking General Curtis LeMay, methodically pulverized Japanese cities using the latest air weapon, a large, technically sophisticated, heavily-armed bomber, the B-29 Superfortress. On March 9th and 10th, this command sent waves of B-29's over Tokyo. The bombing mission left 80% of the city in ruins. Since *Behind the Rising Sun* opened on July 21, 1943, Hollywood scooped the history books by twenty months.

No wonder the GI seemed frustrated. Maybe he couldn't understand why two Occidental actors—J. Carrol Naish and Tom Neal—were picked to portray Japanese nationals in *Rising Sun.* Didn't any of the film's crew recognize the absurdity of their silly appearances, especially the plastered-down, oblique-eye makeup? How could Tom Neal, a clean-cut, boy-next-door American hero, convince anyone that he was a Japanese fighter-pilot ready to die for his emperor? As for J. Carrol Naish, didn't he play that tough Marine officer in *Gung Ho*? Wasn't he the lieutenant fighting on a South Pacific island, blasting Nipponese soldiers out of their pillboxes?

Behind the Rising Sun wasn't the only film depicting a fictitious bombing of Japan. Two other titles, RKO's *Bombardier* (released on May 13, 1943) and Warner Brothers' *God Is My Co-Pilot* (released on February 21, 1945), added to the myth that American aircraft attacked their enemy's island fortress long before LeMay's B-29s staged their massive two-day raid. Both motion pictures capitalized on the news stories that glamorized Colonel Doolittle's April 18, 1942, bombing, but in each instance every facet of that daring event was distorted.

Richard Wallace's *Bombardier* highlighted the summer 1941 adventures of the clean-cut Caucasian American cadets earning their wings in a newly created aviation slot that required precision, agility, and discipline. Alongside the pilots and navigators, the bombardiers were commissioned officers and their training, spearheaded by pudgy Major Pat O'Brien, acknowledged the importance of strategic airpower. Pearl Harbor accelerated their role and weeks later, a squadron of B-17s headed toward Japan on a daring night raid which destroyed an important enemy military base and dozens of oil tanks.

As a propaganda film, *Bombardier* downplayed its fictitious storyline and, employing subtlety and nuance, purported that the events presented were factual. Every GI knew that Doolittle's bombing raiders attacked Tokyo, not some nameless Japanese military outpost and its surrounding storage depot. But most film watchers readily accepted this nocturnal bombing as fact—just another example of American aviation prowess. After all, if Pat O'Brien—replete with oxygen mask and flight jacket—sat in the cockpit, what could happen? Victory, for the Home Front viewer, was irrevocable.

As an Army major in this film, Pat O'Brien probably tarnished the image of the fighting man. He was fat, sloppy, sometimes clumsy, inept, or awkward. His jowls were low and pronounced, his stomach protruded, and his double and triple chins (depending on the camera angle) made him a comical figure—a young Falstaff. Walking around the base with his swagger stick tucked under his elbow, wearing military shirts at least three, maybe four sizes too large, and prancing about in his cavalry boots, he looked like a balloon in a uniform. His saluting seemed arduous; his hand somehow never reached the cap and he seemed out of breath by the mere effort of raising his arm. No wonder the overseas GI audiences gave the film the raspberry.

While *Bombardier* distorted the truth about the air attack against Japan, Warner Brothers acknowledged that its version of the Tokyo bombing raid—*God Is My Co-Pilot*—was fictional. The film's opening credits contained a short blurb admitting that a large force of pursuit and bomber planes did not attack Tokyo from the Kunming section of China in June 1942. Even with this disclaimer, American audiences perceived the picture as true, since the storyline featured a real life double-ace, Colonel Robert Lee Scott (played by Dennis Morgan), a Georgian-born officer who shot down ten Japanese Zeroes. To strengthen the "truth" of *Co-Pilot*, an elaborate aerial scene depicted large numbers of

American aircraft flying off for a massive attack. Eventually the planes became minuscule and finally dropped out of sight. Such a patriotic ending—coupled with stirring martial music—inspired audiences to forget the opening trailer's denial.

What other titles ticked off this moviegoing GI? Maybe he sat through Howard Hawks' *Air Force*, a film that paid homage to the men who staffed the elaborate B-17 aircraft by describing the events that befell one crew which left their California base on December 6th, flying westward to Hawaii. The Pearl Harbor attack changed their flight plan, forcing the airmen to land elsewhere. After a series of narrow escapes, including the rebuilding of the aircraft with cannibalized parts, the crew headed southward to the safety of Australia. Along the way, they participated in an elaborate, impromptu bombing of a Japanese fleet, destroying numerous enemy vessels.

What scenes in *Air Force* annoyed the GI audiences? Perhaps the men in khaki marveled at the superhuman strength of Sergeant John Garfield, who singlehandedly picked up one of the aircraft's turret machine guns, placed it against his right hip, and fired away at several approaching Japanese Zeroes. During this salvo, the impenetrable Sergeant Garfield, unperturbed by the weapon's recoil, blasted an enemy aircraft out of the skies. How did this happen? Didn't Howard Hawks, an experienced director who specialized in aviation films, understand that this weapon was bolted inside the aircraft to curtail its strong backfire? Was Mr. Hawks oblivious to Sir Isaac Newton's Third Law of Motion? As for John Garfield, where did he develop such extraordinary vision? Was he secretly devouring large portions of carrots?

What about that bombing attack of the Japanese fleet on December 8th? According to Howard Hawks, a squadron of B-17s and Navy torpedo planes rendezvoused in the South Pacific and sank several destroyers and one aircraft carrier. Historically, of course, this entire episode was a pipe dream. After the Japanese attacked Pearl Harbor, they went after other military installations—including Guam, Wake Island, and the Philippines—wrecking most of America's armament. For a government that once preached isolationism, the United States was in a precarious situation, reminiscent of George Washington's bleak Valley Forge days. To even remotely suggest that twenty-four hours after one of its worst military defeats the Army Air Corps could

retaliate with a major victory indicated Warner Brothers' phantas-
magoric interpretation of military history.

For the jubilant audiences watching *Air Force* back on the
Home Front, thousands of miles from the combat zone, this film
pandered to the emotional needs of those who craved reassurance
that their side would win. How many moviegoers, in February
1943, realized that this closing victory scene represented another
example of distortion, prevarication, and fiction-as-fact from the
propagandist's typewriter? Our side had taken the offensive, the
film purported, and for most Americans that news provided the
exhilaration to boost morale. When Captain Gig Young dropped
those bombs on the Japanese carrier, the enemy ship's slow
descent to the bottom of the ocean reverberated all the way back to
Main Street.

Once in a while, the GI filmgoer watched scenes that elicited
the old-fashioned horselaugh. In Warner's *Edge of Darkness*,
Errol Flynn—as a Norwegian freedom fighter—pulled the pin
from a hand grenade with his teeth and tossed the weapon with
such accuracy that it killed many German soldiers. Didn't Mr.
Flynn realize that most GIs lacked the alveolar strength to grasp
the weapon by the molars? Didn't Warner Brothers understand
that the hand grenade wasn't a baseball? Of course they did, but
what difference did it make? Errol Flynn wasn't the only actor
exhibiting extraordinary dentoid skills.

Captain Flynn also used his teeth to extricate the safety pin
from its metal coupling without experiencing periodontal discomfort in *Objective Burma*. Other fighting men employing their
bicuspids and molars included Private William Bendix (*Wake
Island*), Sergeant Humphrey Bogart (*Sahara*), Commander John
Wayne (*The Fighting Seabees*), Russian Sergeant Paul Muni
(*Counter-Attack*), Colonel Randolph Scott (*Gung Ho*), and Sergeant Alan Hale (*Desperate Journey*). Probably the most famous
scene of this kind appeared in *Gung Ho* when Private Harold
Landon, trapped in a ditch with his fellow Marines by heavy
Japanese machine-gun fire, removed his gear and shirt simulta-
neously, disengaged the pins from two grenades with his teeth,
and raced through the jungle towards the pillbox, hurling the two
explosives into the enemies' dirt-laden lair.

Other motion pictures contained scenes that exaggerated the
fighting man's prowess or expertise. Aviators, for example, could

operate any type of aircraft without any previous flying experience or preflight instructions. In *A Guy Named Joe*, civilian pilot
Irene Dunne jumped into a parked bomber, turned an ignition
switch, and merely flew off to attack a secret Japanese military
base. The pretty aviatrix eschewed any maps or navigational aids.
In *Action in Arabia*, newspaperman George Sanders—with only
six hours of flying lessons—hijacked a small Axis plane and made
some three-point landings in the Syrian desert. Likewise, Errol
Flynn (*Desperate Journey*), Robert Stack (*To Be or Not to Be*),
Jon Hall (*Invisible Agent*), and George Sanders (*Apointment in
Berlin*) commandeered Nazi warplanes and, seconds later, were
airborne. Where did American and British pilots learn the aerody-
namic principles of German aircraft? Were all airplanes alike?
Were the operating instructions on control panels printed in
Esperanto?

Sometimes mock heroics seemed overstated, superficial, or
ludicrous. In *Flight for Freedom*, Navy pilot Fred MacMurray led
an attack squadron against a Japanese flight in the mid-Pacific.
Descending toward his target, the airman fired vindictively upon
his enemy. Pulling away from his kill, MacMurray offered
posthumous praise to his former sweetheart, a fatality of the War:
"This one's for you, Toni!" Other films employed similar paeans
of retribution after Americans killed their foes. Private Anthony
Quinn, machine-gunning his first Japanese (*Guadalcanal Diary*):
"That's for Captain Cross"; Private Richard Jaeckel, in the same
film, shooting a Japanese soldier: *"That's one you taught me,
Tojo"*; Colonel Dennis Morgan (*God Is My Co-Pilot*), blasting a
Zero out of the sky: *"This one's for Johnny Petach"*; and Lt.
Tyrone Power, as a fighter-pilot (*A Yank in the RAF*) destroying
his first Nazi aircraft: *"That's for the corporal."* Later, Power
downed his second German: *". . . that's for Roger."*

No wonder GI audiences snickered. These tributary pronounce-
ments sounded more like beer commercials than the language of
battle. Maybe the ground pounders were fed up with stereotypes
that portrayed them as candidates for the cover of *Life* magazine.
How many times would the same role show up in a war film? How
often would the "kid" appear innocent and flustered about the
global conflict, only to find comfort with the father figure, an
older, more experienced man proffering homilies about the Four
Freedoms? How about the Ivy League liberal, the Brooklynite,

and the chaplain—each one standing on his private soap box, expounding in his own inimitable way, "loose lips sink ships?"

Other visual clichés flooded the storylines. How about the married GI with a picture of his newly-born child tucked inside his helmet liner, or the farmer-turned-soldier examining the soil on the foreign battlefield? Sometimes the GI carried a chip on his shoulder; other times, he retreated into isolation, preferring to remain a loner. Other dogfaces spent their idle moments keeping diaries as reference material for the great American novel they would write once back home. Occasionally, a European refugee popped up, now an enlisted man in Uncle Sam's Army, to detail the horrors of life under National Socialism to a younger charge. How many GIs wrote their "last" letter, asking the chaplain to mail it if they didn't "come back" from some hazardous mission?

The same scenes appeared over and over again. How many times would audiences watch the makeshift medical operation performed in the heat of battle, the bomber crew that bailed out in enemy territory, the wounded GI who visited his sweetheart with some extremity in a cast, or the elongated "escape" or "chase" from the Axis foes? Similar stereotyping included the elaborate aerial dog fights that tested America's flying mettle, the solo rescue of a friend trapped in no man's land, the occasional romance with a foreign woman, and the austere burial eulogy, performed with solemn patriotic dignity.

What else? Propaganda films highlighted the we-are-your-brothers-in-arms motif to strengthen the Allied forces concept. Other scenes showed GIs treating their mascots with tender loving care. The American flag—a tangible symbol of democracy—flew majestically as the fighting man entered the combat zone. Sometimes, minor disagreement served a useful purpose as various photoplays elaborated the ongoing conflict between the bomber pilot and the pursuit flyer. Who flew the better aircraft? Only Pat O'Brien or Randolph Scott knew for sure. One thing was certain: a speech of praise at the beginning or ending of any film raised the audiences' emotional state to its highest level.

The issues of the war seemed overstated. How many times were GIs told that their fight preserved religious freedom, protected the American way of life, stopped the spread of fascism? How many movies elaborated on the "we didn't start this war, but we're going to finish it" theme? How about the many scenes where tough combat veterans vowed that no one could mock the flag, the President or the Congress and get away with it? What about revenge for Pearl Harbor?

The Axis enemies received their share of stereotyping. American moviegoers hissed when they learned that German and Japanese foes graduated from American universities. Other scenes depicted the enemy as a meticulous dresser, emblazoned with suede gloves, monocles, and swagger sticks. The sadistic medical officer was common, as was the staff member with "friends in high places." Axis villains spoke with heavy, comical accents and bragged about their skill in torture. Off to the side, a small, slimy interrogator awaited instructions while other adversaries explained to their captives that they were "liberators," not "conquerors." The Japanese routinely disemboweled themselves, adhering to the strict code of hara-kiri, while the Italian soldier sang loud arias, utilizing comical gesticulations. Sometimes a young, blond Nazi youth, not fully corrupted by Hitlerism, remembered his catechism days and those important Christian ideals.

So many of the storylines exaggerated the glamorous side of military life that most GIs, sitting in their PX theaters, wore their chukka boots to the screenings. In Warner Brothers' *Flying Fortress*, two American flyers arrived in London, ostensibly to fight for the RAF but, instead, chased pretty girls and began a pleasant, social life. Later, the twosome returned from a bombing mission over Germany, which required B-actor Richard Green to crawl onto the wing of his crippled B-17—at 10,000 feet—to make some repairs! Did Walter Forde, the film's director forget his primer on velocity? Didn't he realize that one gust of wind would send the hapless airman earthbound?

If an American pilot displayed such airborne dexterity, why couldn't an ordinary factory worker do the same? In Universal's *Saboteur*, mild-mannered Robert Cummings confronted his Nazi nemesis on top of New York's famed Statue of Liberty. For the California assembly worker, with no Alpine training, it was a routine outing. In a few seconds, Mr. Cummings saved his girl friend and routed his foe, with no loss of equilibrium in this famous end-of-the-film scene. Similar nimbleness highlighted the theme of Warner's *The Gorilla Man*. In this potboiler, a British commando exhibited such extraordinary skill climbing walls that he rivaled his anthropoid ancestor.

Other scenes aggravated the GI audience, but this was the nature of propaganda films. The foot soldier realized the futility of the frontal bayonet attack against his enemy's fortified defense line but Home Front viewers saw it differently. When John Wayne and his fighting seabees charged the Japanese stronghold, nothing could stop these construction men turned fighters. Put handsome Tyrone Power in charge of a daring midnight commando raid and moments later the Nazi's oil tanks burned incessantly. Let Brian Donlevy loose in the Pacific theater and, within minutes, a Japanese ship rested in its watery grave. While the GIs scoffed at these mock heroics, stateside civilian moviegoers applauded their men in uniform. Did anyone—beside Hollywood—realize that propaganda's efficacy rested on discrete subjectivity? The film-makers understood the rule: show only one side of the coin.

As a film watcher, *Time* magazine's unidentified GI offered a legitimate complaint against Hollywood's stereotypical portrayal of the War. Clearly, the motion picture industry adhered to the OWI's regulations that mandated a positive view of the Allied achievements. If the GI showed annoyance at Hollywood's presentation of military service, it was because he knew the truth. Like Kilroy, the GI was there. He knew the difference between life on the battlefield and life on the screen. He realized, for example, that while the American military system preached democracy, it was prudent not to sign your name to any public complaint.

Hollywood, of course, reduced the War to simplistic terms because the industry understood the components of film propaganda. Stereotypes, clichés, myth, flag-waving, and adulation—these concepts permeated the Hollywood propaganda of World War II, and Home Front audiences, needing daily reassurance that their side was winning, flocked to the shows in record numbers. For Tinseltown, its productions adhered to these rules: sustain morale, follow FDR's dicta, and foster patriotic feelings.

If the disgruntled GI didn't like what he saw on the screen, he was in good company. Other ground pounders understood the fine distinctions that separated military life from cinematography. Most of the GIs knew that while glorification of the Allied cause was the order of the day, certain subjects were taboo. No motion picture would ever show the blunders associated with the War. What Hollywood production would highlight the miscalculations that led to the August 1942 debacle at the French port of Dieppe?

Would John Wayne star as one of the casualties in the Great
Slapton Sands Disaster of 1944? Who would command the 82nd
Airborne Division in its July 11, 1943, raid over the Sicilian port
of Gela, an event that resulted in 229 dead paratroopers when
American sailors, unclear about the situation, blasted away at their
own men?

Other events never made it to the silver screen. No film depicted
American Marines shooting Japanese prisoners in a manner that
resembled target practice. No Hollywood productions showed
headless, American bodies strewn on Pacific island beaches, with
isolated arms or legs bobbing nearby. What director would approve
a storyline about the fear associated with the Normandy D-Day
landing as dozens of wounded American GIs, in their death throes,
cried out for their mothers? Who would fly one of the American
bombers that attacked American forces in the ill-planned Operation
COBRA on July 24, 1944, near the French town of Saint-Lô, that
killed 136 infantrymen including a prominent Lt. General?

Years later, of course, Hollywood changed its course and fired
salvos against the American military system in dozens of motion
picture themes that were unthinkable during the War. Stanley
Kubrick's black, Cold War comedy, *Dr. Strangelove*, ran the Air
Force into the ground with its depiction of such loony characters
as General Jack Ripper and his commander-in-chief, President
Merkin Muffley. Francis Ford Coppola's *Apocalypse Now* captured the darker side of America's Special Forces running amuck
in Southeast Asia as Marlon Brando and his Montagnard warriors
badgered the Army's command staff. Mike Nichols added more
fuel to the fire with his bleak satire, *Catch-22*, an antimilitary film
that described the circuitous logic found in Army Air Corps
regulations. Adapted from the best-selling novel by Joseph Heller,
Catch-22's caricature of U.S. officers as megalomaniacs, solely
interested in aggrandizing their own careers, redefined American
attitudes about war and the men who manage it.

Who would have thought in the flag-waving days of World War
II, when Hollywood accepted FDR's dictum to provide entertainment and propaganda, that the motion picture industry's pendu-
lum would swing so far in such a short period? Who could
envision the ephemeral nature of America's propaganda films? In
those four short years, the nation's moviemakers created a type of
picture that sustained morale, glorified the fighting man, and

vilified the enemy. Back in 1944—when Randolph Scott and his Marine Raiders seized Makin Island—could director Ray Enright imagine that his rousing title, *Gung Ho*, would appear on a new Hollywood film, a 1986 comedy depicting the shenanigans of automobile workers as they resisted the work rules imposed upon them by their new employer, a Japanese manufacturing company? How about Henry Hathaway? Would he believe that the title of his Flying Tigers, blast-them-from-the-skies, 1942 adventure film, *China Girl*—now freed of copyright restraint—would be used a second time in a 1987 Romeo and Juliet tale, about two lovers from New York's Chinatown and Little Italy?

Other titles found their storyline in the legacy left behind by the World War II propaganda films. Paramount's high-flying Navy adventure, *Top Gun* (1986), glamorized the lifestyle of the pilots who roared down the flight deck of elaborate aircraft carriers in their sophisticated F-14 Tomcats, ready to blast America's ene- mies out of the sky. With good-looking Tom Cruise in the computer-guided canopy, *Top Gun* served as an effective recruit- ing film, pandering to the John Wayne instincts found in many male adolescents. United Artists' *The Final Countdown* (1980) was another pitch for volunteers needed to service the Navy's nuclear-powered aircraft carriers. This time fighter-pilots emerged in and out of the twilight zone, traversing between 1941 and 1979. Another Navy recruitment film, Orion Pictures' *Navy Seals* (1990) glamorized the unlikely adventures of this hand- picked attack unit, composed of America's elite swimmers. In this seagoing yarn, frail-looking Charlie Sheen proved that any young man could join the Navy and see the world.

As contemporary propaganda films, these three examples wax pale when placed beside their predecessors—the black-and-white films of 1941-45. As the disgruntled GI stated, the war pictures were distorted and inaccurate, but such shortcomings went unno- ticed because, unlike these later titles, the propaganda storylines appealed to the emotions of millions of Americans on the Home Front. When the United States marched off to fight its second world war, in the dark hours of early 1942, few could predict the outcome and numerous questions frightened most people. Would the U.S. win this war? Did we have the proper manpower and military materiel? How long would the conflict last? Were we safe from enemy attack?

Of course they were. When John Wayne vowed retribution for the Bataan Death March, Americans felt reassured. When Spencer Tracy headed the Doolittle Raiders westward to bomb Tokyo, the Home Front cheered. When Dennis Morgan placed God in his copilot's seat, Americans offered their silent prayers. How about Claudette Colbert's husband? Didn't he return safe and unharmed on Christmas Day? What about Bogart? Didn't he capture more than 100 Nazis singlehandedly? Give Cary Grant some recognition. He was the skipper who slipped his submarine inside of Tokyo bay to wreck the Japanese defense system. Don't forget Errol Flynn. Didn't he drive the Japanese out of Burma?

For most moviegoers on the Home Front, the Hollywood motion picture industry provided the encouragement needed to sustain morale during the country's somber days of defeat, and when the tide turned, glorified the many battles that brought the armed forces closer to V-J Day. Many components contributed to the Allied final victory in August 1945 and the propaganda films ranked high on this list. For most Americans, savoring the 1990s world of computers, lasers, and cable television, World War II events probably seem long ago and far away. But every so often, a familiar, black-and-white film flickers on some large-size television screen, housed in an elaborate home entertainment center. It is Howard Hawks' 1943 adventure, *Air Force*. Don't worry, this storyline promises, America will never lose the War. Hollywood was right. Fifty years later, television viewers still cheer Captain John Ridgely and the crew of the *Mary Ann* as they roar down the runway, flaps up, machine-guns poised, heading for the wild, blue yonder.

SELECTIVE FILMOGRAPHY

WORLD WAR II PROPAGANDA FILMS: DECEMBER 7, 1941-AUGUST 15, 1945

ABOVE SUSPICION. MGM; directed by Richard Thorpe. Released: April 28, 1943. A half-spoof, half-serious story about Nazi espionage in and around the Fatherland during the ambiguous pre-Pearl Harbor days. Fred MacMurray is convincing as an Oxford don who takes his bride, comely Joan Crawford, on a Continental honeymoon that is really an intelligence mission for the Crown. A convoluted plot turns this melodrama into a typical suspense film complete with guttural-sounding Basil Rathbone as a diabolical Axis villain. Best scene: Joan Crawford eyes a group of young Nazi marchers parading by (husband to wife: *". . . if they don't take it easy, they'll be burned out before they're twenty one."*).

ABROAD WITH TWO YANKS. United Artists; directed by Allan Dwan. Released: July 24, 1944. An insignificant B-comedy depicting the daily antics of two Marines, handsome Dennis O'Keefe and salty William Bendix, stationed in Australia, who spend most of their time trying to smooth-talk some down-under beauties, while their buddies are sequestered in the training camp, preparing for an offensive island invasion. Negative propaganda value since the film's theme, goldbricking, would rile up any serviceman seated in the movie audience. Silliest scene: the two gyrenes take French leave, in front of some pompous ladies (O'Keefe to group: *"I would like to ask you to come along, but you know how it is. I'm a one-man dog."*).

ACROSS THE PACIFIC. Warner Brothers; directed by John Huston. Released: August 18, 1942. A slow-moving formula film starring hard-as-nails Humphrey Bogart as a "cashiered" Ameri-

can Army officer who becomes a "turncoat" working for some
Japanese spies aboard a freighter on the high seas. Romance is
furnished by Mary Astor. Sydney Greenstreet is excellent as a
stealthy Japanese agent whose mission is to blow up the Panama
Canal. The strategic waterway is saved by Bogart's deft use of the
machine-gun. Limited propaganda value since most of the Orientals in Greenstreet's entourage are caricatured as inane and docile.
Even Greenstreet slips: (overweight Greenstreet to Bogart: " . . .
the Japanese make great servants.").

ACTION IN ARABIA. RKO; directed by Leonide Moguy.
Released: February 18, 1944. An overblown, seventy-three-
minute B-meller warning of the dangers of Hitlerism in the
volatile Middle East. George Sanders stars as a suave New York
newspaperman hot on the heels of some Nazi intrigue in the
Syrian capital. The smooth-talking journalist, with the help
of rough-and-tumble Robert Armstrong, thwarts an Axis plot to
turn the desert tribes against the Allied cause, rescues an important sheik, and woos a sophisticated American tourist. Funniest scene: George Sanders dancing with pretty Virginia Bruce
(Sanders to partner: *"Damascus, the oldest city in the world. And
here am I right in the middle of it, suffering from the oldest
emotion."*).

ACTION IN THE NORTH ATLANTIC. Warner Brothers; directed by Lloyd Bacon. Released: May 17, 1943. An extended
salute to the men of the Merchant Marine, responsible for
transporting needed war materiel across the Nazi submarine-
infested waters of the North Atlantic Ocean. Raymond Massey is
seaworthy as the captain of a liberty ship on her maiden voyage,
and Humphrey Bogart, the tough, laconic first officer, reminds his
multiethnic crew that final victory depends on the precarious
supply line. When attacked by a German U-boat, the ship initially
flounders, but after some heroic Yankee seamanship and a little
help from the Soviet Air Force, limps its way into the Russian port
of Murmansk. A good, solid propaganda film that depicts the
many forms of cooperation between the Allied powers. Best
scene: Seaman Sam Levene expostulates his wartime philosophy
(Levene to crew: *"I got faith! In God, President Roosevelt, and
the Brooklyn Dodgers—in the order of their importance."*).

ADVENTURES IN IRAQ. Warner Brothers: directed by D. Ross Lederman. Released: September 27, 1943. A far-fetched B-adventure starring John Loder and Warren Douglas as two American civilian pilots who are forced to make a crash landing in neutral Iraq, there to be captured by a pro-Nazi sheik. Later, after a series of comic-strip adventures, they are rescued by the Army Air Corps, proving once again that American prowess is undaunted (John Loder, berating his former Saracen captors: *". . . we'll be at home as soon as we wipe your friend Hitler off the map."*). Of minimal propaganda value since the B-storyline contains one implausible scene after another, downplaying the strategic importance of the Middle East.

ADVENTURES OF A ROOKIE. RKO; directed by Leslie Goodwins. Released: August 20, 1943. A lighthearted, easygoing B-production starring the comedy team of Wally Brown and Alan Carney, whose slapstick routine closely resembled the mannerisms and dialogue of the more famous Abbott and Costello duo. When inducted into the Army, the two rookies provide merriment for their platoon and frustration for their drill sergeant, but still maintain enough comportment to suggest that a hostile war is raging overseas. Later, in *Rookies in Burma,* the jokesters are shipped to the Far Eastern Command where silly-looking, bucktoothed Japanese soldiers capture them on their first patrol. Soon, they escape from the POW camp and, after a series of loony-tune adventures, return to their own lines with valuable enemy secrets, receive decorative medals, and then peel over a ton of potatoes. Of minimal propaganda value except to caricature the Oriental enemy (Private Brown to Private Carney: *". . . boy, we sure made monkeys out of those Japs, didn't we?"*).

AIR FORCE. Warner Brothers; directed by Howard Hawks. Released: March 20, 1943. A realistic tribute to the men who flew the B-17s; one of the ten best films made about the War. An impeccable cast starring John Ridgely as an experienced pilot on route to Pearl Harbor on December 7th. Forced to alter their course, the crew—a microcosm of American strength and virtue—begins a long air odyssey to safety. Superb concretion of anger, hatred, and frustration toward the enemy, played off with Yankee idealism and fortitude (Marine officer to pilot: *". . . I got*

400 Marines and they're fighting mad. There's going to be some Jap tail feathers flying around this island or I'm crazy.''). Aircraft commander's deathbed scene (as crew simulates take-off) has virtually no propaganda equal. Likewise, the stoic heroism of Sergeant Harry Carey, on hearing of the death of his pilot son, blends poignancy and dignity. Religious overtones and the lugubrious strains of martial music highlight this outstanding movie. One of the best (and unique) scenes: flight mechanic George Tobias keeps tightening the engine bolts as their rebuilt airplane edges down the runway, while Japanese bullets whiz nearby.

ALL THROUGH THE NIGHT. Warner Brothers; directed by Vincent Sherman. Released: January 28, 1942. A low-key Runyonesque adventure tale glamorizing the offbeat lifestyle of some smooth-talking bookies bilking unsuspecting marks hanging around New York's fabled Times Square area. Humphrey Bogart, the leader of this carefree gang, spends most of his time collecting payoffs, while his young sidekick, Jackie Gleason, proffers an occasional wisecrack. Inadvertently, they stumble upon a elaborate Nazi spy ring working out of Yorkville. After some rough-and-tumble adventures, the German agents are routed in a classic end-of-the-film car chase. A good propaganda film expounding the need for vigilance (Bogart to police sergeant Barton MacLane: *"I uncovered a nest of fifth columnists.''*).

APPOINTMENT IN BERLIN. Columbia; directed by Horace McCoy. Released: July 26, 1943. A convincing, anti-Nazi thriller starring urbane George Sanders as another "cashiered" British intelligence officer "working" for the Nazi radio network, but unlike Lord Haw Haw, His Majesty's agent broadcasts coded messages back to his superiors. Many close calls and near-discoveries create a taut storyline as Sanders stays always one step ahead of the Gestapo. When unmasked, Sanders cannot escape. His heroic death and the moving eulogy back in London show the British people at their finest hour. Best acting scene: Sanders "denounces" his homeland ("drunken" Sanders to bobby: *"Munich makes me ashamed to be an Englishman.''*).

ASSIGNMENT IN BRITTANY. MGM; directed by Jack Conway. Released: March 11, 1943. An underdone soap opera which in a funny way lauds the work of the French underground. Smooth Jean Pierre Aumont is competent as a British agent sent to the Brittany coast to locate a secret Nazi submarine base. When not sweet-talking pretty Susan Peters, the Englishman hides from Gestapo chief George Coulouris. After much travail the British commandoes, using Aumont's information, destroy the Third Reich's nautical lair (Aumont to underground workers: " . . . *others like me will come here, expecting friends.* "). Solid propaganda value because the film reaffirms the vulnerability of the German occupation of the French coastline.

BACK TO BATAAN. RKO; directed by Edward Dmytryk. Released: May 31, 1945. A powerful tribute to the guerrillas who fought in the Philippine jungles to pave the way for Douglas MacArthur's successful "I-Shall-Return" invasion. Only John Wayne could portray the tough, wiry American in charge of an ill-trained, ill-supplied volunteer army, which soon becomes a thorn in the Japanese side (Wayne to men: " . . . *this is a dirty war we're fighting and we gotta fight it the right way.* "). Anthony Quinn is convincing as second-in-charge, while Beulah Bondi, a tangible reminder of American womanhood, is outstanding as cook, nurse, and earth mother. Many inflammatory scenes— including the infamous Bataan Death March—depict the Japanese as savage, bestial, and inhuman. One of the finest propaganda scenes in any movie: Vladimir Sokoloff, a timid, Philippine school teacher, refuses to desecrate the American flag and is brutally hanged, shrouded in that national emblem.

BACKGROUND TO DANGER. Warner Brothers; directed by Raoul Walsh. Released: June 9, 1943. A solid, pro-Russian tract starring on-again, off-again American gangster George Raft as a United States government agent sabotaging a Third Reich espionage ring in uncommitted, politically-neutral Turkey. When not praising the Soviet Union or eluding Nazi villains, the smooth-talking Mr. Raft woos pretty Russian spy Brenda Marshall (Raft to friend: " . . . *I'm an American! America is at war, Russia is one of our allies.* "). A strong cast, including Sydney Greenstreet and Peter Lorre as Axis spies, enhances this storyline. Best propaganda scene: ingenue Brenda Marshall recites Abraham Lincoln's Gettysburg Address.

BATAAN. MGM; directed by Tay Garnett. Released: May 28, 1943. Another last-stand motion picture depicting the heroic but terrible defeat of Bataan, where American GIs prefer death to surrender. One of the ten best films; a tribute to American fortitude and strength with a powerful "we have lost the first battle but not the War" message. All-male cast stars handsome Robert Taylor as a rugged Army sergeant who, along with a motley team of volunteers, fights a rearguard action to delay an enemy offensive. Many virulent, anti-Japanese remarks (youthful Robert Walker, aiming his machine gun into the jungle bush: *"All I wanna do is get me a Jap! Just one Jap!"*). One of the best of any propaganda scenes: wounded pilot George Murphy crashes his crippled airplane into a bridge to prevent Nipponese forces from crossing a strategic ravine.

BEHIND THE RISING SUN. RKO; directed by Edward Dmytryk. Release: July 21, 1943. Starring multifaceted character actor J. Carrol Naish and clean-cut, all-American boy Tom Neal as two unconvincing Japanese nationals—father and son—caught up in the jingoistic war frenzy in pre-Pearl Harbor Tokyo. One of the most distorted films of the War, highlighted by a fictitious bombing attack that, according to the storyline, obliterated the Japanese capital. Most gruesome scene: Japanese soldiers tossing Chinese babies into the air, then impaling the infants with their bayonets (J. Carrol Naish, proffering some paternal advice: *" . . . torture is an old art with us, my son. We have much use for it these days."*).

A BELL FOR ADANO. Twentieth Century-Fox; directed by Henry King. Released: June 21, 1945. A noncombat, nonviolent military melodrama (based on the book by John Hersey) which stars John Hodiak as a benevolent Army field officer, with William Bendix as his sergeant. Their platoon becomes the small occupation force in a remote southern Italian town, responsible for resolving the numerous problems created by years of fascist rule. The Italian nationals—all wholesome, apolitical, religious, and pro-American—only want their fishing industry revitalized and their church bell returned. Pretty Gene Tierney spends her free time making eyes at the handsome major. After much travail, the United States Army finally restores order, dignity and democracy to a former enemy (Hodiak to townspeople: *"... but, no more fascism—we, Americans, want to bring only good to this town."*). Best scene: the villagers offer prayers of thanksgiving when their new church bell is delivered. A good propaganda film that, in its own subliminal way, sugarcoats the Italian contribution to the Axis belligerency.

BERLIN CORRESPONDENT. Twentieth Century-Fox; directed by Eugene Forde. Released: August 17, 1942. A low-key, anti-Nazi film starring Dana Andrews as a hard-hitting American news commentator, broadcasting from Berlin a few weeks before the December 7th attack on Pearl Harbor. Actually a U.S. plant who sends out coded intelligence reports, the good-looking Andrews is thrown into a Nazi prison when war breaks out. After a series of contrived adventures, he escapes back to England, aided by pretty Virginia Gilmore. Much of the propaganda value is negated by the comic antics of Nazi buffoon Sig Rumann. Worst actor and scene: Martin Kosleck, a head Gestapo officer, as a Nazi Lothario who, unsuccessfully, tries to steal Dana Andrews' girl (Kosleck to girl: *"I'm not such a bad sort as you seem to think."*).

BETRAYAL FROM THE EAST. RKO; directed by William Berke. Released: February 25, 1945. Another B-quickie hacked out to warn Americans about the omnipresent dangers of Japanese fifth columnists who are intent on wreaking havoc on the vulnerable Panama Canal. Granite-faced Lee Tracy is nondescript as an overaged Army buck private now working clandestinely for Uncle Sam's intelligence forces; shapely Nancy Kelly provides the needed romance and encouragement. Hawaiian-born Richard Loo is convincing as yet another samurai sword-waving Japanese fanatic promising harm to all blue-eyed, fair-skinned Occidentals. (Lt. Commander Loo to Yankee foil, Lee Tracy: *"The Japanese will destroy all Americans; as I will destroy you."*). Funniest scene: a large crowd of red-blooded Americans—all wearing jackets and ties—attend a professional football game and cheer vociferously for their home team.

BLACK DRAGONS. Monogram; directed by William Nigh. Released: March 12, 1942. Another 60-minute B-production that capitalizes on the ubiquitous war theme. Popular horror movie star Bela Lugosi, now a Nazi plastic surgeon hiding in the United States, changes the faces of six Japanese agents so that they look like American industrialists; they hope to wreck the defense industry. The FBI, always vigilant, breaks up this Axis plot (B-actor, Clayton Moore, offering his help to this federal agency: *". . . in the present emergency, we can't afford to lose any of the much needed business leaders."*). Of marginal propaganda value except to remind audiences that their enemies were still trying to infiltrate the Home Front.

BLONDIE FOR VICTORY. Columbia; directed by Frank R. Strayer. Released: October 9, 1942. A pleasant Fourth-of-July, V-for-Victory B-comedy featuring some of America's favorite funny paper characters: Blondie, Dagwood, Mr. Dithers, Cookie, and their canine, Daisy, who join up in the fight against the Axis menace. Penny Singleton, in another one of her Blondie movies, organizes the housewives of America into special groups to help with the war effort (Blondie to her bow-tied husband, Arthur Lake: *"Dagwood, there's no longer anything as important as victory work. Mr. Dithers isn't your boss any longer—Uncle Sam is!"*). Good propaganda value, showing the civilians back home doing their share. Best scene: the women's fashion show, where the numerous distaff uniforms are proudly displayed.

BLOOD ON THE SUN. United Artists; directed by Frank Lloyd. Released: April 26, 1945. A fast-moving adventure reaffirming that American democracy and freedom of the press go hand in glove. Rough and tumble James Cagney is perfect as a hard-hitting newspaper reporter working for a U.S.-owned, English-language daily in Tokyo during the uneasy pre-Pearl Harbor days. The redheaded legman gets wind of a journalistic scoop, but falls prey to the Japanese Secret Police. After a complex plot—involving murder, torture, and intrigue—Cagney exposes Nipponese treachery in his newspaper column and the fourth estate prevails. Good propaganda, even with Cagney's abusive remarks (Cagney to girl friend, disparaging the Japanese: *"The scenery is all right; but some of the inhabitants I object to. The higher up you go, the lower grade people you meet."*).

BOMBARDIER. RKO; directed by Richard Wallace. Released: May 13, 1943. An oversimplified salute to the men who drop the bombs on Axis targets. Pat O'Brien and Randolph Scott star as two Air Corps pilots who argue aimlessly and sometimes illogically about the skills and legerdemain required to accurately hit enemy installations. A combat assignment dissolves their disagreements and both men fly off to bomb Tokyo. Scott's heroic death, an act of instant martyrdom, reaffirms the duty-to-country motif. Best propaganda scene: the Japanese defile the U.S. Red Cross earthquake relief aid sent to them, years before Pearl Harbor. The worst line of dialogue: (girl friend to O'Brien, after hearing mobilization orders: "... *you must be the happiest man on earth, Chick. Get those Japs!"*).

THE BUGLE SOUNDS. MGM; directed by S. Sylvan Simon. Released: December 17, 1941. A half-comical, half-serious look at some of the minor problems of adjusting to military life. Perennial B-stars Wallace Beery and Marjorie Main are paired in another story where the bulbous-faced bumpkin—now a sergeant in Uncle Sam's Army—has trouble adapting to "modern times." When War comes, the call to colors is stronger than any personal feelings and soon the overweight Beery breaks up a spy ring operating right outside the post's gate. Silliest scene: the long time NCO is told to forget his cavalry training (Army colonel, Lewis Stone to nonplussed Beery: *"Sergeant, it isn't necessary to make horsemen out of these new men."*). Marginal propaganda value except to show army life in a positive manner.

CAIRO. MGM; directed by W. S. Van Dyke. Released: August 17, 1942. A half-baked B-melodrama starring shipwrecked newspaperman Robert Young, who unknowingly outwits some Nazi agents in the Middle East capital while courting opera singer Jeanette MacDonald. Some rousing patriotic songs, including the popular "We Did It Before and We Can Do It Again," plus a few old-fashioned American homilies, enhance the convoluted storyline (Ethel Waters, an American-born maid, now working in Cairo, reminiscing about happier times back in Harlem: *"I'll settle for a nice colored boy who speaks something besides French or goes around in a nightgown, in which case he turns out to be an Arab."*).

CALL OUT THE MARINES. RKO; directed by Frank Ryan and William Hamilton. Released: January 5, 1942. Another easygoing B-filler glamorizing the comical adventures of some clean-cut Marines on stateside duty in sunny California. Victor McLaglen and Edward Lowe are wonderful as two noncoms of the Sergeants Quirt-Flagg variety. Along with some PFC buddies, they frequent an expensive night club on a regular basis. Ever alert, the two jarheads discover a Nazi spy ring operating near the kitchen and, after a Mack Sennett car chase, the fifth columnists are handed over to officialdom (Sergeant McLaglen to Axis agent: *". . . you should have known you couldn't lick the Marines."*). A good, solid recruitment film that includes numerous scenes of handsome Marines dancing cheek-to-cheek with attractive girls.

CAPTAINS OF THE CLOUDS. Warner Brothers; directed by Michael Curtiz. Released: January 20, 1942. A technicolor acclamation for the men of the Canadian Air Force, combined with an appeal for more volunteers. Carrot-top, cocky James Cagney and baritone songster Dennis Morgan are paired as flying partners who allow a personal argument, centering around comely Brenda Marshall, to wreck their long-time friendship. The Battle of Britain finally unites these experienced airmen and Cagney's many double-dealing, underhanded deeds are redeemed by his heroic, martyr's death. Churchill's rousing "We Shall Never Surrender" speech strengthens the propaganda value, as does the recruiting officer's clarion call for more fighter-pilot enlistments (RCAF officer to potential aviators: *". . . modern air fighting is a young man's game."*).

CASABLANCA. Warner Brothers; directed by Michael Curtiz. Released: November 27, 1942. An outstanding Academy Award winner starring Humphrey Bogart as a tough, cynical owner of a glamorous nightclub in neutral Morocco. Not included in the ten best list because most of the propaganda value is obscured by the intricate political situation existing between Berlin and Vichy. Cast is superb and the storyline is a perennial favorite. Best quote is not about Sam, but comes from Claude Rains when he miscalculates basic geography (Rains to Bogart, discussing the location of Casablanca: *"What waters? We're in the desert."*). Best scene: Paul Henreid conducts *La Marseillaise*. Reevaluation of film, over fifty years later, suggests that Bogart relinquishes former lover Ingrid Bergman because of his latent homosexuality (Bogart to new-found friend Claude Rains, strolling away together to start a new life: *"Louis, this might be the beginning of a beautiful friendship."*).

CHARLIE CHAN IN THE SECRET SERVICE. Monogram; directed by Phil Rosen. Released: January 6, 1943. Another B-action yarn in which the master of Oriental sagacity, Charlie Chan, assigned to Washington's elite Secret Service corps, sifts through an eclectic array of suspects to locate the murderer of a prominent naval scientist. Sidney Toler portrays the Chinese detective competently, while Benson Fong, as Number One Son, offers lighthearted comic relief as the twosome discover hidden doors, a military code book, and a self-activating firearm. After some initial cat-and-mouse deductive investigating, a fifth column Nazi ring is exposed and, this time, the agents grab their woman. Of limited propaganda value except to demonstrate, once more, that enemy spies cannot confute the inscrutable Charlie Chan (Chan to Secret Service colleague, explaining why he works for this agency: *" . . . may learn something of Germans and Japanese here."*).

CHINA. Paramount; directed by John Farrow. Released: March 19, 1943. Another low-key tribute to the Chinese people, stressing that with the help of American know-how, the Oriental nation will defeat the invading Nipponese. Alan Ladd is convincing as an American oil man selling this vital fuel to the Japanese, on the Chinese mainland, a few weeks before the December attack. When war is declared, the good-looking opportunist, with the help of sweet-talking Loretta Young, is transmogrified into a flag-waving super-patriot (strong man Ladd, moments before he is shot by a Japanese general: *" . . . and in the end, it's that pattern of freedom that's going to make guys like you wish you'd never been born."*). Funniest scene: the contrived fist fight between Alan Ladd and William Bendix.

CHINA GIRL. Twentieth Century-Fox; directed by Henry Hathaway. Released: December 9, 1942. Starring song and dance man George Montgomery, who takes on a new role as an American

Flying Tiger pilot who chases after a Eurasian beauty, Gene Tierney. There is much action in the skies over the war-torn Chinese mainland as the volunteer airmen—a small tight-knit group representing the best of American ingenuity—take on the Nipponese air force. A solid propaganda film stressing the many narrow escapes for the good-looking Montgomery while emphasizing the numerous Japanese atrocities (pilot to friends: '' . . . *they kept shooting at him after he bailed out, while he was coming down in a parachute.*'').

CHINA SKY. RKO; directed by Ray Enright. Released: May 16, 1945. Another tribute to the Chinese people and their unremitting resistance against the barbaric Japanese invaders. Randolph Scott works long hours as an American doctor caring for the sick and helpless Chinese villagers, while Anthony Quinn—the guerrilla chieftain—leads successful forays against the enemy. Many Japanese atrocities, including the bombing of hospitals, enhance the propaganda value, but oblique-eyed Anthony Quinn labors as an Oriental. Frequent praise for the Chinese contribution to the Allied war effort (Quinn, adjuring his townspeople for more victories: *"China is trading space for time. But the guerrillas do not retreat! We shall hold the pass!"*).

THE CLOCK. MGM; directed by Vincente Minnelli. Released: March 22, 1945. An over-puffed, gee-whiz fairy tale/love story that in its own innocent way portrays the American GI as weak, ineffectual, and insecure. Robert Walker is vapid as an Army corporal with a forty-eight-hour pass; his timidity and indecisiveness prevent him from leaving New York's elaborate railroad center, Pennsylvania Station. Totally frightened, the young hayseed takes refuge on a public stairway, until Judy Garland comes to his aid. Soon the twosome, now head over heels in love, run through a bureaucratic obstacle course that enables them to marry without the standard waiting period. Character actor James Gleason is excellent as the friendly milkman offering wholesome homilies to the lovers. Propaganda value is nil because the portrayal of an inept Army corporal could only diminish the prowess of the American fighting man. Typical Pollyanna scene: (Robert Walker, making plans for civilian life: *"I got it all figured out; after the War, I'm going to be a builder, a carpenter."*).

COMMANDOES STRIKE AT DAWN. Columbia; directed by John Farrow. Released: December 18, 1942. A solid tribute to the Norwegian people's unremitting fight against the Nazi invaders and the quislings in their small coastal towns and villages. Paul Muni is superb as a humble fisherman who stoically endures the Germans' draconian policies of plunder, brutality, and executions. He organizes a small group of men who escape to England, and then, alongside a contingency of British commandos, return to their homeland in a daring raid that destroys a strategic German air base while rescuing most of the townspeople. Muni's heroic death during this lightning attack reaffirms the dignity, intransigence, and strength of the Scandinavian people and their ongoing resistance to the Third Reich. Best propaganda scene: Major Robert Coote explains his military strategy (Coote to Muni: " . . . *these commando raids are tough and quick. Every man is trained to move like clockwork."*).

THE CONSPIRATORS. Warner Brothers; directed by Jean Negulesco. Released: October 17, 1944. Another spy-versus-spy tale. Hedy Lamarr teams up with sophisticated Paul Henreid and the twosome keep one step ahead of some nasty fifth columnists in neutral Portugal. As a freedom fighter, fleeing from the Nazi atrocities in his Dutch homeland, Henreid seeks vengeance on the aggressors (former schoolteacher Henreid, describing the brutal takeover of his Dutch town: " . . . *one of my pupils, a fourteen-year-old boy, jumped to the blackboard and wrote three words on it—long live liberty. A German officer shot that boy!"*). Good solid cinematic propaganda.

CORREGIDOR. PRC; directed by William Nigh. Released: March 25, 1943. A drowsy B-melodrama using the fall of Corregidor as the backdrop for a routine love triangle involving three Americans stationed in the Philippines at the onset of the War. Otto Kruger is convincing as an M.D. who hopes to win the heart of colleague Elissa Landi, who is more interested in mustachioed Donald Woods. Of limited interest, it lacks any propaganda value because the real horror of the defeat is oversimplified and the plot is enmeshed in one cliché after another (Elissa Landi's prophecy: " . . . *we'll come back, we'll build up everything that has been destroyed."*). Only salvaging merit: the distinguished poet Alfred Noyes reads a testimony to the American spirit.

CORVETTE K-225. Universal; directed by Richard Rosson. Released: September 27, 1943. A big salute to the men of the Canadian Navy who sail the corvettes into the danger-laden waters of the North Atlantic. Randolph Scott is well cast as the commander of K-225, while Barry Fitzgerald and Andy Devine, as experienced crew members, reaffirm the dogma that Hitlerism must be eradicated. After many harrowing adventures, Scott guides his crippled ship into the safe harbors of Ireland. Many anti-Nazi remarks (Scott, describing German atrocities to his superior: *" . . . that U-boat machine-gunned every one of those men to death and we had to sit there and take it."*). Best scene: the Corvette K-225 is honored for its heroism as it returns to port.

COUNTER-ATTACK. Columbia; directed by Zoltan Korda. Released April 3, 1945. A strong, pro-Slavic film glorifying the hard-fought Soviet victories on the eastern front. Paul Muni is convincing as a Red Army commando and part-time lexicographer who captures high-ranking Nazi officers during a Russian military offensive. Many tributes and accolades are heaped upon Soviet leadership and daring (Russian general to staff, ordering the counterattack: *" . . . in five nights, our tanks will move across the surface of the water like crossing a parade ground."*). Important propaganda film necessary as a tangible reminder, to American audiences, that the USSR, a former adversary, is an integral part of the Allied forces.

COWBOY COMMANDOES. Monogram; directed by S. Rob Luby. Released: July 12, 1943. An entertaining B-Western where the good guys wear white, carry sixshooters and ride horses into the sunset, while the bad guys dress in black, display swastikas, and travel in dilapidated pickup trucks. Crash Corrigan and his sidekick Alibi Terhune are rough-and-tough cowboy commandoes who smash a surreptitious Axis ring working right on their homestead. Harmless fun reiterating that Nazis can be anywhere (B-actor Steve Clark to cowpokes: *" . . . hard fighting and fast shooting against a low-down bunch of saboteurs."*). Best scene:

Johnny Bond sings the popular Western song, "I'm Going to Get der Fuehrer Sure as Shooting."

CRASH DIVE. Twentieth Century-Fox; directed by Archie Mayo. Released April 22, 1943. A rip-roaring salute to the sailors who man the Navy PT boats, and to their brothers-in-arms, the submarine crews. Tyrone Power is perfect as an officer/gentleman whose charm and skill make him the ideal leader of a PT command. When transferred to a submarine assignment, headed by Dana Andrews, he easily adapts to underwater life and, subsequently, admits that all ships are important (Power to admiral: *"It isn't one branch of the service, it's all branches. It isn't all ships, it's men."*). Superb use of martial music complements this exciting film. Best scene: Tyrone Power and his attack team blow up the Nazi oil tanks.

THE CROSS OF LORRAINE. MGM; directed by Tay Garnett. Released: November 12, 1943. A solid melodrama starring Jean-Pierre Aumont and Gene Kelly as two Frenchmen who escape from a German POW camp. After many close calls, they return to their home village where they organize a massive uprising against the Nazi captors. An inflated tribute to Gallic intransigence and perseverance, with constant praise for the national leaders (Aumont to Kelly: *"There are thousands of fighting Frenchmen working with General de Gaulle."*). Best scene: battalion priest Sir Cedric Hardwicke's small prayer of thanksgiving for the meager bread rations the Germans dole out to the hungry prisoners.

CRY HAVOC. MGM; directed by Richard Thorpe. Released: November 9, 1943. A puffed-up melodrama in which an all-female cast, starring Margaret Sullavan as a senior American nurse, is trapped on the Bataan peninsula as Japanese offensive forces creep closer and closer. Working around the clock to provide medical care to wounded GIs, the nurses—a cross-section of distaff American life—are heroic and dedicated. Their eventual capture—and impending violation—by the sadistic Japanese soldiers was designed to arouse stateside audiences to greater hatred towards their Oriental enemy. As propaganda, the denouement is riveting, but some of the scenes are 1940-type soap opera dilemmas (nurse Ann Sothern, justifying her flirtation with a married man: *" . . . so what! We're all free, White, and twenty-one!"*).

DANGEROUSLY THEY LIVE. Warner Brothers; directed by Robert Florey. Released: December 24, 1941. A lackluster warning about the dangers of fifth columnists hiding out in upper-middle-class America. Bad-mouth John Garfield stars as a young M.D. whose amnesia patient, sweet-looking Nancy Coleman, ropes him into becoming an eyewitness to the dirty dealings of a Nazi spy ring headed by Raymond Massey. At the end of an elaborate and sometimes disjointed plot, the couple are united and the FBI places the culprits in irons. Limited propaganda value since the spies are more like American gangsters than Axis agents. Worst scene: Nancy Coleman berates her man-in-white for not believing her contradictory tale of kidnapping (Coleman to Garfield: *" . . . even a doctor has no right to be so stupid!"*).

DAYS OF GLORY. RKO; directed by Jacques Tourneur. Released: April 27, 1944. Another important pro-USSR film. Gregory Peck— in his screen debut—portrays a Russian partisan whose hit-and-miss sorties slowly grind the Nazi war machine to a halt. Hiding in their forest lair, the Slavs are courageous, patriotic, and pro-American. Many Nazi brutalities, including the savage hanging of an innocent sixteen-year-old boy, illustrate the nightmare of Operation Barbarossa. Ballerina Tamara Toumanova, while unconvincing as a night raider, supplies the romance for the handsome Gregory Peck. A solid propaganda tract which, in its own way, helped to solidify the Uncle Sam/Uncle Joe pact. Most ambiguous scene: Gregory Peck's sadistic pleasure in watching a Nazi parachutist, falling slowly to the ground, blasted by an ack-ack shell (girl friend to Peck, confused by his apparent glee: *" . . . as if to kill something gave you—forgive me—gave you happiness."*).

DESPERATE JOURNEY. Warner Brothers; directed by Raoul Walsh. Released August 18, 1942. Starring Errol Flynn and an all-male cast as a British aircrew who bomb a German installation deep within the Fatherland, are shot down and begin a long, desperate journey back to their own lines. They are chased by nefarious Gestapo officer Raymond Massey. Patterned after the typical Western film—including such stock shots as the chase, the capture, the escape, and the recapture/re-escape—the film is laden with one implausible situation after another. Propaganda value is limited because of the numerous comical overtones and antics (captured airman Ronald Reagan, when questioned about his nationality: *"I'm one-half American, one-half Jersey City."*).

DESTINATION TOKYO. Warner Brothers; directed by Jerry Wald. Released: December 21, 1943. A superb adventure film glorifying the quiet heroism of the men who work beneath the waves in the Silent Service. Cary Grant is the ideal father/commander who steers his submarine, the *Copperfin*, into the heavily mined waters of Tokyo bay to pave the way for the Doolittle bombing raid. An all-male cast represents every cross-section of American life (except Blacks), and the what-we-are-fighting-for motif is beautifully juxtaposed. Many anti-Japanese remarks (Grant to crew: *"The Japs don't understand the love we have for our women; they don't even have a word for it in their language."*). Best scene: the makeshift operation in which Navy corpsman William Prince removes the appendix from one of his buddies, using only a first aid manual and a few rudimentary instruments.

THE DOUGHGIRLS. Warner Brothers; directed by James V. Kern. Released: August 30, 1944. A just-for-laughs farce that caricatures the more serious problem of the crowded housing conditions in wartime Washington, D.C., when important dollar-a-year executives arrive to do their part for victory. The three doughgirls—Ann Sheridan, Alexis Smith, and Jane Wyman—resolve many social quandaries including the you're-not-legally-married dilemma, while subliminally stressing the importance of cooperation to achieve harmony on every issue. Eve Arden's portrayal of a Russian hero sergeant on tour in the United States enhances the propaganda value by heaping praise on Soviet military achievements. Best scene: the head of War Wives Relief Corps hits the nail on the head with her succinct explanation of one small, but vital job (Irene Manning to the group: *" . . . it's babies, day nurseries for war workers. Every baby we take care of releases a woman for war work; and every woman releases a man."*).

DRAGON SEED. MGM; directed by Jack Conway. Released: July 18, 1944. A long, drawn-out testimony to the Chinese people, their sufferings and travail under the Greater East Asia Co-Prosperity Sphere. Katharine Hepburn and Walter Huston seem awkward portraying Chinese peasants whose simple life style is deracinated by the enemy invasion. A complex plot—involving torture, abuse, traitors-in-the-midst, and national honor—produces a vacillating storyline. The Japanese, stereotyped as ruthless and barbaric, are no match for the descendants of Confucius (rebel leader Turhan Bey to his followers: *" . . : we must work together as the fingers on one hand. We must strike down this enemy and kill him."*). Most effective propaganda scene: the Chinese burn their fields rather than let the Japanese harvest the crop.

EDGE OF DARKNESS. Warner Brothers; directed by Lewis Milestone. Released: March 23, 1943. An elaborate tribute to the fighting spirit of the Scandinavians and their strong ties with American democracy. Errol Flynn and Ann Sheridan star as Norwegian patriots resisting the brutal Nazi occupation of their small fishing village. A diversified plot warns of the ever-present dangers of the quislings and their Axis superiors. The propaganda value is enhanced by the voices of Churchill and Roosevelt (his stirring "Look-to-Norway" speech), coupled with the powerful strains of the Lutheran hymn, "A Mighty Fortress Is Our God." Errol Flynn is convincing as an undaunted underground leader (Flynn to cohorts, denouncing mob rule: *" . . . no, this is not the way! Every man must speak his mind."*). Best scene: the transformation of the pacifist minister into a fighting soldier.

ENEMY AGENTS MEET ELLERY QUEEN. Columbia; directed by James Hogan. Released August 26, 1942. A low-grade B-thriller in which a bunch of insidious-looking Nazi agents—attempting to heist some valuable Dutch diamonds—is thwarted by the famous American detective, aided by some passing U.S. Marines. William Gargan is convincing as the punctilious gumshoe, while Nikki Porter supplies female support. Solid propaganda, especially when glamorizing the fisticuffs of the hard-fighting gyrenes (Detective Gargan, praising Marine sergeant

James Burke: *" . . . with the aid of the Marines and the Navy, you've just captured a Nazi spy ring."*).

ESCAPE IN THE DESERT. Warner Brothers; directed by Edward A. Blatt. Released May 1, 1945. An updated version of the classic B-Western. Nazi prisoners of war flee into the barren Arizona desert, terrorize a wholesome family, and are finally routed when a modern-day posse captures them in a classic end-of-the-film shoot-out. Philip Dorn, as a Dutch freedom-fighter on a sightseeing trip in the old southwest, wearing a suit and tie, stretches the limits of plausibility as the traditional Western hero, but Nazi leader Helmut Dantine performs contemptuously as the Axis scourge willing to kill innocent civilians blocking his bid for freedom. Pretty Jean Sullivan, as the Dutchman's new girl friend, provides the romance in the soft moonlight. A good propaganda film, in its own right, emphasizing that German POW's are still a menace to the American way of life. Best scene: Philip Dorn extemporizing on Nazi justice (Dorn to Axis fugitives: *" . . . when the Germans begin to talk of justice, they must realize they have lost the war."*).

THE FALLEN SPARROW. RKO; directed by Richard Wallace. Released: August 17, 1943. A slow-moving melodrama starring perennial bad boy John Garfield as an American idealist who fought the Axis in Spain as a member of the Abraham Lincoln Brigade. He is captured, tortured, and allowed to escape back to New York where he soon becomes enmeshed in murder, intrigue, and espionage. An involved plot structure sustains interest and suspense in this thriller, but much of the propaganda value is lost because the complexities of political life in Spain are not well defined. Romance is provided by redhead Maureen O'Hara, whose personal life is controlled by Nazi agents (heartbroken Maureen O'Hara, rejecting Garfield's marriage proposal: *"I have a daughter, three years old. She's in Germany as a hostage."*).

THE FIGHTING SEABEES. Republic; directed by Edward Ludwig. Released: January 19, 1944. A strong we're-all-in-this-together statement that glorifies the essential, but sometimes unglamorous adventures of the Navy's Construction Battalion—the Seabees—whose members are responsible for installing the many support systems necessary for victory. John Wayne is outstanding as a construction boss turned fighting man who builds airfields on Japanese-held islands under dangerous conditions. Dennis O'Keefe is convincing as the traditional Navy officer coordinating military matters (O'Keefe to off-again, on-again friend John Wayne: *" . . . you're not here to fight Japs; you're here to fight time."*). Good, solid propaganda reaffirming that every man's job is a vital link in the victory chain.

THE FIGHTING SULLIVANS. Twentieth Century-Fox; directed by Lloyd Bacon. Released: February 3, 1944. A beautiful, overwhelming, poignant, sensitive, heart-touching, wonderful motion picture, based on a heroic but tragic event that stunned Americans. An encomium to the strength, dignity, and righteousness of American youth, it is heavy with corn, using every Pollyanna device known, superb in every detail, the greatest tearjerker of the War. Thomas Mitchell is magnificent as the hard-working, God-fearing, sod-busting, pure American father of the five Sullivan brothers, who are born and bred in the Norman Rockwell world of Waterloo, Iowa. After Pearl Harbor, the five sons join the Navy and, after a misguided directive, are permitted to serve on the same combat ship, the *Juneau.* During a Japanese attack, off Guadalcanal, the vessel is destroyed and all five sons die. One of the greatest propaganda scenes in motion picture history: Ward Bond, a Navy officer, must inform the parents (Bond to confused parents, Thomas Mitchell and Selena Royale: *" . . . all five. The Navy Department deeply regrets to inform you that your sons Albert, Francis, George, Joseph, and Madison Sullivan were killed in action in the South Pacific."*). One of the ten best films of the War.

FIVE GRAVES TO CAIRO. Paramount; directed by Billy Wilder. Released: May 4, 1943. A distorted account of the volatile Egyptian campaign, it includes a secret Nazi oil cache buried deep in the desert and a German officer's abortive search for this important fuel. Erich von Stroheim—complete with monocle and suede gloves—is excellent as the draconian Field Marshal Erwin Rommel while Franchot Tone, a British tommy working as a spy, spends most of his time courting a pretty French maid. An Italian officer is more interested in singing famous arias, but most of the

Nazis are bestial and their blatant killing of an innocent woman depicts their wantonness (Corporal Tone, standing at sweetheart's gravesite: " . . . *we're after them now, coming from all sides. We're going to blast them.* ").

THE FLEET'S IN. Paramount Pictures; directed by Victor Schertzinger. Released: January 19, 1942. A lighthearted B-musical, this recruitment film features the whimsical antics of a group of happy-go-lucky sailors on a four-day pass in San Francisco. Petty Officer William Holden spends most of his time in an elaborate gambling ploy that stipulates he must kiss pretty Dorothy Lamour or his shipmates will lose money, jewelry, and prestige. After a series of convoluted stop-and-go mishaps, arranged by his pal, Eddie Bracken, the bluejacket attains the prized osculation, winning both the girl and the bet. Of limited propaganda value except to show that once again the Navy comes through. Best song: Betty Jane Rhodes' version of "The Fleet's In" (Miss Rhodes to audience: *"Hey there, Mister, you better hide your sister, 'cause the fleet's in."*).

FLIGHT FOR FREEDOM. RKO; directed by Lothar Mendes. Released: February 4, 1943. A far-fetched roman à clef purporting that famous aviatrix Amelia Earhart died while on a top-secret mission, for Army Intelligence, over a Japanese-controlled Pacific island, circa 1937. Rosalind Russell (called Tonie Carter) is less than convincing as an experienced flyer, while her boy friend, Fred MacMurray, tries to bill and coo her at every available moment. Presence of military officers adds a soupçon of propaganda value (admiral to Rosalind Russell: *" . . . when war comes, we'll be able to defend ourselves against attack and strike back at the nerve center of their empire."*). Best scene: sinister-looking Richard Loo, a Japanese agent planted as a hotel clerk, discovers her plot.

FLIGHT LIEUTENANT. Columbia; directed by Sidney Salkow. Released: June 29, 1942. An off-course, mushy flying potboiler that lacks the momentum to get off the ground. Pat O'Brien is unconvincing as a onetime aviation whiz who is grounded while his son, Glenn Ford—personifying the best of American youth— earns his wings as any Army flight lieutenant and is assigned to

test experimental aircraft. When a new model seems too dangerous to fly, the worried father, disregarding military regulations,
goes airborne to reveal the structural flaws; his death reaffirms
duty to country. Little propaganda value except to show the
clean-cut American nature of cadet training. Funniest line: (ten-
year-old son to his father, Pat O'Brien: *". . . anything you do is
jake with me."*).

FLYING FORTRESS. Warner Brothers; directed by Walter
Forde. Released: July 13, 1942. A jejune B-melodrama depicting
the not-so-glamorous adventures of two American flyers—
Richard Greene and Donald Stewart—who join the RAF during
the dangerous Battle of Britain days. Arriving in London, they set
out to seduce English girls and bomb German cities (Greene to
girl: *". . . well, here I go to bomb Berlin at last; boy, am I
happy!"*). Silliest scene: co-pilot Greene, crawling on the wing of
his damaged B-17, a Flying Fortress, while the aircraft bounces up
and down, high in the sky. Pure hokum.

FLYING TIGERS. Republic; directed by David Miller. Released:
September 23, 1942. A loud, blast-them-from-the-skies formula
film deifying the heroic exploits of an American volunteer
group—the Flying Tigers—who openly fought the Japanese long
before war was declared. Tough, laconic John Wayne is perfect as
the squadron commander, the legendary Pappy Boyington, whose
oddball group of unorthodox fliers wreck the Japanese at every
turn. Good-looking, velvet-tongued John Carroll is outstanding as
a recusant-turned-believer, who must learn the hard way that it
takes a team effort to win the War. Much praise for Chinese
leaders makes this an ideal propaganda film. Typical scene: a
Flying Tigers pilot explains his reason for fighting the Japanese
(volunteer to buddies: *". . . . back home, most of us will kill
rattlesnakes whether there's a bounty on them or not."*).

FOLLOW THE BOYS. Universal; directed by Eddie Sutherland.
Released: March 27, 1944. A solid musical tribute to the USO
entertainers who freely and generously provide mirth to the troops
all over the world. George Raft, himself an accomplished dancer,
stars as a 4-F impresario who organizes a spectacular show for the
GIs (narrator to audience: *". . . I am a solider-in-greasepaint*

serving a free country and freedom-loving men.''). Torpedoed by the Japanese in the South Pacific, George Raft's sudden death is a sad reminder of other Hollywood celebrities who became casualties of the War. Numerous personalities, great songs, and superb merriment combine to create maximum propaganda. Most embarrassing scene: Louis Jordan, singing his famous "Is You Is Or Is You Ain't My Baby?" to a segregated, all-Black squad.

FOR WHOM THE BELL TOLLS. Paramount; directed by Sam Wood. Released: July 15, 1943. An elaborate, technicolor hagiography of the famous Ernest Hemingway antifascist novel depicting the adventures of an Abraham Lincoln Brigade member who comes to Spain to fight against Franco's Axis-supported forces during the turbulent, politically sensitive Spanish Civil War. Gary Cooper is excellent as the American idealist assigned to blow up a bridge to expedite a Loyalist offensive. Ingrid Bergman, cast as a Spanish waif, shares her sleeping bag with the handsome stranger. After a series of suspenseful adventures, the guerrillas reach their target and destroy their objective, but Gary Cooper, wounded during the hasty retreat, sacrifices himself to save his new friends. An excellent propaganda film with numerous religious, symbolic, expiable, and allegorical overtones. Best scene: the saboteur explains his leftist philosophy (Cooper to Loyalist: *"I'm here for the Republic!"*).

FOUR JILLS IN A JEEP. Twentieth Century-Fox; directed by William A. Seiter. Released: March 17, 1944. A dreary and occasionally patronizing attempt to glorify the "suffering" of a group of American entertainers on a USO overseas tour. Four Hollywood stars—Kay Francis, Carole Landis, Martha Raye, and Mitzi Mayfair—sing lackluster songs and babble jejune dialogue, and the entire storyline collapses under its cloying pretentiousness. One segment—depicting an Army general, Paul Harvey, pulling rank on a subordinate to take a girl home—labels the commander a fascist. Worst scene: Martha Raye's pathetic attempt at humor (Raye, to anyone who will listen: *" . . . we're rugged women, we want to be right at the front with our men.''*). A hopeless, contrived production; one of the worst films of the War.

GOD IS MY CO-PILOT. Warner Brothers; directed by Robert Florey. Released February 21, 1945. Another paean to the Flying

Tigers, starring light-opera singer Dennis Morgan and Abraham
Lincoln look-alike, Raymond Massey, as volunteer pilots battling
the Japanese in the wide-open China skies. Replete with homilies,
reeking with pious sentimentalities, and laden with historical
inaccuracies, the film is saturated with anti-Japanese remarks
(wingman Dane Clark, singing an out-of-tune limerick: *"... your
mother was a turtle, your father was a snake, and you're a good
Jap."*). The worst performance: Alan Hale as an Air Corps
chaplain.

THE GORILLA MAN. Warner Brothers; directed by D. Ross
Lederman. Released: December 11, 1942. A harmless, inconsequential B-quickie, so replete with one cliffhanger after another
that the storyline resembles pieces of the typical Saturday matinee
serial. B-actor John Loder portrays a British commando whose
skills at climbing walls have earned him the sobriquet, "The
Gorilla Man." When the good-looking officer is framed for
murder—by two Nazi mad scientists posing as medical doctors—
he must move fast to prove his innocence, thwart an impending
espionage plot, catch a German psychopathic killer, and win the
heart of pretty Marian Hall. Of minimal propaganda value except
to depict Nazi agents as unsavory elements operating as fifth
columnists (Captain Loder to girl friend: *"... this whole thing's
a plot; the work of enemy agents trying to discredit me."*).

GUADALCANAL DIARY. Twentieth Century-Fox; directed by
Louis Seller. Released: October 27, 1943. A quiet tribute to the
heroism, sacrifice, and dignity of American determination to pave
the way to Tokyo. Preston Foster, William Bendix, and Lloyd
Nolan star as members of the Marine assault force that captured
the first island in the Solomons against a cruel, crazed enemy.
Complete with numerous stock characters—including the underage recruit, the taxi driver from Flatbush, and the indomitable
father figure—the film reaffirms that American democracy will
prevail. Semidocumentary flair adds realism and enhances the
propaganda value (narrator to audience: *"... the Japanese behind
those weapons are fanatics; chained to their weapons, they'd
rather die at their post than surrender."*). Best scene: the Marines
blast out their adversaries, hiding in some deep mountainous
caves. Another title in the ten-best series.

GUNG HO. Universal; directed by Ray Enright. Released: December 20, 1943. One of the ten best titles of the War. Starring Randolph Scott and J. Carrol Naish as father-figure Marine Corps officers who take a group of raw recruits, hone them razor-sharp, and lead them to victory in the famous raid on Makin Island. Numerous subplots, depicting the occasional levity of drill camp life, show the American fighting man as wholesome and pure. Scott is superb as the tough commander and spiritual comforter (Scott to men, after, winning the battle: *"Raiders, you have shown the way. Our course is clear; it is for us at this moment—with the memory of the sacrifice of our brothers still fresh—to dedicate our hearts, our minds, and our bodies to the great task that is still ahead."*). Best propaganda scene: B-actor Private Harold Landon racing through the jungle, dodging hundreds of bullets, to throw two hand grenades into a Japanese pillbox.

A GUY NAMED JOE. MGM; directed by Victor Fleming. Released: December 24, 1943. A poorly conceived and badly executed film idea. Spencer Tracy stars as a dead bomber pilot whose know-it-all spirit roams around a South Pacific military base giving advice to Van Johnson, a younger, less experienced flyer. Johnson, however, cannot see or hear his sage, but he does manage to walk away with the dead man's former girlfriend, Irene Dunne. As the Supreme Being, dispensing earthly instructions, Lionel Barrymore is perfectly cast, while character actor James Gleason shines as the wing commander. Some interesting flying scenes with the usual anti-Japanese dialogue (pilot to buddies: *". . . get those meatballs, boil them in oil."*). Most unlikely scene: Irene Dunne, a civilian pilot, jumps into an unguarded pursuit plane, flies off to a Japanese military depot, and destroys this important target, without any maps or preflight instruction.

HAIL THE CONQUERING HERO. Paramount; directed by Preston Sturges. Released: June 7, 1944. Another slapstick comedy by the master director that in a offbeat way pays homage to the soft-spoken values of the Marine Corps and their indomitable motto, *semper fidelis*. Eddie Bracken is perfectly cast as a meek recruit who is medically discharged after one month of service, but is too embarrassed to return to his family and friends. After meeting combat-veteran, top sergeant William Demarest, the allergy-prone civilian is hoodwinked into a series of farcical events that culminate in an elaborate welcome home ceremony for the small town's conquering hero. It includes the key to the city, the return of his ex-girl friend, and a shoo-in job as the next mayor. Unable to keep the charade going, the guileless Bracken confesses everything, and to his astonishment, he is quickly vindicated. A good propaganda film that basically reaffirms middle America as a nation of loyal, patriotic, church-going individuals. Most wholesome scene: Eddie Bracken recites a long litany of Marine Corps sacrifices (Bracken to buddies: "... *Wake Island, Guam, Bataan, Corregidor, Guadalcanal. They bled and died.*").

HANGMEN ALSO DIE. United Artists; directed by Fritz Lang. Released: March 23, 1943. A fictitious account of the assassination of the Nazi "protector" of Czechoslovakia, Reinhard Heydrich, by an ardent national and the vile reign of terror that followed. Brian Donlevy is convincing as the patriot/killer, who is aided by his countrymen to escape the Axis brutality, while Anna Lee supplies warmth and comfort. Of strong propaganda value since it depicts the horror of life under German occupation and reaffirms the need for strength until final victory arrives (B-actor Byron Foulger, calling for greater sacrifices by the Czech underground: "... *we must answer terror with terror; theirs is the murder of hostages, ours is the slowing down of the German war machine.*").

HERE COME THE WAVES. Paramount; directed by Mark Sandrich. Released: December 18, 1944. A morale-building musical spotlighting the legendary Bing Crosby as a popular but overage vocalist who—after some slick wheeling and dealing—is permitted to join the Navy as an ordinary seaman. The crooner falls for pretty Betty Hutton, while his bunkmate, curly-locks Sonny Tufts, chases her twin sister (also Betty Hutton) and the foursome sing many songs together. Good propaganda value since it shows that the tars of the Navy, while carefree and happy in their spare time, are ready for the business of war (Sonny Tufts, after being assigned as a dance teacher for the upcoming USO show: "... *what? Drilling a lot of dames, when I could be drilling Japs?*"). Best song: the popular recruitment plea, "Join the Navy."

HITLER'S CHILDREN. RKO: directed by Edward Dmytryk. Released: January 6, 1943. Starring cowboy hero Tim Holt as a crew-cut German adolescent who embraces Hitlerism while in school, and soon after graduation becomes a military officer responsible for perpetuating the New Order in his Bavarian hometown. When his high school girlfriend, sweet-looking Bonita Granville, is whisked away to a medical center—to produce a pure Aryan offspring—the handsome Holt, realizing the errors of his ways, plans an elaborate escape for both of them. The scheme is thwarted and they both suffer martyrs' deaths (Holt to crowd, after being gunned down "*. . . long live the enemies of Nazi Germany!*"). Most vivid propaganda scene: the flogging, by a Nazi troglodyte, of the fair-skinned Bonita Granville.

HITLER'S MADMAN. MGM; directed by Douglas Sirk. Released: June 10, 1943. Another emotional and poignant account of the brutal destruction of the Czech village of Lidice on June 10, 1942, when every male over the age of sixteen was shot as a reprisal for the assassination of the German protector, Reinhard Heydrich. John Carradine's portrayal of the sadistic, inhuman, draconian Nazi leader is outstanding, while Alan Curtis and Patricia Morison, as two partisans, supply the needed patriotic fervor to encourage their villagers to acts of sabotage against the German occupation force. A solid propaganda film, replete with strong religious overtones, prayers, and hymnals, and further enhanced by the dramatic reading of Edna St. Vincent Millay's testimonial poem, "The Murder of Lidice." Best scene: a Czech quisling explains why America cannot win the War (official to subordinate: *Americans, they are soft, spoiled by democracy. We'll mop them up like that. Read Mein Kampf. One day Hitler will take over America and put it in order.*").

HOTEL BERLIN. Warner Brothers; directed by Peter Godfrey. Released: March 2, 1945. An updated version of the 1932 classic, *Grand Hotel*, with a large celebrity cast clustered in an elegant hotel in the German capital as Allied bombs explode nearby during the closing days of the War. Excellent propaganda as the film reiterates America's promise to treat the German people with dignity and compassion. Raymond Massey is solid as a Nazi officer who commits suicide to save himself from the Gestapo.

Peter Lorre, as a former professor and anti-Nazi, justifies the Allied attacks (Lorre to colleagues: *" . . . we are getting no more than we deserve."*). Best warning scene: high-ranking Nazis escape to America to continue an underground fight against the Allies.

ICELAND. Twentieth Century-Fox; directed by Bruce Humberstone. Released: August 12, 1942. A harmless, topsy-turvy winter yarn employing a simplistic storyline. The U.S. Marines arrive in Iceland for combat training, but one corporal, John Payne (accompanied by crony Jack Oakie), is excused from duty and is able to ride around in a private jeep and flirt with girls. In a matter of days he wins the heart of Olympic medalist Sonja Henie and the two of them skate happily ever after. Some good patriotic songs— including the risqué "You Can't Say No to a Soldier"—coat the film with a veneer of tolerance. Corniest scene: Corporal Payne, waving the Red, White, and Blue, initially tries to brush off the amorous advances of the pretty skater (Payne to Sonja Henie: *" . . . well, you know how it is when Uncle Sam calls—duty first!"*).

I'LL BE SEEING YOU. United Artist; directed by William Dieterle. Released: December 20, 1944. A hard look at the adjustments a returning shell-shocked GI must face when he confronts his family, friends, and new social circumstances. Joseph Cotten is outstanding as a battle-decorated casualty, trying to forget the months he spent stateside in a mental ward. Ginger Rogers, plagued with many problems, provides the romance. Propaganda value reaffirms that the price of liberty is not cheap in terms of personal suffering and hardship. Most wholesome scene: the holiday meal blessing (character actor Tom Tully, reciting the benediction: *" . . . please look after all our dear ones and all the boys who are fighting for our country. Amen."*).

IN THE MEANTIME, DARLING. Twentieth Century-Fox; directed by Otto Preminger. Released: September 22, 1944. A lighthearted B-comedy depicting the daily activities of a group of Army officers and their wives billeted in a boarding hotel near their military base. Jeanne Crain is wholesome as a newlywed who must learn the hard way the importance of cooperation in communal living; her husband, Lieutenant Frank Latimore, smiles approvingly. Of limited propaganda value except to show the Norman Rockwell world of clean-cut officers and their wide-eyed brides tilling in their victory gardens, wearing high heel shoes. One small scene, however, showing the married couple cuddled up in their double bed, probably slipped past the Hollywood censors. Most wholesome scene: B-actress Gale Robbins explains why the women have joined their husbands in such incommodious quarters (Miss Robbins to friend: "... *we love our men and we want to be near them.*").

INVISIBLE AGENT. Universal; directed by Edwin L. Martin. Released: August 7, 1942. An enjoyable B-melodrama starring handsome Jon Hall as the grandson of the famous Invisible Man. Using the secret formula his grandfather perfected, he becomes the Invisible Agent, working for U.S. forces. Dispatched into Germany, the unseen spy rescues pretty Ilona Massey while retrieving an important code book and disrupting enemy military operations (voice of Invisible Agent to frightened Nazi:" ... *you're drowning in the ocean of blood around this barren little island you call the New Order.*"). Good propaganda value, depicting the mutual mistrust between Japanese and German agents. Best scene: the Invisible Agent parachutes into the Fatherland but only the empty harness is seen by the confused Nazi sentries staring at the sky.

JACK LONDON. United Artists; directed by Alfred Santell. Released: November 22, 1943. A typical Hollywood biography formula film that traces the career of the popular American writer, Jack London, from oyster boat pilot to acclaimed war correspondent who exposes the atrocities committed by the Japanese in their 1905 attack against Russia. Michael O'Shea depicts the iconoclastic socialist writer as demure, pleasant, and soft-spoken. Redhead Susan Hayward provides romance and literary inspiration. As an added bonus, President Teddy Roosevelt waves the flag with his tough talk against Japanese imperialism. Best scene: author Michael O'Shea explains the territorial ambitions of the Yamato government (O'Shea to U.S. official: "*I saw it with my own eyes, Japanese treachery, Japanese barbarism.*") Solid propaganda film with much praise for the Russian people.

JOAN OF OZARK. Republic; directed by Joseph Santley. Released: July 15, 1942. Another 80-minute B-romp highlighting the comical misadventures of an Ozark hillbilly, Judy Canova, who inadvertently kills a Nazi carrier pigeon carrying a coded message. Soon a fifth column agent chases her through the Missouri backwoods but the fast-footed Miss Canova, after teaming up with smooth-talking Joe E. Brown, leads the Nazi into the waiting arms of the FBI. Of minimal propaganda value except to remind audiences that vigilance is the best defense against the Axis forces hiding in America. Best scene: Joe E. Brown lampoons the Fuehrer (Brown to officials: *"I am going to have peace! A piece of Poland, a piece of Norway, and a piece of Czechoslovakia."*).

JOAN OF PARIS. RKO; directed by Robert Stevenson. Released: January 9, 1942. A B-melodrama starring comely Michelle Morgan as a young French girl who, along with her parish priest, Thomas Mitchell, helps a group of downed British airmen hide from the Gestapo. After a long cat-and-mouse game with Nazi intelligence agents, the Allied flyers leave for England but Michelle Morgan, unable to escape, dies at the hands of her captors. Her martyrdom, coupled with the many religious sermons, strengthens the propaganda value (Michelle Morgan to the Germans, moments before her death: *". . . you can't stop them, nothing can stop them. They've beaten you."*).

JOE SMITH, AMERICAN. MGM; directed by Richard Thorpe. Released: January 7, 1942. A gee-whiz, no-kidding testimony to the average guy, the Joe Smiths of America, who work in the defense plants, manufacturing the materiel necessary for victory, and exercise frugality to pay their $28.83 monthly FHA mortgage. Robert Young is two-dimensional as a $1.00 an hour factory technician assigned to assemble a top-secret bombing device. His wife, toothsome Marsha Hunt, safely guards her prized dining room table from excessive wear. When kidnapped by Nazi agents, the good-looking Young endures torture rather than reveal classified information. Eventually, he escapes and with local police—plus some auditory, olfactory, and tactile skills—helps round up the Nazi spy ring. A good propaganda film that in its own corny way restates the dignity and worth of the American family (Robert

Young to pals: *" . . . we don't like anybody who pushes us around."*).

JOURNEY FOR MARGARET. MGM; directed by W. S. Van Dyke. Released: October 28, 1942. A wholesome story depicting the strength, fortitude, and dignity of England's Finest Hour—during the Luftwaffe attacks against their homeland. Robert Young and Laraine Day are wonderful as an American married couple working in London during the dangerous days of the Nazi blitz. Soon, they adopt a young war orphan, Margaret O'Brien, and begin a long bureaucratic odyssey to bring the child to the safety of the United States. Propaganda value is enhanced by the many scenes highlighting the wanton killing of civilians during the nightly bombing raids (British worker, shaking his fist at German aircraft overhead: *"I'd like to get my hands on you, you dirty Nazi swine."*).

KEEP YOUR POWDER DRY. MGM; directed by Edward Buzzell. Released February 15, 1945. A dreary, torpid, self-righteous soap opera, which purports to pay tribute to the distaff volunteers of the Women's Army Corps—the WACS—who, like their male counterparts, are involved in all facets of military life. Lana Turner and Laraine Day are two cadets who slowly learn that their personal differences are inconsequential against the larger issue of America-at-war. After graduating from the all-White Officers Candidate School, the young ladies are reconciled and soon begin training other recruits. Of dubious propaganda value since elitism, goldbricking, and favoritism are strong themes. Worst scene: angry Lana Turner catfighting with Officer Candidate Day: (Turner to Day: *". . . listen, you old, vicious, smug double-crosser. From now on as long as I'm in this Corps, I will never speak to you again."*).

KEEPER OF THE FLAME. MGM; directed by George Cukor. Released December 16, 1942. A strong warning to the American people about demagoguery, domestic fascism, and mind control, while praising the virtues of freedom of the press. Spencer Tracy shines as a dogged journalist investigating the accidental death of a noted industrialist—a supposedly solid citizen—whose numerous youth organizations have enrolled thousands of students.

Soon the redheaded legman, with the help of Katharine Hepburn, uncovers a full-blown plan to launch a fascist coup by a demented group of American storm troopers. Within hours, newspaper headlines inform the public, proving once again the strength of the fourth estate. Best scene: Katharine Hepburn's denunciation of Hitlerism: (Hepburn to Tracy: *"I saw the face of fascism in my own home; of course they didn't call it fascism. They painted it Red, White, and Blue and called it Americanism."*). A solid propaganda film that borrowed freely from the cinematic techniques in Orson Welles' *Citizen Kane.*

LIFEBOAT. Twentieth Century-Fox; directed by Alfred Hitchcock. Released: January 11, 1944. Another controversial story from the pen of John Steinbeck, it describes the drama of a group of American shipwrecked survivors adrift in a small boat in the mid-Atlantic after their tanker was torpedoed by a Nazi submarine. John Hodiak, Tallulah Bankhead, Henry Hull, and William Bendix are outstanding as rescued passengers, but Walter Slezak steals the show as the U-boat commandant who is also pulled out of the water when his ship is destroyed. After some acrimonious debate, the German officer is placed in charge and secretly steers toward an Axis convoy. When his plan backfires, the crew members bludgeon the Nazi to death. Of limited propaganda value since the film's premise—survival under duress— is obfuscated by the survivors' lynch-mob behavior. Typical scene: Henry Hull, as an American magnate justifying their actions (Hull to crew: *" . . . you can't treat them as human beings; you got to exterminate them."*).

LITTLE TOKYO, U.S.A. Twentieth Century-Fox; directed by Otto Brower. Released: July 8, 1942. A B-filler highlighting the exploits of a dedicated Los Angeles detective and his problems in breaking up a Japanese spy ring—the Black Dragon Society— which is operating surreptitiously in the California city. Preston Foster is competent as the lawman trying to convince his superiors of fifth column activities, and pretty Brenda Joyce provides the distaff support. Of limited propaganda value except to show that American know-how will always prevail in ridding the nation of its foreign secret agents. (Foster, after punching Nipponese spy Harold Huber: *" . . . that's for Pearl Harbor."*).

THE MAJOR AND THE MINOR. Paramount; directed by Billy
Wilder. Released: August 27, 1942. A slow-moving comedy that
harmlessly pokes fun at military school regulations. Ginger
Rogers plays an out-of-work ingenue who impersonates a twelve-
year-old girl to purchase a half-fare railroad ticket from New York
to her rural hometown, Stevenson, Iowa. When railroad officials
catch on to her scam, she is rescued by a fellow passenger, Major
Ray Milland. Unaware of the ruse, he brings her to his academy
where numerous young cadets fall head-over-heels for the comely
"preteen." Unable to keep the charade working, the impecunious
Miss Rogers tiptoes away, rather than allow a scandal to ruin the
major's career. Later, the two are united at a symbolic railroad
station, and after a two-minute courtship, they agree to marry.
Only propaganda scene: Ginger Rogers explains her future husband's mission (Miss Rogers' braggadocio: "... *he's going to
war so that this country will be spared what happened to
France.*").

MARINE RAIDERS. RKO; directed by Harold Schuster. Released: July 11, 1944. An overblown attempt to pay homage to the
Marine Corps, imbued with clichés, stereotypes, and the omnipresent responsibility of command. Pat O'Brien is competent as a
combat officer who, during an important island invasion, keeps
both his eyes on his young charge, Robert Ryan. The Japanese,
hiding deep in the jungle and seen only by moonlight reflection,
commit many atrocities until the Marines, fighting a hand-to-hand
battle, push their enemy back into the sea. Propaganda value
enhanced by the numerous acts of American heroism in contrast to
the savagery of war (Ryan to buddy: "*I knew what they did in
Hong Kong, in Nanking, and Bataan. But, I guess I wasn't close
enough.*").

THE MASTER RACE. RKO; directed by Herbert J. Biberman.
Released: September 22, 1944. A nondescript B-letdown that, in
an overblown and sluggish manner, warns of the dangers of neo-
Nazism. Reptilian-looking George Coulouris portrays a
Schutzstaffel colonel—posing insidiously as a Belgian patriot—
hoping to plant the seeds of unrest and discontent against the
American occupation forces that now govern most of liberated
Europe (Coulouris, giving instructions to his Nazi cronies: "...

preserve our master race. In our hands, hatred can be turned into the most potent of any weapon.''). Poor propaganda value since the enemy, the fifth columnist Nazis, are downtrodden and ragged in appearance.

MINISTRY OF FEAR. Paramount; directed by Fritz Lang. Released October 19, 1944. A major disappointment under the auspices of a renowned director. Ray Milland seems puny as an innocent bystander, recently released from a British mental institution, who becomes the lucky winner of an ordinary-looking cake at a local charity raffle. Soon, he is entwined with wartime espionage where spy chases spy, agent kills agent, and police look for the wrong man. However, with the help of blonde Marjorie Reynolds, the Allied cause remains intact. Virtually no propaganda value except to demonstrate the recalcitrant nature of the British people (civilian to Milland: *''. . . keep the curtains drawn, the blasted Nazis will be over in a bit. I hope our lads give them a proper pasting.''*).

THE MIRACLE OF MORGAN'S CREEK. Paramount; directed by Preston Sturges. Released: January 5, 1944. A madcap classic, one of the funniest films ever made. Featuring young, wide-eyed, talkative Betty Hutton, who drunkenly marries a GI cad. The next morning, after the soldier has tiptoed away, she cannot remember the stranger's name. Later, shy, good-natured, and 4-F Eddie Bracken ''volunteers'' to remarry the girl, and the storyline's denouement is scintillating comedy. William Demarest is irate as Betty Hutton's father, while state governor Brian Donlevy— proud of the ''miracle'' taking place in the small town of Morgan's Creek—orders an official holiday. Little propaganda value except to show most American GIs as friendly, wholesome, and clean-cut. Typical scene: the brouhaha when various levels of authority show up to arrest the confused Bracken, but his faithful girlfriend, undaunted by officialdom, dismisses his predicament: (Betty Hutton to sister: *''I'll love Norval till my dying day.''*).

MISS V. FROM MOSCOW. PRC; directed by Lothar Mendes. Released: January 21, 1943. A warmed-up B-leftover in which pretty Russian spy Lola Lane, using the code name Miss V. from Moscow, crosses the enemy lines into France, and gleans much valuable information from a Nazi dullard who is infatuated by her charms. Soon, she is sending important messages to the Allied command. Subsequently, she accepts death before capture by the Gestapo (Axis villain John Vosper to his underlings: *". . . instead of a Russian bear in our trap, we have a very beautiful woman!"*). Another film glorifying Soviet achievements and suffering.

MISSION TO MOSCOW. Warner Brothers; directed by Michael Curtiz. Released May 22, 1943. An outspoken and controversial pro-Russian tract; often called the greatest propaganda film ever made. An elaborate panegyric lauding the USSR while watering down the evils of communism. Walter Huston is ideal as the East Coast lawyer and Bible-quoting orator who is handpicked in 1936 by old Doctor-Win-the-War as the U.S. ambassador to Moscow. After a short tenure, the venerable Huston returns as a devoted Slavophile, praising Stalin and the Red Army (Huston to the mustachioed Georgian leader: *"I believe, Sir, that history will record you as a great builder for the benefit of mankind."*). Overflowing with inaccuracies and oozing with distortions, the film was a hard-line rationalization for the second front, and whitewashed every communist misdeed including the infamous Hitler/Stalin pact, the purge trials, and the invasion of Finland. Most Russian leaders are caricatures, worshipping the tenets of American democracy, while the peasants, well-scrubbed and happy, spend most of their time kissing the ring on Walter Huston's capitalist finger. Not included in the ten best list because the propaganda, while superb, is intellectual, not visceral, requiring an intimate knowledge of Soviet history to be effective.

MR. WINKLE GOES TO WAR. Columbia; directed by Alfred E. Green. Released: July 19, 1944. An easygoing, homespun, human interest story describing the quiet dignity of a shy forty-four-year-old bank teller who is drafted into the Army, completes combat training, and is sent to a South Pacific island, where he destroys a Japanese pillbox with a slow-moving bulldozer. Edward G. Robinson is splendid as the taciturn milquetoast who becomes an acclaimed war hero. Another overage buddy, Robert Armstrong, only wants to strangle a Japanese soldier to revenge his brother's death on Wake Island. A good propaganda film that reaffirms the wartime philosophy that all men must work in unity (Private

Edward G. Robinson explains why he refused a discharge: *"... a company is everybody doing a job together."*). Strangest scenes: Private Robinson and his new army pals complete their basic training without receiving a soldier's first military rite of passage—the regulation haircut.

MRS. MINIVER. MGM; directed by William Wyler. Released: May 13, 1942. Winner of five academy awards. An overrated, overblown Hollywood production starring Greer Garson and Walter Pidgeon as a stiff-upper-lip English couple frightened by the daily Nazi air raids on London and its environs. A pseudo-gallant, upper-middle class life style—complete with sports car and prize-winning roses—is supposed to demonstrate the permanence of the British Empire, but seems, rather, to advocate snobbery and the caste system. Best scene: Greer Garson confronts a downed German flyer in her kitchen (Mrs. Miniver, explaining to her husband the dexterity employed to capture this Luftwaffe pilot: *"I just took it [his gun] away from him and called the police."*). Propaganda message enhanced by strong moralizing and many anti-Nazi remarks.

THE MOON IS DOWN. Twentieth Century-Fox; directed by Irving Pichel. Released: March 10, 1943. An offbeat film version of the famous and controversial John Steinbeck novel depicting the Nazi takeover of a small Norwegian mining village and the hardships inflicted upon innocent civilians. Sir Cedric Hardwicke's distinctive British accent sounds strange coming from a high-ranking German officer, but Lee J. Cobb is more down-to-earth as the town doctor. Of dubious propaganda value since some of the Axis soldiers are portrayed sympathetically, while the resistance movement seems mute and ineffective (town mayor Henry Travers to Sir Cedric: *"... free men can't start a war but once it's started they can still fight on in defeat."*).

MY FAVORITE BLONDE. Paramount; directed by Sidney Lanfield. Released: March 18, 1942. An all-American Bob Hope comedy, in which the master jokester pokes fun at the Arsenal of Democracy's enemies and reassures audiences that officialdom is hard at work routing its Axis foes. Only Bob Hope, as American as apple pie, could break up a spy ring, court fast-talking, blonde

Madeleine Carroll, and win a government citation. Good propaganda value combined with harmless fun (ski-nose Hope, giving a Nazi spy the once-over: *". . . rigor mortis, junior."*).

MY FAVORITE SPY. RKO; directed by Tay Garnett. Released: May 6, 1942. A high jinks B-musical starring one of radio's popular big band leaders. Kay Kayser is funny as an uncoordinated Army officer working undercover to expose some fifth columnists who send out cryptic messages via the orchestra's counterpoint score. After a series of foot-in-the-mouth laughs, the lanky musician, with the help of comely Ellen Drew, breaks up the Axis espionage ring—showing that music calms the savage beast. Of minimal propaganda value except to remind audiences that everyone must do his share to keep Old Glory waving (Kayser to friends: *"I'll fight for my country anytime they need me."*).

NAZI AGENT. MGM; directed by Jules Dassin. Released: January 21, 1942. A strong indictment of those Nazi agents who were working in the German consulate offices during the shaky days before war with America was declared. Conrad Veidt is superb as a mild-mannered, soft-spoken U.S. citizen who inadvertently kills his twin brother and then assumes the bon vivant Nazi spy's role. Soon, with his new identity, he disrupts all espionage work and, with the help of the FBI, the saboteurs are routed. Ann Ayars, as a French national, supplies the necessary romance, while character actor Martin Kosleck is another reptilian Third Reich bureaucrat. Best scene: Conrad Veidt expounding on democratic principles (Veidt to Germans: *". . . the good people of the world are rising to crush you—and everything you stand for—once and for all"*). Solid propaganda because the film's premise—that fifth columnists are everywhere—was timely and accurate.

NONE SHALL ESCAPE. Columbia; directed by Andre Detoth. Released: January 28, 1944. A low-key, quasi-science fiction story. Sometime in the future, Germany has surrendered and the Allied tribunal begins the arduous task of punishing war criminals, with the promise that "none" of the sadistic leaders "shall escape." When called before the bar of justice, Alexander Knox exhibits numerous fiendish qualities as the Nazi commandant who brutalized a small Polish village. Marsha Hunt stoically explains the Third Reich's policy of murder, rape, filial betrayal, deportation, and anti-Semitism. A good, solid propaganda tract that, in a roundabout way, anticipates the 1945–46 Nuremberg Trials. Best scene: the town's rabbi calls for rebellion (Rabbi Richard Hale to his followers: *"I say to you, let us choose to fight here, now."*).

THE NORTH STAR. RKO; directed by Lewis Milestone. Released: October 13, 1943. An exaggerated pro-Soviet statement, with the sufferings and hardships of Comrade Ivan oozing out of every frame. Dana Andrews' midwestern twang sounds strange coming from a Ukrainian national who rallies his family when their small village is attacked by the Nazi juggernaut in June 1941. Walter Huston is sincere as the country doctor who activates the Soviet's scorched-earth policy (Comrade Dean Jagger to peasants: *". . . as villagers, you must destroy everything."*). Sadistic SS chief Erich von Stroheim, as the fiend who drains blood from small Ukrainian children to replenish his wounded Germans, personifies Nazi bestiality in its vilest form. A strange footnote: years later, during the McCarthy Witch Hunt, *The North Star,* denounced as Red propaganda, was truncated and reissued as an anti-Soviet film entitled *Armored Attack.*

NORTHERN PURSUIT. Warner Brothers; directed by Raoul Walsh. Released: October 25, 1943. A hibernal adventure about a Nazi spy ring operating in Canada's uncharted wastelands. Errol Flynn, bundled warmly, stars as an assiduous Royal Canadian Mounted policeman who, true to tradition, gets his man following an elaborate trek across many ice-cold miles. Strong warning about fifth column activities stresses the need for eternal vigilance. Nazi agents, led by good-looking Helmut Dantine, are insidious and threatening (Nazi to cohorts: *"I heard that the hostage system works very well in Europe. It can work just as well here."*). Most tasteless scene: last ten seconds, when Flynn, finished with the storyline, spoofs his recent "in-like-Flynn" rape case.

OBJECTIVE BURMA. Warner Brothers; directed by Raoul Walsh. Released: February 17, 1945. A controversial and exaggerated pro-American tract which suggests that the U.S. Army, spearheaded by former swashbuckler Errol Flynn and an all-male cast, captured the whole of Burma. In a distorted and somewhat embarrassing film script there is almost no reference to the British. Probably the most gruesome scene in any propaganda film occurs when the mutilated bodies of dead American GIs are discovered by their commander (newspaperman Henry Hull, describing the Japanese atrocities: *". . . they're degenerate moral idiots; stinking little savages. Wipe them out I say, wipe them off the face of the earth!"*).

ONCE UPON A HONEYMOON. RKO; directed by Leo McCarey. Released: November 4, 1942. A harmless and sometimes inappropriate screwball comedy, with shapely Ginger Rogers as a former New York burlesque queen who unknowingly marries a Nazi stooge in prewar Vienna, but is soon shown the light by handsome American journalist Cary Grant. After a series of sometimes funny, sometimes silly adventures, the twosome slip away from the clutches of the ever-encroaching Gestapo. Many underhanded, sarcastic remarks thrown at the Third Reich (Ginger Rogers to Nazi husband Walter Slezak: *". . . darling, I wouldn't trust those two swastikas any further than I could throw Goering."*). Limited propaganda value.

PARIS AFTER DARK. Twentieth Century-Fox; directed by Leonide Moguy. Released: October 6, 1943. Another low-budget melodrama that glorifies the sub rosa world of the French resistance forces operating in the City of Lights, chipping away at the Third Reich occupation. George Sanders' polished English accent sounds strange coming from a French doctor who quietly heads an underground ring, disrupting factory production and ordering Allied air strikes. As his head nurse, Brenda Marshall smuggles secret messages between arrondissements, while her husband, Philip Dorn, becomes a wartime casualty, sacrificing himself for the glory of France. A solid propaganda film that restates the Allied message that the invasion of France is coming soon. Best scene: Brenda Marshall broadcasts her prophecy over the clandestine radio network: (Marshall to countrymen: *". . . on the day of our liberation, you will hear the church bells of France ringing from every city, every village."*).

PASSAGE TO MARSEILLES. Warner Brothers; directed by Michael Curtiz. Released: February 17, 1944. A blatant pro-Free

French melodrama that takes many nasty swipes at the Vichy government. Humphrey Bogart's tough guy accent seems strange coming from a liberal Parisian journalist who is sent to the infamous penal camp, Devil's Island, on trumped-up charges. When war breaks out, Bogart—along with five other convicts—escapes to England, joins the bomber squadron, and, nightly, attacks the German installations on the Continent. Bogart's martyr's death reinforces the propaganda value even though the confusing, three-tier flashback obfuscates some of the political issues. With Peter Lorre, Claude Rains, and Sydney Greenstreet in supporting roles, the film is a copycat version of the director's earlier triumph, *Casablanca*. Best scene: the escapees swear their allegiance (character actor Vladimir Sokoloff administering the oath:*". . . I will do everything in my power to reach France, our mother country."*).

THE PIED PIPER. Twentieth Century-Fox; directed by Irving Pichel. Released: July 8, 1942. Another strong testimony to British fortitude and determination, starring the venerable Monty Woolley as an aristocratic Englishman vacationing on the French Riviera when war breaks out in Europe. His long odyssey back to London brings many adventures as he becomes the "official" escort to a motley assortment of orphan children. As the modern Pied Piper, he guides his young charges to safety (Woolley to group: *". . . young or old, an Englishman's place at a time like this is in England."*). Many anti-Nazi scenes, including the strafing of civilians on French roads, enhance the propaganda value. Best scene: Woolley returns to his fashionable London club and downplays his quiet heroism.

PITTSBURGH. Universal Pictures; directed by Lewis Seiler. Released: November 30, 1942. A strong tribute to American factory workers, exhorting them to even greater levels of wartime production. John Wayne and Randolph Scott are strong but obstinate Yankee individualists who change the city of Pittsburgh into an important mill center. Pearl Harbor dissolves all their personal differences and both men encourage guns-before-butter as their plant churns out new and better war materiel (Scott to workers: *"Let's face the facts, gentlemen. We're all in this together—every man and woman in our factory should have the same goal as our soldiers.''*).

PRIVATE BUCKAROO. Universal; directed by Eddie Cline. Released: June 11, 1942. A happy-go-lucky B-musical starring the popular singing trio, the Andrews Sisters, big-band leader Harry James, and comedian Joe E. Lewis, who entertain American fighting men stationed at a local training base. Many rousing songs and dance routines turn this lighthearted feature into a flag-waving extravaganza as young American GIs, coming from all walks of life, are united in their effort for total victory (trumpeter James, to a group of recruits: *''. . . we're supposed to be fighting the Japs, not ourselves.''*). Best musical number: the Andrews Sisters sing ''Don't Sit Under the Apple Tree.''

THE PURPLE HEART. Twentieth Century-Fox; directed by Lewis Milestone. Released: February 23, 1944. *The best propaganda film of World War II.* A stirring, rousing, heroic testimony to the men of the Army Air Corps, it is a fictitious account of the April 18, 1942, Doolittle bombing raid of Tokyo and the capture, kangaroo trial, and execution of one hapless crew. Dana Andrews is superb as a B-25 pilot who, along with the other airmen, refuses to reveal military information. But Richard Loo's performance as a fanatical, crazed, sadistic Japanese officer is a tour de force. Heightened use of martial music punctuates the victory-through-death motif (Andrews denouncing Japanese justice: *''This is your war, you wanted it, you asked for it, you started it! And now, you're going to get it. And it won't be finished until your dirty little empire is wiped off the face of the earth.''*). Best propaganda scene: the Japanese, hearing of a new victory in the Greater East Asia Prosperity scheme, break out in a crazed celebration ritual in their civil courtroom.

REMEMBER PEARL HARBOR. Republic Pictures; directed by Joseph Santely. Released: May 11, 1942. A rushed-through B-melodrama, with rough-and-tumble cowboy star Red Barry (now known more properly as Donald M. Barry) changing his Western jeans for Army khakis. After initially being duped by some enemy agents, he eventually thwarts a Japanese invasion of

some unknown Philippine island. An artificial script vitiates most
of the propaganda value even though there is much hoopla with
the call to colors (B-actor Ian Keith, prophesying American
determinism: "... *we, who are here under General MacArthur,
will let the world know when the enemy does come in thousands—
or tens of thousands—that we are ready!*").

REUNION IN FRANCE. MGM; directed by Jules Dassin. Released: December 2, 1942. An overstated melodrama using the
Fall of France and the Nazi takeover as a backdrop. Joan Crawford
is superficial as a one-time French aristocrat who loses all her
material possessions to the Third Reich's seizure. A silly triangle—involving Philip Dorn, a loyal Frenchman posing as a
collaborator, and strong, silent John Wayne, a downed RAF pilot
escaping back to England—only creates muddle and understate-
ment. Most of the time Miss Crawford, suffering stoically in
gowns by Adrian, either bemoans her predicament or enjoys haute
cuisine (Joan Crawford, mumbling her hard luck story: "... *it's
simple enough. My house has been taken away from me. My
money is gone and I owe for my breakfast this morning.*").
Funniest scene: John Wayne, dressed as a chauffeur.

ROSIE THE RIVETER. Republic; directed by Joseph Santley.
Released: April 5, 1944. An elaborate B-musical that idealizes the
overalls-clad women aircraft workers, who spend long hours at
their grinding wheels, spinning lathes and drill presses, turning
out needed war materiel, but find time to sing a medley of patriotic
tunes. Jane Frazee is perfectly cast as the pretty riveter who
encourages her friends to higher levels of airplane production,
while her fiancé, handsome Frank Albertson, a member of Uncle
Sam's fighting forces, beams with exuberant pride. Best scene:
Jane Frazee "announces" her wedding date (Miss Frazee to
friends: "... *I don't know—winning the war is more important.*"). A solid propaganda film that heaps dollops of praise on
the defense workers, citing their contributions on the long road to
victory. Best song: Betty Hutton's rendition of the risqué, "I'm
Doing It for Defense."

SABOTEUR. Universal Pictures; directed by Alfred Hitchcock.
Released: April 23, 1942. A typical, humdrum chase melodrama

which pits the efforts of a nondescript American mechanic, falsely accused of murder, against a sophisticated, well-tuned German fifth columnist ring that is disrupting wartime production. Robert Cummings looks silly wearing a necktie in every scene, but after an elaborate California-to-New York trek, he finally corners the Axis saboteur on top of the Statue of Liberty, while comely Priscilla Lane smiles approvingly. Of minimal propaganda value since the FBI, the local constabulary, and the Navy yard police are portrayed as ineffectual organizations, unable to thwart espionage. Corniest scene: Robert Cummings prophesying the Allied victory (Cummings to Nazi spies: *"... we'll win, if it takes from now until the cows come home."*).

SAHARA. Columbia Pictures; directed by Zoltan Korda. Released: September 29, 1943. One of the ten top pictures of the War. An assorted group of American GIs and British tommies, led by tough, tank Sergeant Humphrey Bogart, routs the Germans in the hot, waterless North African desert. Bogart is perfectly cast as a rugged but fair NCO fighting for the preservation of Jeffersonian democracy (Bogart to crew: *"... when I go to Berlin, I'm gonna be riding that tank. The same one that's standing there with the name Lulu Belle written on it."*). Best scene: the moment of truth, when Bogart realizes he cannot abandon an innocent Italian prisoner of war in the middle of the desert.

SECRET AGENT OF JAPAN. Twentieth Century-Fox; directed by Irving Pichel. Released: March 16, 1942. A fast-moving B-quickie indicating that British intelligence surreptitiously operated in the port city of Shanghai weeks before the December 7th attack on Pearl Harbor. Preston Foster, an escaped American criminal, is convincing as a convivial nightclub owner, while Lynn Bari, a courier for the Crown, gathers secret codes and models haute couture. After some cat-and-mouse maneuvering with the Japanese occupation forces, the twosome, with the help of the Chinese underground, flee to the hinterland with important information, while the Nipponese, unaware of their ruse, look elsewhere (Foster to friend: *"... you're in Jap town now—you gotta roll with the punches."*). A good propaganda film that served as the B-model for dozens of other pictures.

SEVEN DAYS ASHORE. RKO; directed by John Auer. Released: April 12, 1944. A simplistic, seventy-five-minute B-comedy starring the slapstick team of Alan Carney and Wally Brown as Merchant Marine seamen on a seven-day pass in friendly San Francisco. Along with their buddies, the twosome chase many girls, pose as eccentric millionaires, help a friend marry his sweetheart, and sing a medley of popular or patriotic melodies. When their leave expires, the Jacks receive a gala musical sendoff as they board their ship, bound for the Pacific theater. Of limited propaganda value except to laud the clean-cut crews who man the cargo vessels that deliver the materiel for victory. Best musical scene: Carney and Brown explain their raison d'être (duo singing to the crowd: *". . . we have our fun in every port, but we're around to hold the fort."*).

SEVEN MILES FROM ALCATRAZ. RKO; directed by Edward Dmytryk. Released: November 10, 1942. Another sixty-two-minute B-cliffhanger describing the transformation of two convicts, James Craig and Frank Jenks, who escape from Alcatraz by swimming to a lighthouse seven miles away. After a series of Merrie Melodies adventures, including the standard rescue from a locked cellar, the two men overpower some Nazi agents minutes before the Germans rendezvous with a secret U-boat. Acclaimed as heroes, the two jailbirds receive a shorter sentence for their patriotic work and a big kiss from pulchritudinous Bonita Granville. Of limited propaganda value except to suggest that prisoners also can wave the Red, White, and Blue (convict Frank Jenks, expatiating the Third Reich shortcomings: *"These Nazis are hotheads. They've been waving their arms in the air so long, they're dizzy."*).

THE SEVENTH CROSS. MGM; directed by Fred Zinnemann. Released: July 24, 1944. A maudlin, self-righteous melodrama which argues, feebly, that not all Germans are corrupt, only followers of Hitlerism. Redhead Spencer Tracy is lackluster as a German national who in 1936 escapes from a concentration camp, endures many harrowing adventures, and finally reaches the safety of Holland, aided by an old school chum, Hume Cronyn. Laden with molasses, the film creeps along, enmeshed by its tendentiousness. Many anti-Nazi scenes (prisoner cursing his military captors: *"... someday, others will answer for me. They'll shout it back at you."*). Worst scene: Tracy looks up his old girlfriend, now married to a Third Reich official, who tells the fugitive to beat it.

SHERLOCK HOLMES AND THE SECRET WEAPON. Universal; directed by Roy Neill. Released: December 28, 1942. A conventional B-mystery in which the master of deductive reasoning, Sherlock Holmes, uncovers a Nazi spy ring operating in war-torn London. Basil Rathbone is superb as the famous pipe-smoking, violin-playing sleuth, while wing-collared Nigel Bruce is ideal as Dr. Watson. Strong propaganda film reaffirming the dogged spirit of the British people (Holmes to Watson: *"... this blessed plot, this earth, this realm, this England."*). Later, in *Sherlock Holmes and the Voice of Terror*, the twosome wreck another Axis saboteur. Eventually, they travel to America where they help the FBI recover some important secret information in *Sherlock Holmes in Washington*.

SINCE YOU WENT AWAY. United Artists; directed by John Cromwell. Released: July 19, 1944. One of the worst films of the War. An elaborate, puffed-up Hollywood production bewailing the effects of the War on an upper-middle class American family living in safety on the Home Front, while the breadwinner has left for combat. Claudette Colbert is unconvincing as the faithful wife struggling to maintain normalcy. A plethora of subplots— including the problems of hiring maids, new boarders, the daughter's teenage crush on an older man—run this film into the ground. Racism, snobbery, and White America are strong themes; the "common" man is often disparaged (Jennifer Jones, disapproving of her younger sister's boyfriend: *"... besides, he isn't even an officer."*). Even the classic railroad station scene—where lovers Robert Walker and Jennifer Jones are separated—cannot salvage this tacky film.

SO PROUDLY WE HAIL. Paramount; directed by Mark Sandrich. Released: June 22, 1943. An overblown tribute to the women in the Army Nurses Corps who were trapped in Corregidor during the early days of the War. An all-star cast includes Claudette Colbert, Paulette Goddard, and Veronica Lake as

modern-day Florence Nightingales who care for sick and
wounded GIs, while enemy bombs fall dangerously nearby. After
many setbacks and a near capture, the nurses are rescued by the
U.S. Navy. Many nasty remarks about the Japanese (distraught
American nurse Veronica Lake, promising vengeance for the
Pearl Harbor death of her fiancé: *"I'm going to kill Japs, every
bloodstained one I can get my hands on."*).

SOMEWHERE I'LL FIND YOU. MGM; directed by Wesley
Ruggles. Released: August 6, 1942. A fast-moving, stop-the-
presses, journalistic adventure tale that glamorizes the unconven-
tional methods used by the fourth estate to track down their story.
Clark Gable is outstanding as a flamboyant foreign correspondent
whose peripatetic wanderings bring him to Manila on December
7th. With Lana Turner at his side, the ace reporter sends out one
dispatch after another describing American heroism against the
Japanese troops attacking Corregidor, and, even though the battle
is lost, he prophesies an American victory (Gable, pounding out
his byline: *". . . 300,000 Japanese were tied in knots long enough
for the U.S.A. to get its Sunday clothes off and go to work."*). A
solid propaganda film restating the importance of a free press in a
democratic society.

SONG OF RUSSIA. MGM; directed by Gregory Ratoff. Released: December 29, 1943. A strange combination of music and
praise for the Soviet people. Robert Taylor is charming as a
famous American conductor—a Tchaikovsky devotee—on tour
in the USSR the day the German invasion starts. He soon
witnesses the strength and dignity of his new-found Russian
friends. Comely Susan Peters supplies the needed romance as the
handsome musician tries to escape from the Nazi scourge and the
Red Army mobilizes (Russian freedom-fighter John Hodiak to
Taylor: *"We'll make them pay in blood for every home they've
ravaged."*). Best propaganda scene: the avuncular voice of the
Man of Steel, Joseph Stalin, calling his nation to arms against the
German invaders.

STAND BY FOR ACTION. MGM; directed by Robert Z. Leon-
ard. Released: December 10, 1942. An easygoing melodrama
saluting the men of the Navy who work less-than-modern ships.

Brian Donlevy is convincing as a long-time seafarer who must make do with an outdated escort vessel in the Pacific theater. Robert Taylor is competent as his executive officer, but Walter Brennan—who sailed on the ship during the Great War—steals the show as a strong example of American pride, determination, and fortitude. By following military regulations, the U.S. Navy sinks an important Japanese vessel (Donlevy to crew: " . . . *risking the life of any one man must be subordinated to risking the lives of many."*). Good propaganda value enhanced by onetime Captain Kidd, Charles Laughton, as top Navy official. Best scene: Laughton's oration on revolutionary hero, John Paul Jones.

STAR SPANGLED RHYTHM. Paramount; directed by George Marshall. Released December 31, 1942. An all-star variety show featuring the top players from a leading production company in a manner that is entertaining, lighthearted, and patriotic. Betty Hutton shines as a telephone operator whose topsy-turvy antics convince a young sailor, Eddie Bracken, that his security guard father is an important film executive. With the help of Bing Crosby, Bob Hope, Fred MacMurray, Dorothy Lamour, Paulette Goddard, Dick Powell, William Bendix, Rochester, Robert Preston, Ray Milland and numerous celebrities, Miss Hutton keeps the charade rolling until the Navy tars are back on the high seas. A solid propaganda film with continuous praise for God, country, and flag. Best propaganda scene: Bing Crosby expounds American determinism (the crooner to audience: " . . . *there aren't any Germans, Italians or Japs that are going to push us off our hard won, homemade Rand McNally maps."*).

THE STORY OF GI JOE. United Artists; directed by William A. Wellman. Released: June 18, 1945. A beautiful testimony to the quiet lifestyle of Pulitzer Prize winner Ernie Pyle, the beloved war correspondent who was killed in combat. Burgess Meredith is outstanding as the journalist who became the common soldier's best friend and whose newspaper dispatches reflected the hopes, aspirations, and fears of the fighting man (dogface to Meredith: *"Why wasn't I born a 4-F, instead of good-looking?"*). Young Robert Mitchum is perfect as the Army officer in charge of the squad that the writer adopts. Best propaganda scene: the justification for the Allied bombing of the sixth-century Monte Cassino

Abbey (GI to buddy: *"I'm a Catholic and I say bomb it! I've got a wife and kid. Think I wanna die for a piece of stone?"*).

SUBMARINE ALERT. Paramount; directed by Frank Mc-Donald. Released: June 28, 1943. A typical B-yarn about spies, espionage, and Japanese submarines operating a few miles off the strategic Western Coast. Richard Arlen is lackluster as a radio engineer who, after a series of improbable adventures, helps the FBI break up an Axis spy ring, minutes before an American cargo ship is torpedoed. Pretty Wendy Barrie provides the romance. Typical anti-German, anti-Japanese remarks (B-actor John Miljan to Axis captors: *". . . I don't bargain with rats."*). Flag-waving ending adds to the propaganda (Richard Arlen, now an American GI: *". . . we know our way of life is best. We're fighting to keep it."*).

TARZAN TRIUMPHS. RKO; directed by William Thiele. Released: January 20, 1943. Another contribution to the Allied victory effort. Only Olympic-winner, chest-pounding, vine-swinging Johnny Weissmuller could portray the invincible Tarzan, whose peaceful lifestyle is interrupted when a gang of Nazis, headed by the ubiquitous character actor, Sig Rumann, invades his jungle domain. Aided by natives, elephants, and Cheta, the Ape Man makes quick work of the Axis scourge (Tarzan to native: *". . . take gun, kill Nazis."*). Good propaganda while entertaining, since the film's premise, German stealthiness in Africa, stresses the global nature of the War. Later, the monosyllabic Weissmuller, with some equestrian help, routed the Nazis a second time in *Tarzan's Desert Mystery*.

TENDER COMRADE. RKO; directed by Edward Dmytryk. Released: December 29, 1943. A World War II soap opera starring Ginger Rogers and Robert Ryan as former high school sweethearts who marry but are separated when the husband enters the Army at the onset of the War. Soon, the pretty Ginger Rogers shares an apartment with four other women and they experience many Home Front problems: rationing, hoarding, shortages, and opportunism (Ginger Rogers to roommates: *". . . I think anyone who hoards is a heel."*). Eventually, the good-looking Robert Ryan becomes a combat fatality but his off-screen death only strengthens the righteousness of God and country. Best scene: Mady Christians berates the neighborhood butcher for showing favoritism to certain customers by winking at the rationing laws.

TEXAS TO BATAAN. Monogram; directed by Robert Tansey. Released: October 13, 1942. Another B-Western, stamped with the Monogram imprimatur, in which a trio of Texas cowpokes— the Range Busters—are hard at work transporting needed horses from the wide-open prairie to American military installations in the Philippines during the uneasy pre-Pearl Harbor days. B-actors Dave Sharp and John King personify the best of Western ideals while routing fifth columnist attacks (cowboy Sharp to pals: *". . . if the cavalry needs horses in the Philippines, we'll get them there."*). Propaganda value is marginal except to show Americans as clean-cut and righteous. Most wholesome scene: tenor John King sings the popular ballad, "Home on the Range," to a wide-eyed group of native Filipinos.

THAT NAZTY NUISANCE. United Artists; directed by Glenn Tryon. Released: May 28, 1943. A cheap, B-comedy poking fun at Hitler, Mussolini, and Tojo in a manner that, retrospectively, seems tasteless. Spoofster Bobby Watson, who strongly resembled the Fuehrer, double-crosses (and, even, triple-crosses) his Axis pals over and over again in this pseudo-burlesque. Joe Devlin, as Mussolini, can't stand his German cohort (Devlin to Watson: *"I'm a gonna die justa because you made me your Axis partner."*). The talented Watson was stuck with his Hitler look-alike part for the rest of the War: *The Devil with Hitler* brought the German leader down to earth (from the hereafter) to perform one good deed (he doesn't); *Hitler—Dead or Alive* portrayed the silly antics of three American hit men attempting to assassinate the Fuehrer; *The Miracle of Morgan's Creek* placed Watson on screen for a mere ten seconds depicting the Fuehrer as a cartoon character. His one serious role was in *The Hitler Gang,* an in-depth analysis of the psychic disorders found in Nazism.

THEY CAME TO BLOW UP AMERICA. Twentieth Century-Fox; directed by Edward Ludwig. Released: May 7, 1943. An oversized B-production that capitalized on newspaper stories about Nazi saboteurs landing on American shores, by submarine, to blow up defense installations. George Sanders plays another perfidious Axis villain, but he is no match for tough FBI man Ward Bond. Good propaganda since the film's message—the need to guard America's vast coastline—contained much truth. Abundant praise heaped upon J. Edgar Hoover's agents (hard-working G-man Ward Bond to colleague: "*. . . we've got to pull them faster than they've pulled on us, if this bureau is going to mean anything in the war effort.*").

THEY GOT ME COVERED. RKO; directed by David Butler. January 4, 1943. Another Bob Hope madcap yarn involving stateside spies, enemy agents, intrigue, and the ubiquitous chase scene in the nation's capital. Fast-talking Bob Hope, with pretty Dorothy Lamour (sans sarong) tagging along, once more defends Yankee democracy from the Axis scourge. Good propaganda depicting the wholesomeness of American life, while providing some important escapist entertainment (burlesque queen Marion Martin proffering a small malapropism: "*. . . but there's just one thing that little Gloria ain't going to do and that's front for a bunch of swastickers! There's a lot of freedom in this country and I wanna go on enjoying it.*").

THIRTY SECONDS OVER TOKYO. MGM; directed by Mervyn LeRoy. Released: November 15, 1944. A magnificent motion picture containing a superb mixture of pathos, heroism, corn, and homespun philosophy. Spencer Tracy is outstanding as the real-life hero, Colonel Jimmy Doolittle, who led the daring Tokyo raid in 1942. Van Johnson also shines as the clean-cut American boy determined to protect home and hearth. Replete with inaccuracies, distortions, and fiction-as-fact (which heighten the propaganda effect), the film is one of the ten best, highlighting the important work of the Chinese villagers and their fight against the Japanese (Van Johnson to his Oriental doctor: "*. . . you saved my life, Doc. We'll be back; maybe not us, ourselves, but a lot of guys like us. And, I'd like to be with them—you're our kind of people.*"). Best scene: Van Johnson's stalled plane, blocking traffic on the aircraft carrier *Hornet,* finally starts.

THIS ABOVE ALL. Twentieth Century-Fox; directed by Anatole Litvak. Released: May 14, 1942. A hearts-and-flowers soap opera in which Tyrone Power, a disillusioned Englishman witnessing the Battle of Britain, is taught by pretty Joan Fontaine that before England can be reformed, the nation must first be saved. The Adonis-like Power is too wholesome to portray this down-and-out limey whose frustrations with the rigid social caste system have made him an army deserter. Of limited propaganda value since the storyline is more concerned with the two lovers than with the nature of the enemy. One of the sudsiest scenes ever: Tyrone Power sees the light and promises to reform (Power to girl friend: *" . . . that of all the things on earth, God has made no more beautiful, more noble a thing than a man and woman who truly love each other."*).

THIS IS THE ARMY. Warner Brothers; directed by Michael Curtiz. Released: July 29, 1943. A flag-waving, Red, White, and Blue, breast-pounding musical extravaganza—one of the best of its kind—which restates the basic American virtues, freedoms, and principles. Heavy with old-fashioned banality and syrupy moralizing, the film's incidental storyline, the entertainment of troops, skips quickly from one cliché to another, while the rousing music of Irving Berlin calls every American to arms. Magnificent propaganda sparkling with an all-star cast: (Joe Louis, now a PFC, to his friends: *" . . . all I know is I'm in Uncle Sam's Army and we're on God's side."*). One of the most effective propaganda scenes ever made: plump Kate Smith, the doyenne of popular vocalists, sings the overpowering "God Bless America," while every listener—ears glued to home radios—sits or stands solemnly in rapt attention.

THIS LAND IS MINE. RKO; directed by Jean Renoir. Released: March 17, 1943. A realistic look at the many hardships that life under Nazi occupation brings to a small Gallic village. Oversized Charles Laughton is miscast as the town's schoolteacher who secretly harbors a crush on redheaded Maureen O'Hara. Many plots including sabotage, betrayal, quislings, and resistance allow the storyline to teeter between patriotism and melodrama, while the shooting of civilian hostages served to arouse moviegoing audiences against Axis brutality. Best scene: Laughton's insistence that clandestine acts are necessary (Laughton to underground worker: *" . . . it increases our misery, but shortens our slavery.''*). Propaganda value tarnished by buffoon antics of Nazi chief Walter Slezak.

THREE RUSSIAN GIRLS. United Artists; directed by Fedor Ozep and Henry Kesler. Released: December 30, 1943. A vapid B-quickie which in a haphazard way heaps praise upon the fighting spirit of the Soviet allies. Kent Smith is anomalous as a Nebraskan engineer, working as a test pilot for the Red Air Force in early June 1941. When the Nazi attack begins, the good-looking Smith is shot out of the skies near Leningrad. Nursed back to health by pretty comrade Anna Sten, the American civilian appreciates Russian life and women. Soon, the twosome are holding hands and cementing Russo-American alliances. Good propaganda—in its own strange way—because the story purports that American volunteers were assisting the USSR before the war started (Kent to sweetheart: *"I'm leaving for Murmansk to-night.''*).

THUNDERBIRDS. Twentieth Century-Fox; directed by William A. Wellman. Released: October 19. 1942. A low-key, technicolor salute to the civilian instructors of the Army's famed Arizona Thunderbird training school, where British, Chinese, and American cadets learn to fly the pursuit planes that will lead the attack against the Axis. Preston Foster is fair-minded as a former Lafayette Escadrille World War I ace who teaches the young men basic aviation rudiments, while finding time to court pretty Gene Tierney. Under his tutelage, a group of British students earn their wings, but one man, John Sutton, wins the hand of the comely Miss Tierney. A good recruitment film, highlighting the versatility of the AT-6 aircraft and, in its unobtrusive way, demonstrating the cooperation existing among the three Allied nations. Most effective scene: the cadets are briefed about their mission (squadron leader Reginald Denny to his entourage: *" . . . this war is going to be won in the air.''*).

TO BE OR NOT TO BE. United Artists; directed by Ernst Lubitsch. Released: February 19, 1942. A half-serious, half-spoof portrayal of the German takeover of Poland that pairs Jack Benny and Carole Lombard as two famous thespians—a husband and wife team—in Nazi-occupied Warsaw. A myriad of subplots—

including the cuckold spouse, impersonation of a Nazi spy, and British underground intelligence—juxtapose both the serious and comical effects of Axis aggression. Character actor Sig Rumann is perfect as the inept Gestapo colonel who constantly puts his foot into his mouth. However, some of the gags fall flat (Benny to friend: *"I'm a good pole, I love my country and I love my slipper."*). Of marginal propaganda value since the Nazi leaders are caricatured as buffoons or incompetents who joke about the War in a manner that lacks propriety or sensitivity. Worst scene: a member of Benny's troupe imitates the Fuehrer on an official visit to the theater.

TO HAVE AND HAVE NOT. Warner Brothers; directed by Howard Hawks. Released: October 18, 1944. A slow-moving melodrama in which fishing boat captain Humphrey Bogart, operating surreptitiously out of an Atlantic port in Martinique, agrees to smuggle some Free French fugitives onto the Vichy-controlled island. Most of the propaganda value is undermined by the ambiguous plot; the *j'accusé* finger is never pointed at the real foe, Nazism, but, off-target, is aimed at a few overweight heavies. Even Bogart confuses matters (lone wolf Bogart to agents: *" . . . you save France, I'm gonna save my boat."*). After preserving democracy, Bogart leaves the island with pretty Lauren Bacall. Best line is not about whistling, but the seductive Bacall's annoyance with Bogey's appearance (Bacall to Bogart: *" . . . why don't you shave?"*).

TO THE SHORES OF TRIPOLI. Twentieth Century-Fox; directed by Bruce Humberstone. Released: March 11, 1942. Another flag-waving tribute to the men who serve in the Marine Corps and their strong commitment to defending the American way-of-life. John Payne stars as a pampered playboy who frivolously enlists in the Corps at its San Diego camp. Soon, his unsavory ways vanish and, under the tutelage of tough Marine sergeant Randolph Scott and pretty Navy nurse Maureen O'Hara, the former wastrel comes to terms with *semper fidelis*. When the Pearl Harbor attack is flashed over the airwaves, the Marines saddle up and march to a waiting transport ship, ready to seek out their Oriental enemy. A good technicolor salute, with authentic footage of fancy parade ground drills that enhances the propaganda value. Best scene: the Corps is cited for its heroic, but tragic, defense of Wake Island (narrator to audience: " . . . *[the Marines] who when trapped on Wake Island in the early days of the present conflict, and asked what they wanted, impudently and gloriously replied, Send us more Japs!"*).

TOMORROW THE WORLD. United Artist; directed by Leslie Fenton. Released: December 18, 1944. A half-cooked soap opera, 1940s style, in which love and kindness nullify the evils of a Nazi education. Fredric March is stuffy as a small-town American university professor who becomes the guardian of a twelve-year-old German youth, whose peripatetic wanderings finally drop him on the scholar's doorstep. Skip Homeier, recreating his Broadway role, is confused, hateful, suspicious, and spends most of his time spouting vicious Third Reich slogans. After pulling many dirty tricks on everyone around him, the lad finally sees the Jeffersonian light (Fredric March to girlfriend Betty Field, discussing the methodology for teaching their new charge the Four Freedoms: " . . . *once he mixes with American kids, he'll find out what's what."*). Good propaganda value since the storyline restates the horror of growing up in Nazi Germany.

TONIGHT WE RAID CALAIS. Twentieth Century-Fox; directed by John Brahm. Released: March 29, 1943. Another B-picture cheering the exploits of the French Resistance. Good-looking John Sutton, a British agent gathering intelligence information on Gallic soil, has trouble convincing pretty French lass Annabella of his noble cause. Aided by rugged French peasant Lee J. Cobb, the suave Englishman completes his assignment, wins the heart of the girl, then relinquishes the romance to the fortunes of war (Annabella, refusing to leave France, when the mission is over " . . . *this is where I belong."*). Of limited propaganda value since the storyline concentrates more on the Romeo-and-Juliet theme than the problems of Nazi occupation.

UNCERTAIN GLORY. Warner Brothers; directed by Raoul Walsh. Released: April 24, 1944. An offbeat, somewhat allegorical tale, that—in a roundabout way—praises Gallic heroism and integrity. Dashing Errol Flynn, a convicted French murderer, in exchange for three more days of life, elects to confess to the

Gestapo (for another man's crime, a patriotic saboteur) in lieu of civil execution. Paul Lukas is the chief inspector who orchestrates this bizarre plan and keeps watch over the mustachioed Flynn as he spends his last days wooing a country maid. Flynn's final surrender—an act of expiation—exemplifies French courage and loyalty (farmer to Flynn, pointing to an old horse: "... *she's like France, too old to beat, too tough to die.*"). Strong propaganda value, reiterating the terror of Nazi domination over innocent civilians.

UP IN ARMS. RKO; directed by Elliott Nugent. Released: February 7, 1944. A high-powered technicolor musical caricature that is more akin to a Saturday afternoon cartoon than a propaganda film. Danny Kaye, in his screen debut, plays a naive hypochondriac drafted into the Army, where his numerous imaginary illnesses play havoc with his friends, sergeants, and commanders. When his unit lands on a South Pacific island, the gibberish-speaking Kaye, after a series of Bugs Bunny adventures, captures a large contingency of Japanese soldiers who were hiding in the jungle. Accredited as a hero, the silly-looking GI receives his military kudos, plus a kiss from his girlfriend, pretty Dinah Shore. Of dubious propaganda value, because the film suggests that military life resembles the shenanigans found in college fraternities, while the Japanese adversary is nothing more than a myopic, chubby bag of wind, waiting to surrender. One of the worst scenes: Danny Kaye explains to a Japanese officer the location of his unit's tanks (Kaye to enemy: "... *we have a great big tank, we keep hot water in it all the time.*").

WAKE ISLAND. Paramount Pictures: directed by John Farrow. Released: August 12, 1942. Another film on the ten best list, a powerful call-to-arms for every American. A cheering salute to the U.S. Marine Corps and its brave, but unsuccessful, defense of Wake Island, a few days after the Pearl Harbor attack. Brian Donlevy is the tough but tender leatherneck commander, who stands by his men until the very end to keep the Japanese hordes off the island. William Bendix is outstanding as the typical gyrene; with his numerous malapropisms and love of Brooklyn he personifies the best of America's manpower. Superb juxtaposition, including pathos, comedy, warmth, kindness-to-animals, and

Japanese treachery, provides a perfect balance on every level. Best scene: the Marines refuse to surrender: (Donlevy's message to Japanese: *". . . tell them to come and get us."*).

WATCH ON THE RHINE. Warner Brothers; directed by Herman Shumlin. Released: July 27, 1943. A powerful anti-Nazi tract, with husband-and-wife team Bette Davis and Paul Lukas, actively engaged in the German resistance movement and reiterating the ever-present dangers of fifth columnists at work in America. A strong plea for U.S. vigilance against the sub rosa world of Axis agents enhances the propaganda value. Lukas, in an Academy Award role, is outstanding as a known enemy of the Third Reich (Lukas to guest: *"I am an antifascist! I work at that!"*). Best scene: Lukas shoots the Nazi spy rather than compromise American security.

WILSON. Twentieth Century-Fox; directed by Henry King. Released: August 2, 1944. A Red, White, and Blue technicolor tribute to the twenty-eighth President of the United States, highlighting the chief executive's career from his 1909 Princeton University days to state governor, and then on to the White House, where he leads the nation to victory during the Great War. Shakespearean actor Alexander Knox portrays Woodrow Wilson punctiliously, while Geraldine Fitzgerald shines as his second wife who assumed much of the President's authority during his convalescence in 1920–21. Thomas Mitchell and Sir Cedric Hardwicke are splendid as politicians involved in every facet of Washington, D.C. life. A good propaganda film which persuasively highlights many of the battlefield victories of World War I as a modern-day analogy. Best scene: the President dresses down the German ambassador, accusing the man of perfidy (Wilson to Count von Bernstorff: *"Won't you Germans ever be civilized? Won't you ever learn to keep your word?"*).

WING AND A PRAYER. Twentieth Century-Fox; directed by Henry Hathaway. Released: July 24, 1944. One of the ten best propaganda films of the War. An elaborate but down-to-earth salute to the men who must chart their lone naval behemoth into the dangerous Japanese-laden waters in early 1942 on a secret offensive mission. Starring Don Ameche, Dana Andrews, and

Charles Bickford as experienced flight officers whose microcosm world aboard a U.S. aircraft carrier in the Pacific Ocean demonstrates American tenacity against their Oriental adversary. A myriad of subplots—including the underage tail gunner, the overage flight mechanic, the flyer who refuses to conform to military regulations, and the kibitzing of a Hollywood star turned carrier pilot—reaffirm the heroic nature of American seapower. Don Ameche is capable as a tough Navy Captain struggling to keep his ship on an even keel (Ameche to officers: *". . . you will not interpret the orders—you will obey them."*), while Dana Andrews, as an easygoing squadron leader, learns the difficulty of command decision. Best propaganda scene: Ensign Kevin O'Shea crashing his pursuit plane into the path of an oncoming Japanese torpedo, saving the carrier from destruction.

WOMEN IN BONDAGE. Monogram; directed by Steve Sekely. Released: November 16, 1943. A low-grade B-exposé, accusing the Third Reich of immoral practices regarding marriage and childbirth. Gail Patrick portrays a German national who is forbidden by Nazi edict to marry her SS trooper boyfriend, because she is nearsighted. Instead, she is interned with other women-in-bondage to produce one child after another, to provide the Fatherland with new manpower for future wars. Strong propaganda, even though the storyline employs platitude after platitude. Most maudlin scene: Gail Patrick, hearing of Allied raids: (Miss Patrick to inmates: *". . . the women of Germany, too, will be able to lift their heads and hearts again."*).

A YANK ON THE BURMA ROAD. MGM; directed by George B. Seitz. Released: January 19, 1942. A B-quickie, one of the first movies hacked out after the Pearl harbor attack, highlighting American prowess. Barry Nelson, a former New York City cabby, is lukewarm as a truck driver, delivering needed medical supplies to Chungking—over the serpentine Burma Road—while routing the Japanese invaders at every turn. Helping out is pretty Laraine Day. Best scene: pseudo-tough guy Barry Nelson promises retribution for December 7th (Nelson to ragtag entourage: *". . . those rats! All right, they asked for it! We'll get a couple of licks in of our own."*). Of dubious propaganda value since the Chinese, caricatured as docile and menial, seem ineffective as a military ally.

CHRONOLOGICAL LISTING OF FILMS

1941

The Bugle Sounds (December 17, 1941)
Dangerously They Live (December 24, 1941)

1942

Call Out the Marines (January 5)
Joe Smith, American (January 7)
Joan of Paris (January 9)
The Fleet's In (January 19)
A Yank on the Burma Road (January 19)
Captains of the Clouds (January 20)
Nazi Agent (January 21)
All Through the Night (January 28)
To Be or Not To Be (February 19)
To the Shores of Tripoli (March 11)
Black Dragons (March 12)
Secret Agent of Japan (March 16)
My Favorite Blonde (March 18)
True to the Army (March 18)
Unseen Enemy (March 25)
Two Yanks in Trinidad (March 26)
Saboteur (April 23)
Rolling Down the Great Divide (April 24)
The Wife Takes a Flyer (April 28)
Yukon Patrol (April 30)
My Favorite Spy (May 6)
Remember Pearl Harbor (May 11)
Mrs. Miniver (May 13)
This Above All (May 14)
Private Buckaroo (June 11)
Holiday Inn (June 12)

She's in the Army (June 16)
The Phantom Plainsmen (June 16)
Submarine Raider (June 20)
Flight Lieutenant (June 29)
Escape from Hong Kong (June 30)
Rubber Racketeers (June 30)
Prisoner of Japan (June 30)
The Pied Piper (July 8)
Little Tokyo, U.S.A. (July 8)
Atlantic Convoy (July 10)
Flying Fortress (July 13)
Joan of Ozark (July 15)
Drums of the Congo (July 22)
Danger in the Pacific (August 6)
Somewhere I'll Find You (August 6)
Invisible Agent (August 7)
Bombs Over Burma (August 8)
Sabotage Squad (August 11)
Careful, Soft Shoulders (August 12)
Iceland (August 12)
Wake Island (August 12)
Berlin Correspondent (August 17)
Cairo (August 17)
Hillbilly Blitzkrieg (August 17)
Across the Pacific (August 18)
Busses Roar (August 18)
Desperate Journey (August 18)
Secret Enemies (August 18)
Enemy Agents Meet Ellery Queen (August 26)
The Major and the Minor (August 27)
They Raid by Night (September 3)
Riders of the Northland (September 4)
Bells of Capistrano (September 15)
Sherlock Holmes and the Voice of Terror (September 16)
Manila Calling (September 18)
Foreign Agent (September 21)
Flying Tigers (September 23)
A Yank in Libya (September 30)
Top Sergeant (October 1)
Blondie for Victory (October 9)

Jungle Siren (October 10)
Texas to Bataan (October 13)
Seven Days Leave (October 15)
The Navy Comes Through (October 15)
Thunderbirds (October 19)
The Devil with Hitler (October 22)
Army Surgeon (October 26)
Journey for Margaret (October 28)
Once Upon a Honeymoon (November 4)
Lady from Chungking (November 9)
Seven Miles from Alcatraz (November 10)
Valley of Hunted Men (November 13)
Lucky Jordan (November 16)
Fall In (November 20)
Casablanca (November 27)
Pittsburgh (November 30)
Reunion in France (December 2)
Madame Spy (December 2)
China Girl (December 9)
Stand By for Action (December 10)
The Gorilla Man (December 11)
Keeper of the Flame (December 16)
Pride of the Army (December 16)
Commandoes Strike at Dawn (December 18)
Quiet Please, Murder (December 24)
When Johnny Comes Marching Home (December 24)
Sherlock Holmes and the Secret Weapon (December 28)
Star Spangled Rhythm (December 31)

1943

They Got Me Covered (January 4)
Night Plane from Chungking (January 4)
Hitler's Children (January 6)
Charlie Chan in the Secret Service (January 6)
Chetniks—the Fighting Guerrillas (January 11)
Tarzan Triumphs (January 20)
Miss V. from Moscow (January 21)
Flight for Freedom (February 4)
Wild Horse Rustlers (February 12)

Secrets of the Underground (February 18)
The Moon Is Down (March 10)
Assignment in Brittany (March 11)
This Land Is Mine (March 17)
China (March 19)
Air Force (March 20)
Hangmen Also Die (March 23)
Edge of Darkness (March 23)
Corregidor (March 25)
Tonight We Raid Calais (March 29)
Hitler—Dead or Alive (March 31)
Sherlock Holmes in Washington (March 31)
The More the Merrier (April 7)
Pilot No. 5 (April 8)
King of the Cowboys (April 9)
I Escaped from the Gestapo (April 15)
Crash Dive (April 22)
Reveille with Beverly (April 23)
Above Suspicion (April 28)
Swing Shift Masie (April 30)
Mr. Lucky (May 3)
Five Graves to Cairo (May 4)
They Came to Blow Up America (May 7)
Pacific Rendezvous (May 8)
Stage Door Canteen (May 12)
Bombardier (May 13)
Action in the North Atlantic (May 17)
Mission to Moscow (May 22)
Spy Train (May 25)
That Nazty Nuisance (May 28)
Bataan (May 28)
Nazi Spy Ring (June 2)
Background to Danger (June 9)
Hitler's Madman (June 10)
So Proudly We Hail (June 22)
Wings Over the Pacific (June 25)
Submarine Alert (June 28)
Yanks Ahoy (June 29)
Marines Come Through (July 8)
Bomber's Moon (July 9)

Cowboy Commandoes (July 12)
The Sky's the Limit (July 13)
Good Luck, Mr. Yates (July 15)
For Whom the Bell Tolls (July 15)
Behind the Rising Sun (July 21)
Appointment in Berlin (July 26)
Watch on the Rhine (July 27)
We've Never Been Licked (July 29)
This Is the Army (July 29)
Salute to the Marines (August 2)
Let's Face It (August 4)
Passport to Suez (August 12)
Hostages (August 12)
Destroyer (August 16)
The Fallen Sparrow (August 17)
Adventures of a Rookie (August 20)
Revenge of the Zombies (August 26)
Black Market Rustlers (August 31)
Submarine Base (September 2)
First Comes Courage (September 10)
Tiger Fangs (September 27)
Corvette K-225 (September 27)
Adventures in Iraq (September 27)
Sahara (September 29)
Paris After Dark (October 6)
The North Star (October 13)
Northern Pursuit (October 25)
Guadalcanal Diary (October 27)
The Strange Death of Adolf Hitler (October 28)
Gangway for Tomorrow (November 3)
Cry Havoc (November 9)
Happy Land (November 10)
Minesweeper (November 10)
The Cross of Lorraine (November 12)
Women in Bondage (November 16)
Jack London (November 22)
The Underdog (November 24)
Tarzan's Desert Mystery (December 6)
Rookies in Burma (December 16)

Gung Ho (December 20)
Destination Tokyo (December 21)
A Guy Named Joe (December 24)
Cowboy in the Clouds (December 24)
Tender Comrade (December 29)
Song of Russia (December 29)
Three Russian Girls (December 30)
Raiders of Sunset Pass (December 30)
There's Something About a Soldier (December 31)

1944

The Miracle of Morgan's Creek (January 5)
Lifeboat (January 11)
The Fighting Seabees (January 19)
Rationing (January 28)
None Shall Escape (January 28)
Passport to Destiny (January 31)
The Fighting Sullivans (February 3)
In Our Time (February 4)
Up in Arms (February 7)
Cowboy Canteen (February 8)
The Imposter (February 10)
Weekend Pass (February 14)
See Here, Private Hargrove (February 16)
Passage to Marseilles (February 17)
Action in Arabia (February 18)
The Purple Heart (February 23)
The Navy Way (February 25)
Sweethearts of the U.S.A. (February 25)
Four Jills in a Jeep (March 17)
Sundown Valley (March 23)
Follow the Boys (March 27)
Two-Man Submarine (March 29)
Rosie the Riveter (April 5)
Hey, Rookie (April 6)
Seven Days Ashore (April 21)
Uncertain Glory (April 24)
The Hitler Gang (April 26)

The Story of Dr. Wassell (April 26)
Days of Glory (April 27)
Johnny Doesn't Live Here Anymore (May 15)
The Eve of St. Mark (May 22)
Ladies of Washington (May 25)
Secret Command (June 5)
The Black Parachute (June 5)
Hail the Conquering Hero (June 7)
I Love a Soldier (June 14)
Marine Raiders (July 11)
Dragon Seed (July 18)
Mr. Winkle Goes to War (July 19)
Since You Went Away (July 19)
Abroad with Two Yanks (July 24)
The Seventh Cross (July 24)
Wing and a Prayer (July 24)
Waterfront (August 2)
Wilson (August 2)
A Wave, A Wac, and a Marine (August 12)
Enemy of Women (August 21)
U-Boat Prisoner (August 22)
The Doughgirls (August 30)
Storm Over Lisbon (September 5)
In the Meantime, Darling (September 22)
The Master Race (September 22)
My Buddy (September 22)
My Pal Wolf (September 25)
The Conspirators (October 17)
To Have and Have Not (October 18)
Ministry of Fear (October 19)
Thirty Seconds Over Tokyo (November 15)
Hollywood Canteen (December 5)
Army Wives (December 6)
The Unwritten Code (December 7)
Sunday Dinner for a Soldier (December 8)
Tomorrow the World (December 18)
Here Come the Waves (December 18)
I'll Be Seeing You (December 20)

1945

The Enchanted Cottage (February 15)
Keep Your Powder Dry (February 15)
Objective Burma (February 17)
God Is My Co-Pilot (February 21)
Betrayal From the East (February 25)
GI Honeymoon (February 26)
Hotel Berlin (March 2)
Sergeant Mike (March 13)
The Clock (March 22)
Counter-Attack (April 3)
Corpus Christi Bandits (April 20)
A Medal for Benny (April 27)
Blood on the Sun (April 26)
Escape in the Desert (May 1)
China Sky (May 16)
Back to Bataan (May 31)
The Story of GI Joe (June 18)
Captain Eddie (June 19)
A Bell for Adano (June 21)
Pride of the Marines (August 7)
Anchors Aweigh (August 14)

SELECTIVE BIBLIOGRAPHY

Basinger, Jeanine. *The World War II Combat Film: Anatomy of a Genre.* New York: Columbia UP, 1986.

Butler, Ivan. *The War Film.* New York: Barnes, 1974.

Cross, Robin. *The Big Book of B Movies, or How Low Was My Budget?* New York: St. Martins, 1981.

Deming, Barbara. *Running Away from Myself: A Dream Portrait of America Drawn from the Films of the Forties.* New York: Grossman, 1969.

Dick, Bernard F. *The Star-Spangled Screen: The American World War II Film.* Lexington: UP of Kentucky, 1985.

Dower, John W. *War Without Mercy: Race and Power in the Pacific War.* New York: Pantheon, 1986.

Farber, Manny. "Movies in Wartime," *New Republic* 7 Sept., 1942: 16–20.

Ford, Nick. *Language in Uniform: A Reader on Propaganda.* New York: Odyssey, 1967.

Furhammar, Leif, and Isaksson, Folke. *Politics and Film.* New York: Praeger, 1971.

Fyne, Robert. "From Hollywood to Moscow," *Film Library Quarterly* 16 (1983): 30–36.

——. "The Unsung Heroes of World War II," *Literature/Film Quarterly* 6 (1979): 148–57.

"GI's Versus Hollywood," *Time,* 11 Sept., 1944: 9.

Goodman, Ezra. "Hollywood Belligerent," *Nation,* 12 Sept., 1942: 213–14.

Guy, Rory. "Hollywood Goes to War," *Cinema* 3.2 (1966): 22–29.

Higham, Charles, and Greenberg, Joel. *Hollywood in the Forties.* New York: Barnes, 1968.

"Hollywood to the Wars," *Time,* 22 Dec., 1941: 46.

Hughes, Robert, ed. *Film: Films of Peace and War.* New York: Grove, 1962.

Jacobs, Lewis. "World War II and the American Film," *Cinema Journal* 7 (1967): 1–22.

Jeavons, Clyde. *A Pictorial History of War Films.* Secaucus, NJ: Citadel, 1974.

Jones, Dorothy B. "Hollywood Goes to War," *Nation,* 27 Jan., 1945: 93–95.

Jones, James. "Phony War Films," *Saturday Evening Post,* 30 Mar., 1963: 64–67.

Jones, Ken D., and McClure, A. F. *Hollywood at War: The American Motion Picture and World War II.* New York: Castle, 1973.

Kagan, Norman. *The War Film.* New York: Pyramid, 1974.

Kane, Kathryn. *Visions of War: Hollywood Combat Films of World War II.* Ann Arbor: UMI Research Press, 1982.

Kelly, Thomas O., II. "Race and Racism in the American World War II War Film: The Negro, the Nazi, and the 'Jap' in *Bataan* and *Sahara.*" *Michigan Academician* 24 (Summer 1992): 571–84.

King, Larry L. "The Battle of Popcorn Bay," *Harper's,* May 1967: 50–54.

Klozoff, Max, Johnson, William, and Corless, Richard. "Shooting at Wars: Three Views," *Film Quarterly* 2 (1967): 27–36.

Koch, Howard. *Casablanca: Script and Legend.* Woodstock, NY: Overlook, 1973.

Koppes, Clayton R., and Black, Gregory D. *Hollywood Goes to War: How Politics, Profits and Propaganda Shaped World War II Movies.* New York: Free Press, 1987.

Lingeman, Richard R. *Don't You Know There's a War On? The American Home Front, 1941–1945.* New York: Putnam's, 1970.

Manvell, Roger. *Films and the Second World War.* New York: Dell, 1974.

Maynard, Richard A. *Propaganda on Film: A Nation at War.* Rochelle Park, NJ: Hayden, 1975.

Miller, Don. *"B" Movies.* New York: Curtis, 1973.

Morella, Joe, Epstein, Edward Z., and Griggs, John. *The Films of World War II.* Secaucus, NJ: Citadel, 1973.

Nichols, Dudley. "Men in Battle: A Review of Three Current Pictures," *Hollywood Quarterly* 1 (1945): 34–39.

Orriss, Bruce. *When Hollywood Ruled the Skies.* Santa Clarita, CA: Aviation, 1984.

Parish, James Robert. *The Great Combat Pictures: Twentieth-Century Warfare on the Screen.* Metuchen, NJ: Scarecrow, 1990.

Peck, Jeff. "The Heroic Soviet on the American Screen," *Film and History* 9 (1979): 54–63.

Perlmutter, Tom. *War Movies.* Secaucus, NJ: Castle, 1974.

Renov, Michael. *Hollywood's Wartime Woman: Representation and Ideology.* Ann Arbor: UMI Research, 1988.

Rogers, Donald. *Since You Went Away: From Rosie the Riveter to*

Bond Drives, World War II at Home. New Rochelle, NY: Arlington, 1973.

Rubin, Steven Jay. *Combat Films: American Realism 1945–1970.* Jefferson, NC: McFarland, 1981.

Shindler, Colin. *Hollywood Goes to War: Films and American Society 1939–1952.* Boston: Routledge, 1979.

Small, Melvin. "Buffoons and Brave Hearts: Hollywood Portrays the Russians 1939–1944," *California Historical Quarterly* 52 (1973): 326–37.

———. "Hollywood and Teaching about Russian American Relations," *Film and History* 10 (1980): 1–8.

———. "How We Learned to Love the Russians: American Media and the Soviet Union during World War II," *The Historian* 36 (1974): 455–78.

———. "War Films Made in Hollywood, 1942–1944," *Hollywood Quarterly* 1 (1945): 1–19.

Soderbergh, Peter A. "The War Films," *Discourse* 11 (1968): 87–91.

Stults, Taylor. "World War II Films as Propaganda," *Film and History* 2 (1972): 23–27.

Suid, Lawrence H. *Guts and Glory: Great American War Movies.* Reading, MA: Addison, 1978.

Tyler, Parker. *Magic and Myth of the Movies.* New York: Simon, 1947.

Wanger, William. "Movies with a Message," *Saturday Review,* 7 Mar., 1942: 12.

White, David M., and Averson, Richard. *The Celluloid Weapon.* Boston: Beacon, 1972.

White, Raymond E. "Hollywood Cowboys Go to War: The B-Western Movie During World War II," *Under Western Skies,* Sept. 1983: 23–66.

Whitehall, Richard. "One, Two, Three," *Films and Filming* 10 (Aug. 1964): 7+.

Woll, Allen L. *The Hollywood Musical Goes to War.* Chicago: Nelson, 1983.

INDEX

ABOUT THE AUTHOR

ROBERT FYNE (B.A., Jersey City State College; M.A., Seton Hall University; Ph.D., New York University) is an associate professor of English at Kean College, Union, New Jersey, where he teaches a Russian film course. Active in several international cinema organizations, Dr. Fyne has read papers at numerous conferences examining Hollywood's World War II propaganda. At the Centre de Recherche d'Histoire Quantitative, Université de Caen, he presented "Hollywood and Europe: The Films of 1940," an essay published in *L'Année 1940 en Europe*. Other papers concerned with wartime propaganda were delivered at the International Conference on the Occasion of the Fiftieth Anniversary of the Opening of the Second World War at Paris, the Fourth World Congress for Soviet and East European Studies at Harrogate, England, and the Third Biennial Project for Books at Cambridge University, England. Dr. Fyne has published articles in leading scholarly journals and film periodicals including *Christian Century, Film Library Quarterly, Literature/Film Quarterly, The Quarterly Review of Film Studies, Alaska Quarterly Review,* and *The Journal of Popular Film and Television*. Other awards included NEH fellowships to Cornell University, Northwestern University, the University of Illinois, and Harvard University plus a summer stipend at the Kennan Institute for Advanced Russian Studies. Presently, Dr. Fyne is the book review editor for *Film & History*.